THE BAILIWICK OF
GUERNSEY

THE QUEEN'S CHANNEL ISLANDS

The Bailiwick of Jersey
The Bailiwick of Guernsey

THE KING'S ENGLAND

Edited by Arthur Mee

In 41 Volumes

THE QUEEN'S CHANNEL ISLANDS

THE BAILIWICK OF GUERNSEY

By
C. P. LE HURAY

fully revised and edited by
J. C. T. UTTLEY, M.A.

Illustrated with new photographs by
A. F. KERSTING

HODDER AND STOUGHTON

Printed in Great Britain
for Hodder and Stoughton Limited,
St. Paul's House, Warwick Lane, London, E.C.4,
by Richard Clay (The Chaucer Press), Ltd.,
Bungay, Suffolk

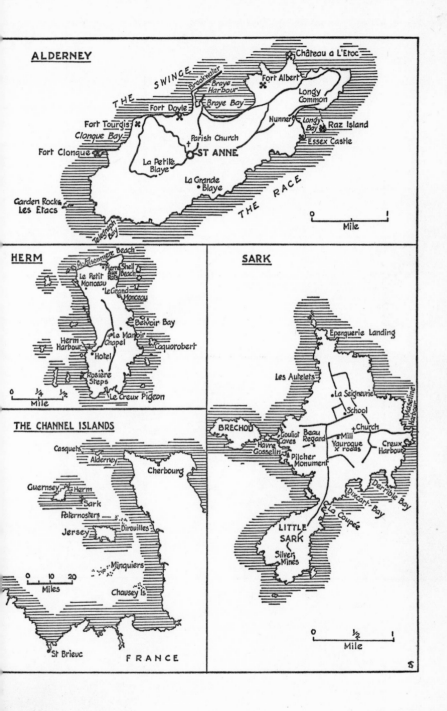

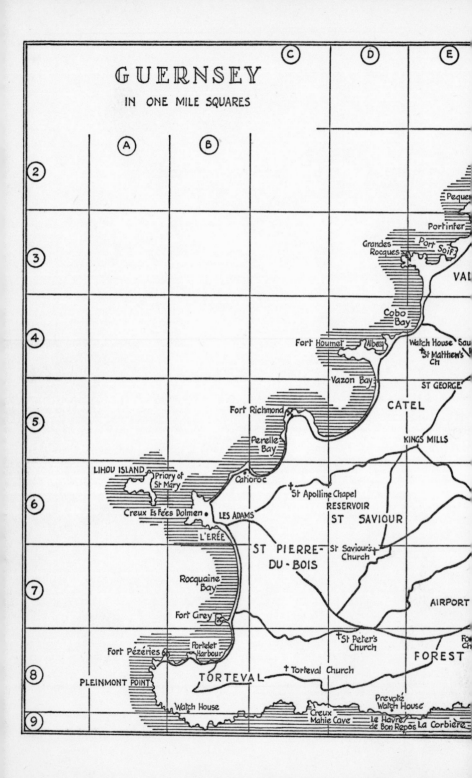

GUERNSEY

IN ONE MILE SQUARES

Ⓐ Ⓑ Ⓒ Ⓓ Ⓔ

② ③ ④ ⑤ ⑥ ⑦ ⑧ ⑨

Pequer
Portinfer
Grandes Rocques
Port Soif
VAL
Cobo Bay
Fort Houmet
Albeq
Watch House Sau
St Matthew's Ch
Vazon Bay
ST GEORGE
Fort Richmond
CATEL
Perelle Bay
KINGS MILLS
LIHOU ISLAND
Priory of St Mary
Catioroc
St Apolline Chapel
RESERVOIR
Creux Es Fées Dolmen
LES ADAMS
ST SAVIOUR
L'ERÉE
ST PIERRE-DU-BOIS
St Saviour's Church
Rocquaine Bay
AIRPORT
Fort Grey
Fort Pézéries
Portelet Harbour
St Peter's Church
FOREST
Fo Ch
+ Torteval Church
PLEINMONT POINT
TORTEVAL
Prevôté Watch House
Watch House
Creux Mahie Cave
Le Havre de Bon Repôs
La Corbière

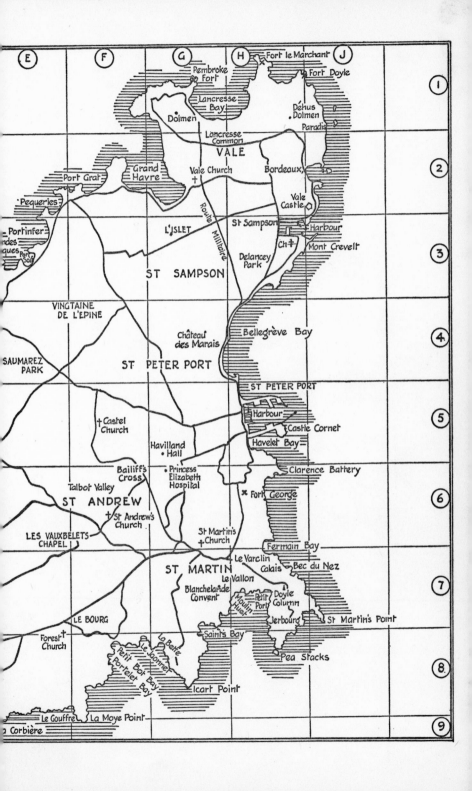

LIST OF ILLUSTRATIONS

INTRODUCTION

In a phrase more poetical than accurate, Victor Hugo once desscribed the Channel Islands as fragments of Europe dropped by France and picked up by England.

A casual glance at the map will show that the Channel Islands extend over an area of approximately 3,000 square miles. Their southern limit is the coast of Brittany from Paimpol to Mont St Michel, their eastern from Mont St Michel to Cape la Hague. A line drawn from Cape la Hague to the Casquets, and from there, passing the rocks on the west coast of Guernsey, just clearing the Roches Douvres and reaching the Brittany coast at les Héaux, where there is a lighthouse, will form the northern and western boundaries. Within these limits are groups of islands, shoals and rocks which, geologically and historically, constitute the most interesting area of the English Channel.

Hugo, in a far more accurate phrase, describes this archipelago as the Ægean of the Channel.

Since the loss of Normandy in the reign of King John the islands have always been regarded as an appanage of the English Crown.

The Channel Islands may claim, in a very special sense, to be part and parcel of the Queen's England. Indeed, the only other portion of Her Majesty's dominions in any way analogous to them is the Isle of Man.

The Norman Conquest of England in 1066, however, made no difference to their status as an outlying corner of the Duchy of Normandy. For them the Conqueror was, and remained, Duke of Normandy. It was not until the opening years of the 13th century, when John lost his French possessions, that the link with England assumed the strength which it has ever since maintained.

John, despised as weak by many historians, exhibited gifts of far-seeing diplomacy in his attitude towards the Channel Islands. He must have realised the strategic value, to an England in rivalry with France, of what was then a most defensible outpost on the very doorstep of the enemy, if given a population loyal to the English Crown. For this he was prepared to pay a fair price, and that price was the valuable set of privileges embodied in the charters which every reigning monarch from his time to the present day was to endorse. Thus the islands, despite even the Papal Bull of Neutrality, were closely affected by the centuries' long struggle between England and France.

The division of the islands into two separate entities, the Bailiwick of Jersey and that of Guernsey, came much later, in the reign of Henry VII. At first there was a Warden of the Isles, appointed by the King, whose duties were primarily of a military nature. He is sometimes referred to as Captain, and very much later as Governor. Frequently non-resident, he appointed a deputy or lieutenant. In the course of centuries the office of governor, sometimes hereditary, tended to become nominal, finally ceasing to exist at all. Today the Lieutenant-Governor in each bailiwick is the commander-in-chief, with very little civil administrative responsibilities.

The Royal Court originated as the ducal court for the islands, presided over first by the Seneschal of Normandy, and later, with the natural increase of business, by his deputy, or Bailiff, one for each of the two main islands. In the administration of justice and island affairs, the Bailiffs were assisted by a body of Jurats, an office of ancient lineage, possibly dating back to the *hommes Jugeurs* of the Norman Empire. The struggle for supremacy between the warden, captain, or governor, as military head, and the Bailiff, as civil head, was a long and bitter one, lasting for centuries. The Lieutenant-Governor of Guernsey still has a seat in the Court of Chief Pleas, held at the three chief feasts of the year, Christmas, Easter, and Michaelmas, but the seigneurs of fiefs and the constables of the parishes, who are compelled to attend, pay homage, not to him, but to the Bailiff.

That they are part of the Queen's England is true of the larger islands, but there are a few minor portions of the archipelago which are definitely French. Some have occasionally been in dispute between England and France. Possession of others by France has never been challenged by the British Crown.

A few miles to the west of Granville is the Chausey group. There is only one island of any size, the Grande Ile, and that is scarcely larger than Herm. The Chausey Islands were at one time of considerable strategic importance to France. They were captured by Jersey privateers in 1744 and held for a considerable time. In fact, the quarries were worked and the stone shipped to Guernsey and Jersey for the building of fortifications. In 1780 Rullecour's fleet, prepared for what became, fortunately, its abortive attack on Jersey, took shelter here during severe weather.

But although by the peace of Aix-la-Chapelle these islands were handed back to France, thus acknowledging their dependency on that country, we do find that their possession was questioned by England in the Middle Ages. When Pope Alexander VI, in 1490, transferred the Channel Islands from the diocese of Coutances to that of Winchester, the Chausey Islands were included. It may therefore be inferred that at that time Chausey was regarded as a dependency of the English Crown. Later, however, the islands reverted to Coutances, and nothing further is heard of this claim.

North-west of Chausey, and not more than 12 miles south of St Helier, lie the Minquiers. This dangerous and very extensive group of rocks has for centuries taken heavy toll of shipping.

The Maîtresse Ile, the largest of this group, towers 72 feet above high water at neap tides and measures approximately 200 by 50 yards. It is a resort of Jersey fishermen, especially during the vraicking season, and has several huts upon it.

Although always regarded as Jersey territory, the Minquiers have produced a number of minor diplomatic clashes between England and France over fishing rights.

Two important groups of rocks, the Ecrehous and the Dirouilles, lie nearly midway between St Catherine's Point, Jersey, and Port Bail on the Normandy coast. Between the two groups there is a fairly safe channel into Bouley Bay, Jersey.

On the Ecrehous are the ruins of an ancient chapel, built in 1203 by the monks of Val Richer, near Lisieux. Even in quite recent times the Ecrehous were not without their hermit, for at the end of last century and the beginning of the present, an old Jersey fisherman, Philip Pinel, lived there alone for over 40 years. He was known as the King of the Ecrehous.

It was he, probably, who defended this portion of British territory against the French when, in 1883, they made an attempt to annex these rocky islets. Fishing rights were again the underlying reason for this attempt at annexation. The international crisis which ensued, though exciting at the time, was fortunately peaceably settled, and Jersey's territorial limits remained unviolated. More recent discussions between the British and French Governments over the status of the Minquiers and the Ecrehous were resolved by the decision of the International Court in favour of Jersey and the British.

In his *Toilers of the Sea*, Hugo falls into a serious error about another group of rocks which lie off the north coast of Jersey nearest to Guernsey. These are the Paternosters, and he places them between Guernsey and Sark, and suggests that a ship stranded on them could signal Icart Point.

His error is emphasised by the fact that he compares their situation with the isolation of the Roches Douvres. These are a dangerous reef, with 12 heads, always uncovered. The whole group extends over an area of about 4 miles by 3 miles. The Douvres lie almost due south of the Hanois and roughly two-thirds of the distance between that point and the coast of Brittany.

The highest rock of the group is nearly 50 feet above the water, and upon this in 1869 the French Government erected a lighthouse, 160 feet in height. This fact in itself established the ownership of the group as French, and this ownership has apparently never been questioned.

Nearly due north of Guernsey lie the Casquets, which are British. The group is roughly 1½ miles in length from west to east and some half-mile in breadth. The lighthouse towers, of which there are three, are on the northern islet, which is about 100 feet above high-water spring tide. These three bear the names of St Peter, St Thomas, and the Donjon respectively.

In 1877 two were abolished as lighthouses and the remaining one improved. This light gives three quick flashes every thirty seconds, and is about 113 feet above high water.

There is also on the Casquets a fog-siren which gives three blasts in quick succession every two minutes.

A light existed on these rocks as early as 1726, but it consisted merely of a coal-fire kept in a glow by the use of bellows. A system of revolving lamps was not substituted until 1790.

In 1823 extensive damage was done to the lighthouse by a storm of unparalleled fury.

On the Casquets there is a small garden in which a few vegetables and flowers are grown. But the rocks are completely barren, and the whole of the earth of this garden was brought in boats from Alderney.

There are two landing-places for boats, but they are seldom accessible at the same time, owing to the incessant swell. The keepers are frequently weather-bound for many weeks. In consequence, the rocks are provisioned for at least three months.

The Casquets were occupied by one or two Germans during the Second World War, and on one occasion a small British commando force effected a landing there. They surprised and captured two or three men, one of whom so little expected such an irruption from without that he was found performing an elaborate head toilet which involved the putting of his hair in a net.

It is generally agreed by historians that the White Ship, *la Blanche Nef*, the loss of which is said to have led an English king never to smile again, was wrecked, not on the Casquets, but just off Barfleur, on the eastern point of the Cotentin or Cherbourg peninsula.

The Hurd Deep, a depression of considerable length in the bed of the Channel, and the dumping place of much ammunition and of many obsolete ships, follows a line parallel to and about 20 miles west of Guernsey and Alderney.

4

GUERNSEY

The Parish of St Peter Port, known as the Town parish, is the most important in the Island, embracing as it does the capital, and with it approximately 40 per cent of the population. At its heart lies the ancient settlement of St Peter Port, with the Town Church, the Markets, the Harbour, and close by the Town Hospital, the Royal Court, The Constables' Office, the Guille-Allès Library, and Hauteville. Off shore Castle Cornet stands proudly on its rock. On the higher ground above the Old Town are the residential areas of the New Town, Cambridge Park, and the Arsenal. While on the heights to the south are the remains of Fort George.

At some period, so remote that there exists no record of it either in history or in tradition, St Peter Port arose in the narrow seaward mouth of a valley, running in a more or less south-westerly direction from the coast.

This valley has been produced by the slow erosive action of two main streams, both less than two miles long and rising in St Martin's parish, which unite at the Pont Renier at the bottom of the Ruettes Brayes, and flow thence in one large stream into the Town Harbour.

In the town itself no traces of these streams can now be seen. This natural drainage has been led in fairly recent times into storm water-sewers.

How narrow was the valley mouth in which the town arose will be best appreciated by taking up a post of observation on the Albert Pier. Beside the southern side of the Town Church, whose altar, it must be noted, was built on the beach itself, is the comparatively narrow street of Church Hill. As recently as 1914 this street was adapted to modern traffic requirements by cutting back still farther the little cemetery behind the Picquet House, a plot of land which rises to a considerable height above sea and road level. Cornet Street, too, which runs southwards, rises very steeply.

It may therefore be assumed that the south end of the church was built against steeply rising ground.

The north end faces the High Street, on the left side of which, going up, is the Commercial Arcade. Early in the 19th century this shopping centre was carved out of the cliff face, and the extent of this excavation can be gauged by climbing the Arcade steps to Clifton or by gazing up Market Hill to the houses which rise, tier upon tier, above Old Rectory House.

5

A stream of considerable size probably ran down between the north end of the church and the site of the pump in Church Square. It entered the sea at the Rue des Vaches (Cow Lane), whose floor level was then considerably lower than it is today. It is not unlikely that a branch of this stream may have washed the outer wall of the church.

Quay Street, once the Rue du Pilori, may have originated as a slipway. Beyond it, to the north, the cliffs began, so that from here to the southernmost wall of the church was the natural fishing harbour which was to develop into the port of St Peter.

North and south of this short length of coast, vulnerable to attack from the sea, save for the artificial defences of the church and, perhaps, a stone rampart, rose steep cliffs, down the face of which tracks soon appeared, made sometimes by man, sometimes by animals. At first these tracks were winding and irregular, for it is an innate tendency of man to avoid natural obstacles. In the course of time these tracks were improved and became recognised paths, the steeper ones developing into flights of steps. The North Pier steps, at the top of the High Street, were probably improved as an approach to the new North Pier when that arm was built in the reign of Queen Anne. But they probably existed long before then. Half-way down these steps from the High Street they fork in two directions. There are patches of cobblestones in the landings of the lower flights, and an occasional worn and rusted iron ring and staple, let into the paving, suggest that boats were once moored here.

A much steeper and straighter flight will be found lower down the High Street. These are partly roofed over. As a cliff-side track they, too, must be of great age.

On the south esplanade, between the Town Church and Havelet, there is only one group of steps. These, subject to numerous turns, as though following the easiest path up the hillside, are flanked with old vaults and derelict buildings of the 18th and early 19th centuries, rather reminiscent of certain scenes in Dickens. They lead into Cliff Street, which, rising steeply, ends at St Barnabas Church, site of the old Tour Beauregard, or, by turning to the right, through a narrow alley, significantly named the Coupée Lane, attain Cornet Street. Alternatively, a turn to the left takes the traveller along the Strand, an elevated and almost level cliff path, running almost parallel with Hauteville, and ending some distance up Havelet at the rear of the Brewery.

To the west of the Town Church lie the market buildings. These fill the narrow valley as far as the foot of the Bordage, and Fountain and Market Streets are the modern equivalents of the tracks on the

6

The harbour

ST PETER PORT

Castle Cornet

The High Street and Town Church, St Peter Port

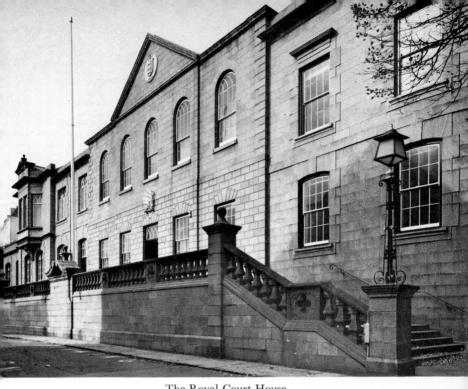

The Royal Court House

ST PETER PORT

The Markets

The church of St James the Less, St Peter Port

side of the stream which once flowed naturally down the valley. On the Market Street side the cliffs are particularly precipitous, and the climb up Constitution or Clifton Steps, not to mention the numerous private flights which end in the Clifton neighbourhood, demands both energy and resolution.

At the foot of the steps in Fountain Street, known as Rosemary Lane, is one of the barriers of the town. There is little doubt that this stone does mark the westernmost boundary of the town of the Middle Ages, for the high wall bordering the steps bears every indication of antiquity. The steps lead right up to the Mignot Plateau, formerly a part of the Tour Beauregard or, by keeping to the left, to Cornet Street, almost opposite the Coupée Lane.

Mill Street, originally known as Haut Pavé, which becomes Mansell Street long before it reaches Trinity Church, represents a path running fairly high up the flank of the hillside. Steps lead down to the base of the valley in Bordage, but another set, nearly opposite, climbs upwards, to form a short cut into what was once the green valley of Vauvert.

In the Bordage the widest set of steps in the island leads up once again to St Barnabas. These steps, however, can be avoided by continuing up the Bordage and turning, by a left-hand hairpin bend, up Tower Hill.

Behind the left-hand side of Bordage rises Pedvin Street and behind that again Hauteville. Pedvin Street itself forms another hairpin bend with Bordage, leading into Hauteville. On the right-hand side are numerous flights of steps, all of them private, scaling the steep face of the cliff at the back of nearly every house.

From Trinity Square—triangular in shape—two roads lead upwards on the right. The older of these follows a valley, Vauvert, already referred to. Victoria Road, bordered by fields little more than a century ago, is of modern construction. The old route in that direction is represented by the Bouillon Steps, another natural track. Farther to the left the tortuousness of Mount Durand shows it also to be an ancient trackway.

Park Street is the continuation of the highway inland. It follows the base of the valley, whereas Park Lane, running parallel to it and on its left-hand flank, is probably the ancient track.

At the western end of this lane is perhaps the most interesting set of steps in the island. These steps, built between high walls, scale a steep cliff-face and terminate at the foot of the Vardes, not far from the Montville estate. The upper landings of these steps are ideal spots from which to obtain a bird's-eye view of the valley in which St Peter Port lies. The most casual glance will reveal how St Peter

7

Port clings precariously to the face of the hillside, as well as the colossal amount of patient labour expended in excavating, terracing, and levelling, so that a steep and narrow valley, with a marshy base, was transformed into an accessible and defensible settlement.

Those who have time to stand and stare should turn their backs upon Charrotterie and gaze along Park Street in the direction of Mount Durand. They will then get an impression of the capital of Guernsey as a Continental town, not of the type of Cancale, but rather of the old Mentone of the azure coast.

Perhaps the finest spot from which to contemplate the slow evolution of the town of St Peter Port, from its earliest beginnings as a settlement of dwellings huddled together to the west of the Town Church to a crowded city sprawling and clinging precariously to the flanks of hills north and west and south, is from the carriage-way of the Montville estate.

This walk, acquired by the States between the two World Wars, with the object presumably of saving it from the speculative builder, who had already made great inroads upon the estate, deserves to be better known both by natives and visitors.

It begins at the foot of the Vardes, a steep hill forming the right-hand prong of the fork at the top of Hauteville. The drive was cut, rather like a shelf, in the flank of a steep hillside in the early days of the 19th century. It emerges near the gardener's lodge in Colborne Road. The house, a typical Victorian dwelling, built by a prosperous Guernseyman of the same period, stood at the Vardes end of the drive. Of it only traces of the foundations now remain, for it was burnt to the ground many years ago, after being struck by lightning.

The hillside above and below the drive was once well wooded, but many trees have been felled. On the left-hand side, going towards Colborne Road, there are one or two items of interest. One is the round stone tower of an old windmill. Another is a tiny plot, overgrown with weeds and surrounded by a high stone wall, pierced in one place by an opening, from which the gate has long since disappeared. This "neglected spot" is the Quaker cemetery. Many years have passed since an interment took place here, and no stones or mounds mark the graves of the departed Friends.

On the right-hand edge of the path the hillside descends precipitously to Charotterie and Colborne Road. At intervals a break in the trees reveals an excellent glimpse of the valley. From a point just inside the Vardes entrance a fine view is obtainable, from left to right, of the spire of St Joseph's, the Victoria Tower, and the turrets of Elizabeth College.

Below the tower of St Joseph's the face of the hillside appears to have been scarped. This is at a point just behind the timber-yard. On the opposite side of the road, too—although a descent into Charotterie is necessary to see this—the face of the cliff is precipitous, and also bears evidence of having been quarried away. The valley here, between the saw-mill and Miller's yard, is very narrow, and the road originally followed a curve dangerous to modern traffic, until the Occupation forces, yielding to military necessity, made some effort to straighten and widen it.

From a point much farther along the drive the narrowness of this gorge can be still better appreciated, and, framed between its two flanks, the spires of St Barnabas and of the Town Church can be clearly seen.

The valley below, however, claims the most attention. At the top end it forks in two directions. The main valley lies between the Ruettes Brayes and Colborne Road. The subsidiary valley accommodates Prince Albert Road, leading to the Queen's Road. The town end of this valley bears the interesting name of la Pierre Percée.

Wide terraces, many of them walled, rise from the valley towards the Mont Durand. The few trees remaining on this hillside suggest the existence here in the past of a considerable woodland.

Between this woodland and the road is a low-lying but relatively level tract of land which is scheduled as a site for States Houses. The large house at its rear was once the seat of the Mansell family, who gave their name to Mansell Street and Contrée Mansell.

This area was once a large and deep reservoir, fed by the streams flowing down Colborne Road, the Ruettes Brayes, and the Pierre Percée. Henceforth, until this water reached the sea in the neighbourhood of the Town Church, it was an important factor in the relatively primitive industrial activities of St Peter Port.

Even before entering this reservoir, the water turned a mill at the Pont Renier, and at the foot of the Ruettes Brayes formed a public *lavoir*. Below the main reservoir it was dammed again and again to drive mills which ground corn or sawed timber. In the neighbourhood of Park Street the blacksmith used it for bonding wheels. Of the Park Street blacksmiths, who were also farriers, only one now remains. But these tradesmen were once far more numerous, even at the beginning of the present century.

The name Charotterie suggests carriage-building and, indeed, the industry flourished in this area as late as the beginning of the 20th century. Of the many establishments which produced not only the box-carts used in vraicking and the wooden ploughs and

9

harrows, but also the heavy wooden wheelbarrow, there now exists but one.

In the Bordage the stream did service for bakers, brewers, and other trades. Lower down still, in the vicinity of the market, it not only turned more mills, but also provided a number of convenient washing-places for vegetables as well as clothes.

The very name of Fountain Street is an indication of the water which must once have flowed through that *venelle*.

But the track which wound steeply along the bank of this stream—Fountain Street, the Bordage, Park Street, and Charotterie—did more than give access to the establishments which it served. It penetrated, up the Ruettes Brayes, into the very centre of the island. It climbed, up the Pierre Percée, to the heights above the town, to the Mont Durand and the Petite Marche, now Queen's Road.

Colborne Road, however, is of recent creation. It was cut, as an examination of one side of it will show, out of the flank of the valley, during the governorship of Sir John Colborne, the successor of that famous road-maker, Sir John Doyle.

Its purpose is evident. It is a convenient approach to Fort George from the town. The only alternative approaches were Cornet Street and Hauteville or Tower Hill and Hauteville, both of which were far narrower and more inconvenient a century ago than they are today. Even now they could scarcely be classed as ideal.

MARKETS. The original site of the Market in Guernsey was Les Landes in the Castel Parish, but by the 14th century at the latest the advantages of St Peter Port had prevailed.

In the first year of his reign, Edward II addressed a letter to Otho de Grandison, the Governor, in which he said:

"That having been informed that the market held at the Landes had been transferred to a fief belonging to a private individual, to his prejudice, the governor was to order public proclamation to be made, that it should be held there as usual, and nowhere else."

But it is unlikely that his order had any effect. For centuries the market was held round every side of the Town Church save that facing the sea, and as far up the High Street as the foot of Berthelot Street. Parts of this area may have been embraced by small private fiefs, but the king's rights to market tolls were apparently admitted, for as recently as 1813, when the States were discussing the purchase, as a market, of what is now known as the French Halles, the following statement was made:

"It is an expense which should fall upon the States, for not only do markets, by their very nature, arise from Royal prerogative, and are established for the benefit of all, but this one is specifically and by concession of His Majesty in Council, placed at the disposal of the States."

That Royal right has never been abrogated, and tangible evidence of this still exists in Market Street, where market goods are weighed on the queen's scales with the queen's weights. The inscription over the entrance, a relic of Victorian days, still reads: "Poids de la Reine".

The question of a covered market first arose in 1726, when a committee of the States was appointed to select a site. Nothing appears to have been done, however, until 1777, when the matter was taken up by private enterprise. A Meat Market Company was formed, and application was made to His Majesty in Council for permission to erect a market. This application in itself proves the existence of royal rights over St Peter Port markets.

This Order in Council, when issued, permitted the States to grant to the company certain duties on all cattle killed. But the States had the option of taking over the market at any time, upon payment of what it had cost the company.

The market was built in 1780, and above it, at a cost of £2,300, rose the new Assembly Rooms, the ancient ones having been in the Pollet. These rooms now constitute the Guille-Allès Library.

Here butchers sold their meat from open stalls, much as they had formerly done in the High Street. This went on until 1822, when the present meat market was built on the opposite side of the street. The cost of its erection, over £4,000, was met by the issue of non-interest-bearing notes, all of which were destroyed as and when they were redeemed from the proceeds of stall-rents. This was a novel financial experiment, which the States were to repeat on several other occasions.

The open space under the Assembly Rooms thus set free was then allotted to retailers of vegetables. These found it draughty, however, and displayed a marked preference for the old stands in the vicinity of the Town Church. Gradually the old meat market became occupied by vendors of eggs, butter, poultry, and fruit imported from Brittany, and assumed, in consequence, the name of the French Halles.

Thus the market was gradually moving away from the High Street. In 1778 certain improvements were effected to the bottom of Cornet Street, and the fish market placed there, but whether this was covered or not is not clear.

The space between the French Halles and the States Arcade, once the Rectory garden (the house flanking Market Steps is still known as Old Rectory House), became the Place du Marché, and here and in the alcoves of the new meat market, higher up the street, the old women sat, under huge umbrellas when rain poured down, and sold Guernsey butter, curds, and eggs.

The States Arcade was set apart for the use of country people, not butchers, who brought in their own ready dressed porkers and calves for sale here. Ten divisions were scrupulously marked out, one for each parish.

The present vegetable market—that part between the fish market and the Market Halls—was the next building to be erected. It was one of the first measures taken by the States to widen and improve Fountain Street. The building was appropriated to the use of fish-sellers, and was fitted with 40 marble-topped tables, for which the guide-books of the period show unbounded admiration. These were subsequently removed to the present fish market, which was the next building to go up.

The erection of the present fish market preceded that of the Market Halls by only a short space of time. Both are built of red granite with blue granite quoins. The buildings, however, differ in architectural style.

The façade of the Market Halls is not unpleasing, but there is insufficient space in front of it to enable one to appreciate the symmetry of its lines. Beneath the Market Halls, with its entrance under the middle turret, is a large subterranean chamber used as a bond store. The floor of this can be but a few inches above that of the ancient valley.

Although the markets form a compact block, their architecture is heterogeneous. But that is perhaps their charm. Native pride in them has never waned, and it was never better expressed than in *Guerin's Almanack*:

"No town, with a similar population, can be better supplied with market accommodation than St Peter Port; it has few equals in Europe. The most sumptuous provision is made in lofty, spacious and well-lighted halls for the sale of fruit and vegetables, fish, meat and poultry."

THE GUILLE-ALLÈS LIBRARY. The building over the French Halles, now the Guille-Allès Library, has already been referred to as the

Assembly Rooms. That building has played an important and interesting part in the social history of the island.

According to Jacob, it was built in 1780, "by a society of gentlemen", at a cost of £2,300, and was opened in 1782. This Society was no new one. It already had premises in the Pollet. But these had become somewhat cramped, and the Society took advantage of the construction of a meat market by a private company to build over it far more commodious premises.

The Assembly Rooms were a rather select club. The rules of that club make interesting reading today. Assemblies, which apparently meant dances, were at first held every Tuesday, and later on alternate Tuesdays. The programme followed one set form. Dancing began with a quadrille, not exceeding five figures, and this was always followed by a country dance.

Ladies must have preponderated, and the rules prescribed what would nowadays be called a system of queueing up for male partners.

Membership was restricted to natives who had themselves subscribed or whose parents had done so. Candidates for membership had to be proposed by the master of ceremonies, and their admission was approved only by the votes of two-thirds of the subscribers present. Only native subscribers were entitled to vote, and a fortnight had to elapse between nomination and election.

Children were never admitted. Officers of the garrison or of the squadron were the only non-natives admitted. These, if in uniform, might wear boots, but—a very necessary precaution—military officers were forbidden to wear spurs.

Every male native subscriber might be called upon to exercise the office of master of ceremonies. Refusal meant a fine of half a guinea, although the provision of an efficient deputy was allowed.

The social need supplied by the Assembly Rooms must have declined as the 19th century advanced. In 1870 the States bought the premises, which during the next decade were used for public entertainments of the type then popular. Chirgwin, the white-eyed Kaffir, appeared there, and a revival of the art of hypnotism by Mesmer attracted large native audiences. Arthur Horton, the notorious Tichborne claimant, also appeared there in the course of his public campaign to collect funds to fight his case.

Clifton Hall, which had not yet become the Salvation Army citadel, probably supplanted the Assembly Rooms as a centre of public entertainment. In any case, the States disposed of the property in 1883 to Messrs Guille and Allès, who proposed to convert it into a public library. The purchase price was £900.

The story of Guille and Allès, founders of the Library, is typical

13

of the 19th century. In 1834, Guille, a lad of 14, went to that land of promise, the United States. There he not only prospered, but educated himself by extensive reading, accumulating before the age of 20 several hundred volumes of standard works.

As time rolled on he and his friend and fellow-Guernseyman, Allès, became associated in business. They had much in common, and prospered exceedingly. Guille paid a visit to Guernsey in 1851, and while here advocated the formation of parish libraries in the *Gazette*, in a series of articles which attracted the attention of the Farmer's Club and gained for him the honorary membership of that body.

But it was not until Guille's second visit, in 1855, that anything definite was done. It was then that a committee, taking the name of the Guille Library Committee, was set up. Guille's collection of books was divided into five sections, and located at convenient places about the island in charge of friends, the largest section being reserved for the town.

The idea was to exchange these cases in rotation, the basic idea of a travelling library today. But this was never carried out. After the volumes had been read in their respective areas they were returned to these places, where they remained unused until 1867, when Guille once more came to the island, this time to remain.

He immediately had all books brought to one central depôt in town. But he opened a branch reading-room at St Martin's, of which he took personal charge. Winter and summer, rain, storm, or sunshine, he was always there to superintend his undertaking. At the end of three years he found the strain too much for his health. The branch was discontinued, and he concentrated his attention upon the central establishment.

Single-handed, he carried on his enterprise until 1881. His was an uphill task, for his fellow-islanders showed little desire to read. Then in 1881 Guille's old associate, Allès, came to his aid.

The renewed association soon bore fruit. In 1882 the old Assembly Rooms were opened to the public. Over the door appeared the most appropriate motto: "Ingredere ut proficias" (Enter that thou may'st profit).

That entrance is not the present entrance, but the one within the French Halles.

It was in 1886 that the Guille-Allès Library assumed its present shape and size. The handsome entrance in Market Street replaced that in the French Halles, and a spacious lobby and staircase led up to the library proper.

Upstairs the area was considerably extended by the purchase

from the parish of some land at the back. This land had originally been the property of the Rectory. The old ballroom became a large, airy reading-room, with the librarian's office at the far end. The lending department, a newsroom, and a magazine-room were accommodated on the same floor.

The roof of the old buildings was reconstructed, and this allowed for the provision of a lecture-room of ample size, whose walls are now adorned with numerous and interesting samples of the work of local artists. On this floor, too, is a large room devoted exclusively to the files of local newspapers, a room devoted to Channel Islands literature, a museum, and the *locale* for the island's learned society, the Société Guernesiaise.

THE ROYAL COURT-HOUSE. It is curious that the Royal Court-houses of both Jersey and Guernsey are situated so inconspicuously as to escape the notice of the casual visitor. That of Jersey is tucked away in a corner of the Royal Square. The Guernsey Royal Court, although built on the heights above the town, and a building of considerable elevation is so hemmed in by other buildings and surrounded by narrow streets, that the severe beauty of its fine granite façade is almost completely lost.

Built in the last year of the 18th century, to replace the old King's Barn, known as the Plaiderie, at the bottom of the Pollet, the cost of its erection was met partly from the sale of the old Cohue, as the Court building was then called, partly from the proceeds of States lotteries, and partly from taxation. Strangely enough, however, the building is the property of the Crown.

At the beginning of the present century the Court-house was vastly improved, as a permanent memorial to the Diamond Jubilee of Queen Victoria, by symmetrical additions at either end and the extension of the terrace. At one end is the Greffe, or records office, a veritable treasure-house of ancient, as well as modern, documents, and a mine of information for the historian. At the other end are the Stamp Office and the Police Court, the latter now presided over by a magistrate.

From the entrance lobby, situated centrally, a broad spiral staircase leads to the Royal Court Chamber, also used for assemblies of the States. This has been completely renovated and decorated to form a dignified hall. Its fittings and its panelling are all in walnut. At one end is a curved raised dais, in the middle of which is the Bailiff's seat. The *Jurats* occupy places on either side of him. At States' meetings these seats are occupied by the president and the *conseillers*, the deputies and *douzaine* representatives being

15

accommodated in the body of the hall, with the Crown Officers in the middle. The Crown Officers and the Bailiff are the only members who wear robes at States' meetings.

Facing the presidential dais is the public gallery, small, but comfortably upholstered, in contrast to the old gallery, which consisted of narrow, uncomfortable deal benches.

The many portraits in oils of distinguished Bailiffs and Lieutenant-Governors, which covered the walls of the chamber until the renovation, have been removed, and are hung in the entrance lobby. Behind the presidential chair, however, still hang the Royal Arms, which, dating back to the time of the Georges, bear quarterings of special interest to students of dynastic history.

Other features of interest in the Royal Court building are the Library, well supplied with law books, the *Jurats'* Room, much used also for committee work, and the Bailiff's Chambers, a suite of rooms worthy of the dignity of the first citizen of the island.

The Royal Court, consisting of the Bailiff and 12 *Jurats*, was until very recently both a legislative and an administrative body. The States, or local Parliament, begins to appear in the records in the later Middle Ages, and has existed with varying degrees of influence ever since. Its chief function at first appears to have been the voting of money, but it was in no sense a representative body. It consisted of the Bailiff as president, the 12 *Jurats*, the Crown officers (*procureur* and *comptrolleur*), and the rector (parish priests) and the constable of each of the 10 parishes. Of these, only the constables were elected, and then only by the suffrage of *chefs de famille*—that is, landed proprietors. A seat was allotted to the Lieutenant-Governor, and he was entitled then, as now, to speak, but not to vote.

The first step towards a more representative house did not come until the end of the 18th century, when the town complained that, although called upon to contribute some two-thirds of the taxation, it had no greater representation than each of the nine country parishes, which between them contributed only one-third.

In 1846, partly as the result of a Privy Council Committee of Enquiry, there was some reform of the States. The constables were replaced by one delegate appointed from among their number by the *douzaine*, or Council, of each parish. In St Peter Port parish separate *douzaines* were set up for each of its four cantons or wards, and each of these cantonal *douzaines* was entitled to send one delegate. In addition, this parish's central *douzaine* sent a quota of two, so that the town now had a representation of six, compared with one from each of the nine country parishes.

The end of the 19th century brought a further broadening of the basis of representation. This took the form of people's deputies, elected on a restricted franchise. Then, in the more democratic climate following the First World War, their number was increased from 12 to 18, elected on a still broader basis.

For it must be noted that until well into the present century taxation was imposed only on property-owners. The capital value of property was assessed in quarters (£25), and such terms as income or rateable value were foreign to fiscal thought and practice in the island.

An attempt to broaden the franchise by allowing individuals to declare that they owned property (personal or real) worth a few quarters was made at the beginning of the century. The end of the First World War saw not only the imposition of income tax, but also a radical change in the system of parochial assessment. Rental value was made the basis of taxation. The names of all ratepayers were automatically entered on the voters' list, and these might vote for parish officials and people's deputies. In theory the franchise for people's deputies—and for people's deputies only—was universal. In practice, non-ratepayers were placed on the voters' list only by making personal application.

The Reform Law of 1948, which followed a post-occupation agitation and a Privy Council Commission, has banished the rectors from the States of Deliberation (the legislative body), but retained them in the States of Election. *Jurats*, as such, no longer have a seat in the States of Deliberation. They are replaced by 12 *conseillers* elected by a reformed and reduced States of Election, a kind of Electoral College. The cantonal *douzaines* of St Peter Port parish are abolished, and each parish *douzaine* now appoints one representative, not for one session only, but for a term of 12 months. The Crown officers retain their seats, but have no vote.

The remainder of the House consists of 33 people's deputies, elected on a basis of universal adult suffrage. The directly elected representatives of the people have, therefore, a majority in the States.

The other body to use the Royal Court is the Chief Pleas, the Crown's Feudal Court, which meets three times a year. The seigneurs, or their representatives, of all fiefs must appear and pay homage, under penalty of a fine. And it is the duty of Her Majesty's Receiver-General to arrange a dinner. Few, apart from the members of the Court, attend this. The *bordiers*, who were formerly entitled to attend, relinquished this right in the middle of the 19th century as a *quid pro quo* for being excused their duties.

17

HAUTEVILLE HOUSE. For 15 years, from 1855 till 1870, Hugo resided at Hauteville, which, by permission of the local authorities, he was later allowed to purchase. A skilful and practical craftsman in all forms of woodwork, Hugo himself transformed it, with panelling and carving, into a house whose atmosphere is recognisable as French the moment the threshold is crossed. It is now the property of the city of Paris.

He could have chosen no more pleasant spot for his residence in Guernsey. From the windows of the upper storeys at the back he looked upon the harbour of St Peter Port, during the period of its development. To the north lay Alderney, flanked by the Casquet Reef and the menhir-like Ortach. Eastwards lay Herm and Jethou, with Sark stretching to the south. Far in the background was Jersey, from which he had fled. And on the skyline extended unendingly the coastline of his beloved France.

Hauteville is a steep slope rising to the south of St Peter Port. It is rather less than a quarter of a mile from the Town Church, and is reached either by climbing Cornet Street or scaling the steps of Tower Hill from the Bordage.

The lower part of Hauteville, between St Barnabas Church (now the Lukis and Island Museum) and Pedvin Street, is narrow, marking as it does the southern limit of the old town. Above this the street is lined by houses of the late Georgian or early Victorian period. Not very far up, near the public pump, is one still called Friends' House. Here during the days of Hugo's exile lived Juliette Drouet.

As a young actress, Juliette called upon the poet one January morning in 1833, to ask if she might be given a part in his play *Lucrezia Borgia*. Hugo was vanquished by her charms, and their love endured until her death in 1883. Hugo frequently dined at Friends' House with Madame Drouet, his sons, and any friends who might be visiting him from France. The friends would, of course, first call and pay their respects to Madame Hugo, after which they would pass on down the street to the livelier social atmosphere of Madame Drouet's *petit salon*.

At first sight, Hauteville House, a few yards higher up, looks gloomy and forbidding. A broad flight of steps and a couple of ever-green trees almost fill the tiny space constituting the forecourt. Over the wide arched doorway, painted a funereal black, waves the tricolor of France. The glass of the fanlight consists of the bases of soda-water bottles diligently collected by Hugo.

But as soon as the house is entered the atmosphere changes. The spirit of the great romantic seems to haunt every nook and cranny of the rambling old mansion. It is a veritable museum of treasures. Victor Hugo had a passion for *bric-à-brac*. The walls of the dining-room are almost hidden by rare old tiles and reliefs. The wonderful carved oak with which the house is filled was all slowly collected, much of it in Guernsey itself, piece by piece, and placed in position, not only by his own direction, but often with his personal co-operation.

When Victor Hugo fled from France he lost all his possessions. In Guernsey he was obliged to gather his household goods all over again. To Jules Janin he wrote: "I have no longer a country, but I want a home." That was what he created in Hauteville House.

One great pillar in the front hall is carved with scenes from *Notre Dame de Paris*. Never was there a house which so completely bears the stamp of its owner. Portraits of him hang everywhere, the best being in the billiard-room. A few of his sketches are still preserved, strikingly individual, done in charcoal, burnt onion, or ink-blots.

On the second storey is the famous oak gallery. This is a very large room, cut into two portions by an open screen. Half-way up the walls is dark wainscoting, heavy beams cross the ceiling, panelled chests alternate with deep window-seats, and heavy doors give entrance. Everything is of oak, and not one square inch of it is free from carving. The figure which surmounts the great candelabra is said to have been carved by Hugo himself.

One half of the room was prepared for the reception of Garibaldi when the Italian patriot was at the height of his troubles. And although he never occupied it, it is still known as Garibaldi's Chamber.

At the very top of the house is Victor Hugo's study. It is a small roof greenhouse. The floor consists of a skylight, giving light to the room below. Here Hugo stood (he never sat to write) at a plain shelf of black walnut and wrote *Les Misérables*, *les Travailleurs de la Mer*, and *l'Homme qui Rit*.

Outside and below lies the small secluded garden, with its trim lawn and those exotic shrubs and trees which flourish so well in the genial climate of the Channel Islands.

Near the study on the top floor is the poet's bedroom. In it stands a narrow couch, like that of a soldier, on which he slept without a pillow. The volumes on the shelves around the room—few in number, for Hugo kept no library—bear the marks of frequent use.

Other rooms which should be mentioned are the Red Drawing-room, the Blue Drawing-room, which opens out into the Conservatory, containing a fine grape-vine, the Dining-room, and the Smoking-room. The last has a Gobelin tapestry upon its ceiling, from which hangs a very ancient Oriental lantern.

The Dining-room has a carved oak ceiling and a chimney-piece filled with Dutch Delft ware. The carved wooden chair in a window recess, guarded by a chain, dates from 1534. Another treasure is a salt cellar, made by a pupil of Michael Angelo. Typical of Hugo are the carved inscriptions, one of which reads: *Life is an exile.*

The Red and Blue Drawing-rooms have much in common. There are tapestries which once belonged to Queen Christina of Sweden, statues which came from the palace of the Doges at Venice, and a fire-screen embroidered by Madame de Pompadour. In the Blue Drawing-room is a large and beautiful mirror, supported by four gilded columns, which formerly adorned the bed of Francis I. On either side of the entrance are cabinets upon which stand Chinese vases of inestimable value.

With the fall of the Empire in 1870, Hugo returned to France. He retained Hauteville House, and although he again visited Guernsey, his days of exile were at an end.

Hauteville House is open to the literary pilgrim, who cannot fail to be impressed by the meticulous knowledge of and real affection felt for Hugo displayed by the curator and guide.

LES BARRIÈRES DE LA VILLE. The six granite stones scattered about the centre of St Peter Port, and known as les Barrières de la Ville or the gates of the town, would probably pass unremarked by either the native of, or the visitor to, the island but for a neatly inscribed brass plaque which crowns the one in the wall, outside the entrance to the General Post Office in Smith Street.

The inscription reads:

"This stone is one of the six stones erected by order of the Royal Court in 1700 to mark the sites of the gates of the town when, in the XIV century, St Peter Port was walled in for defensive purposes."

Each of these barrier stones bears the same inscription, still quite legible, that in Fountain Street being perhaps the clearest. There is some variation in the spelling, *barrière* having sometimes one and sometimes a double R. The Smith Street stone reads as follows:

"Barières de la Ville. Nicholas Careye, James Careye, Conetables, 1700."

The Pollet stone has lost its top, and the word *barrières* is missing.

In 1350, the King, Edward III, ordered a wall to be built round St Peter Port. But, despite the fact that the island had been invaded and the town burnt down three times in 50 years, the order was not obeyed. The cost, it was contended, would be far too heavy.

A year later, Edward III wrote to the Governor, Sir John Maltravers, ordering that:

"our town of St Peter Port, which is a place adapted to such a refuge, should be enclosed with a strong wall".

It is however improbable that this reiterated order was carried out. Traces of the old gates have completely disappeared, and the only evidence of their existence is an occasional and rare reference to them in old contracts.

The evidence for any system of ramparts is even more flimsy. The northern and southern flanks of the valley, at the seaward end of which stood the Town Church, were natural defences. At the southern end stood the Tour Beauregard, on the site of which St Barnabas Church now stands.

At the foot of the Fountain Street end of Rosemary Lane stands one of these *barrières*, and half-way up these steps another flight at right angles leads up to the top of the eminence now known as the Mignot Plateau. It is possible, therefore, that the Fountain Street *barrière*, far from marking a gateway to the town, is in fact an entrance to the Tour Beauregard from the town.

Parts of the walls in these steps may not improbably date back to the time of Edward III. This entrance provided a convenient means of escape to a place where effective resistance could be made to an enemy who had occupied the town. It provided also a useful point of counter-attack. Last, but not least, at its foot was the fountain after which the street was named, providing a useful water supply if, for any reason, that on the Cornet Street side should fail.

From this gate to Tower Hill steps a towering cliff provided natural defence. From the summit, within the Tour, a good view of the marshy valley through which Charrotterie now runs, but then known as Vallée de la Misère, could be obtained.

At the top of these steps is another *barrière*. This must have marked the southern entrance to the Tour. Here now are Cliff Street and Castle Vaudin, with an old flight of steps leading down to the South Esplanade. Parts of these walls are extremely ancient.

The area between these steps and the Town Church which now forms the southern flank of Cornet Street was then a steep cliff, forming a natural defence.

The northern boundary, consisting of steep cliffs, needed no artificial defences. This ran along the back of Market Street, following the heights above what is now called the Commercial Arcade, until it reached the middle of Berthelot Street. Here there may have been another gate, but if a boundary stone stood here, it has long since disappeared.

At the Plaiderie stood another strong point, of which not a vestige remains except its name, la Tour Gand. It must nevertheless have been for the northern end of the town what the Tour Beauregard was for the southern.

The eastern side of the Pollet and of the greater part of High Street needed no artificial defences. They consisted of steep cliffs. If any artificial defences were built, when did they disappear?

In the 17th century, Sir Peter Osborne, that sturdy Royalist, made Fountain Street and parts of the High Street untenable with his guns from Castle Cornet, but he never claimed to have battered down the town ramparts. Again, when the present barriers were set up it is clear from the ordinance that they were intended to replace previous barriers, which had been defaced or lost. Gates and ramparts must have disappeared a long time before.

The ordinance ordering the setting up of the existing *barrières* was passed in 1684. The *barrières* are all dated 1700. Why this long delay of 16 years? The ordinance itself perhaps supplies the answer. Here is a rough translation of it:

"Whereas it has been represented to the Court by the Constables of the Town that the Barriers of the said Town are for the most part defaced and lost, and that it may be necessary that new ones be procured and erected, it is hereby ordained that the said Constables and Douzeniers of the said Town shall betake themselves to the places where the said Barriers stood of old and shall procure and erect new ones, after having made full enquiry as to the places, and shall keep a record of the places where they shall be placed, to be used in case of need."

It seems fairly evident that the constables met with considerable difficulty in discovering the sites of the old *barrières*. And, apart from the fact that most of these have been shifted in quite recent times, though seldom more than a yard or two, we may safely assume that they indicate only approximately the boundaries of mediaeval St Peter Port.

When the Royal Court, at the end of the 17th century, ordered the setting up of the *barrières*, it was inspired by no antiquarian or archaeological sentiments. The decision was made mainly because of the law of inheritance. Under this, the eldest son could not raise his *préciput* (eldership) on the estate of his deceased parents if that estate were situated within the barriers of the town.

This was rational, for the purpose of the *préciput* was the keeping intact of farming property. And farms are not a feature of towns.

The barriers, as fixed by the town constables in 1700, must have remained the legal limits, outside of which alone the *préciput* was leviable, until 1840. During that century and a half vast changes took place. St Peter Port grew in size and prosperity, and the claiming of a *préciput* outside the barriers, but within the new town limits, became a flagrant injustice.

Thus it came about that in 1840 the law of inheritance was amended and new boundaries were fixed for the town. But the old barrier-stones were not removed. The new law regarded the built-up area in and around St Peter Port as the legal barriers of the town. They extended from the Longstore to Havelet, from the sea to the top of Charrotterie, from the middle of Queen's Road to Mount Durand, and, for legal purposes, these have remained the boundaries of the town ever since. Finally, in 1954, the right of Préciput was abolished for the whole island; the stones remain as a reminder of an earlier age.

One other factor, an eminently practical one, also inspired the decision of the Royal Court. In 1683 the States had ordered that no houses within the barriers of the town should be thatched or continue to be covered with thatch. In view of the many disastrous fires which had occurred, this was a very wise decision. But, as it had to be implemented by the constables, it was small wonder that they sought the authority of the Court to define these boundaries, so that there should be no dispute when the removal of thatch was ordered by them.

We may therefore safely assume that the red-tiled roofs of the town date from the year 1700.

The Tour Beauregard was built, as part of the defences of the town, probably in the year 1357. Some of the land attached to it was sold in 1597, during the reign of Queen Elizabeth I. Its usefulness as a fortification must therefore have been considered of little value by the end of the 16th century.

Before the fortress was built, the plateau was probably crowned by a menhir, for old contracts refer to la Roque Graine. Executions for heresy and witchcraft are said to have taken place at the bottom of Tower Hill, where Bordage makes an obtuse bend to the right. This would have been outside the precincts of the tower and the town.

It is not surprising, therefore, that Cerberus, the dog which guards the entrance to the infernal regions, haunts the neighbourhood of the Tour Beauregard. He is known as Tchi-co, and tradition avers

B

that for six weeks before and after Christmas this dog patrols a beat which takes in Cornet Street and Fountain Street—in short, which compasses the old tower.

Strange to relate, Cerberus appears in other parts of the island, most often, but not always, as a dog. A black dog, le Chen Bodu, is said to haunt the Clos du Valle. Another, at the Ville au Roi, is headless. In the neighbourhood of l'Erée, le Varou roams the dunes. Another black dog haunts a portion of the Forest Road.

Other reputed island supernatural phenomena are the Spectre of the Grandes Maisons, of undefined shape, and the beasts, form unspecified, of the Rue de la Bète, St Andrew's, and of the Rue Maze and la Devise de Sausmarez, St Martin's. A small white hare, accompanied by a will-o'-the-wisp (*Feau Belingier*), appears during stormy weather near the boundary fountain in the Hubits, and a spectral goat haunts les Grons, also at St Martin's. The preponderance of spectral dogs is, however, very striking.

At the end of the 18th century Cornet Street was one of the most important thoroughfares of the town. Between its foot and the Town Church was the fish market. Higher up, merchants of divers commodities, printers and bankers, had their establishments.

But from early in the 19th century businesses began to move into the High Street and the Pollet, formerly residential areas, and Cornet Street, frequently anglicised as Horn Street, gradually deteriorated until, in the early years of the 20th century, it became virtually a slum.

Between the two wars much of it, especially on the northern side, was bought and demolished by the States. The result was a considerable widening of the street at its upper end. The lower part of the street suffered badly in Guernsey's one and only German air raid of 1940.

FOUNTAIN STREET, MARKET STREET, AND CLIFTON. Old prints of Fountain Street show that thoroughfare to have been both quaint and picturesque. In the 14th century it was probably no more than half its present length, extending from Rosemary Lane to the Town Church.

There is a dearth of evidence as to the extent of the churchyard, but it is known that Fountain Street reached almost to the south wall of the church, from which it was separated by a narrow passage, the east end of which was probably washed by the tide. As this passage was called la Grille, it is highly probable that it was closed at night by an iron grating.

The disused pump at the Fish Market end of the Vegetable

Market may probably have drawn water from the original fountain from which the street was named. This fountain, and the one in Church Square, opposite the north door of the church, were fed by the streams flowing down the Vallée de la Misère, and were, in consequence, not very deep. It must be observed that until the dawn of the present century the town was amply supplied with public pumps, maintained by the parish constables. Of late years all have been labelled "Unfit for drinking" or "This water must be boiled before drinking". A couple of centuries ago, however, when no alternative supply existed, this water must have been far more seriously contaminated than it is today.

Numerous mills were turned by the streams flowing down the valley. Mill Street was the site of one. Another was the Moulin du Milieu, near the present Market Steps. On the Fountain Street side the stream probably flowed under a bridge of flagstones, called the Pont Archon, near the steps which now lead into the Vegetable Market. It then flowed through the churchyard, where it turned another mill of great antiquity, for it is mentioned as early as the 12th century. In confirming his father's gift of the church of St Peter Port to the Abbey of Marmoutiers, Henry I (Beauclerc) adds, "a certain water-mill in the churchyard of the same church".

The northern flank of Market Street rises slightly less steeply at the eastern than at its western end, as will be apparent by a glance at Constitution and Clifton Steps. This hill, now known as Clifton, was originally called Mont Gibel. This may be a corruption of Gibet, and a gibbet may once have existed here. At the beginning of the 14th century, however, the Courtil du Gibet at St Andrew's, where the apocryphal Bailiff of the Bailiff's Cross is said to have met his doom, was already in existence.

Not until the beginning of the 19th century did buildings begin to climb the face of Mont Gibel. Behind the Assembly Rooms arose the National Schools, which, despite dire prophecies that they would crumble under their own weight and precipitate themselves, together with the debris of the Assembly Rooms, into Market Street, did service in this capacity for nearly 100 years. These buildings, with some minor adaptations, are now used as a concert hall and theatre, and have been renamed the Central Hall. Here island talent in every branch of the arts competes annually in the Eisteddfod.

The old National School, now the Central Hall, must not be confused with la petite école de la Ville, so called to distinguish it from Elizabeth College, la grande école. La petite école dated back to pre-Reformation days. On Easter Day, 1513, a good and pious

25

old couple, Thomas le Marquant and Jannette Thelry, his wife, appeared in the Town Church, before the Bailiff and three *Jurats* (as in the Contract Court today), and formally declared the gift which they had made to St Peter Port of a house and garden on the north side of the chapel of St Julien, that the parish school might be kept in the said house in time to come, bestowing also at the same time two quarters of annual wheat *rente* upon the school-master, who was to repeat to the scholars, and make them repeat, every evening before leaving, an anthem of Our Lady, with a De Profundis and an Ave Maria for the souls of the donors, the souls of all their friends and benefactors, and for all the souls in general for whom God would have us pray.

This school house was rebuilt early in the 19th century, and stood very near where St Julien's Avenue now opens upon Glategny Esplanade. Its lineal descendant is Vauvert School, built early in the present century on the site of Myrtle Lodge.

The stone-and-mortar invasion of Mont Gibel from the High Street end was due to the enterprise of a Jerseyman, le Boutillier, who built the Commercial Arcade, early in the 19th century. This was a stupendous task, involving not only the purchase of a cluster of houses on the High Street—a gigantic financial operation—but also the quarrying away of thousands of tons of gravel and stone, a herculean undertaking with the relatively primitive equipment of those days. The outcome was the disappearance of some of the narrow alleys in the neighbourhood of the church (the steps leading into the Arcade, opposite the north door, may be a relic of one of these, the Rue Tanquerel), the Arcade steps, with their unfinished houses, the financial ruin of le Boutillier, and the abandonment of his design before it was fully completed. The Arcade was intended to have four entrances, "two from the High Street and two from the opposite angles". It was also to be covered with a glass roof.

The Arcade steps and those of Clifton are well worth climbing because of the vistas they reveal not only of the valley which forms the cradle of the town, but also of the Little Russel.

THE TOWN HOSPITAL. A rather delightful glimpse of the Town Hospital can be obtained from the top of Hirzel Street. This is reached by climbing Smith Street and turning to the right by the office of the Lieutenant-Governor. The buildings, plain in them-selves, though architecturally not unpleasing, have the picturesque background of the terraces on the north side of St Julien's Avenue, which at this spot are generously clothed in shrubs and trees. On the right appears a prison-like building: originally a mental home, this has recently been modernised and converted into a home for the destitute.

The main entrance to the Town Hospital is at the base of Hirzel Street, in a narrow lane known as the Rue des Frères, though more commonly as Hospital Lane. This is an ancient track which led from the old friary, which is now Elizabeth College, to the Canichers. From the Canichers access was gained to the sea-front via the Truchot or, by continuing along the Canichers, the coast was reached in the neighbourhood of the Salerie.

The Town Hospital has always been so called, the word hospital being, of course, a survival of pre-Reformation days when the poor were relieved by the religious houses. Officially it has never been called the Workhouse, although it has sometimes been referred to as la Maison de Charité. It has one affectionate nick-name among a certain class. That is the "Pelican".

A glance at the entrance will reveal the reason for this. Over the gate, carved in shallow relief on a stone, is a pelican feeding its young with blood from its own breast. Though bad natural history, this must have ministered to the moral self-esteem of those who were responsible for the erection of the institution.

The Town Hospital was built for the poor of the town. The land was acquired in 1741, and the institution was in use by 1743. Its cost was borne largely by gifts from well-to-do townsmen, and although the upkeep devolved for the most part on the rates, the hospital was, and always has been, well endowed.

The donations board in the Board Room bears the names of many Guernseymen who distinguished themselves in every walk of life, but particularly in commerce. Indeed, that board is an epitome of island commercial history during the 18th and 19th centuries.

The buildings have been extended since 1743. But there is a spaciousness about the quadrangle, with its edging of well-kept flower-beds, which makes the word pauper seem misplaced. There is a seclusion and sense of remoteness, too, reminiscent of an old public school or university college.

In *An Historical Account of Guernsey*, Dicey, writing in 1751, devotes 14 pages to a eulogy of the Town Hospital and its founders. Its success may be gauged by the fact that in this same year some of the country parishes resolved to build a like institution for themselves. Those parishes remaining outside the scheme gradually came in, St Pierre-du-Bois in 1798 and the Forest in 1826.

The Country Hospital, established at the Câtel, followed the lines of the Town Hospital with regard to buildings, but it was generously endowed with land, enabling it to be run as a farm.

27

The third decade of the 20th century saw the end of parochial administration of the Poor Law and the setting up of a central public assistance authority by the States. The Second World War saw the merging of the Town and Country Hospitals into one, the Town Hospital becoming the Public Assistance Institution and the Country Hospital a much-needed Emergency General Hospital for the sick and injured.

This Emergency Hospital has now been superseded by the Princess Elizabeth Hospital at the Vauquiédor, and the old Câtel Institution is now used as a mental home.

It must not be thought, however, that the "annals of the poor" date back only to 1741. As a social problem, poverty began to manifest itself with the decay of feudalism and the beginning of modern times at the end of the 15th and beginning of the 16th centuries. It was then that the open-field system gave way to enclosures, leading to the appearance of hedgerows. But the story of a problem whose solutions, as in England, ranged from church collections to universal social insurance, must be sought in the ordinances of the Royal Court from the time of Queen Elizabeth. This forms one of the most fascinating subjects of local history.

It might almost be supposed that the expression "charity begins at home" was coined when poverty became a problem of which the law was compelled to take cognisance. As far back as the reign of Queen Elizabeth I—in 1537, to give a precise date for this island— the poor and indigent were divided into two categories, local poor and stranger poor. In England the word stranger meant belonging to another part of the country, and this formed the *raison d'être* for the law of settlement. In Guernsey the word had the full implication of foreigner, one who did not belong to the island.

It is curious to find that in the early days of the Elizabethan era there were "foreigners" in Guernsey, foreigners incapable of maintaining themselves and forced to beg for their living. It must be assumed that these were discharged soldiers, or sailors who had forsaken their calling when their ship had touched at Guernsey, and in some cases the dependants of such men.

In any case, as early as 1537 it was ordained that anyone, not having been in Guernsey more than a year and a day, who could not live without begging was to quit the island. Those failing to do so were to be whipped and flogged. It was then the duty of the parish constable to hand them over to the *prévôt*, who would arrange for their deportation. Native poor, however, were permitted to beg, but strictly within the confines of their own parish.

Not until 1566 do we find any reference to the maintenance of the poor as a public charge. Orphans, and those children of parents lacking the means to send them to England "to learn good trades whereby they might in future assist their parents", were to be found good masters in their own parish or, failing this, be sent by the constables to England as apprentices, and this at the expense of the parish.

Meanwhile, poverty was becoming endowed, in a sense, by means of legacies left for this purpose. This necessitated the appointment of trustees to administer these charitable bequests, and in 1577 the Royal Court ordained that deacons of the church (the Presbyterian system then prevailed in Guernsey) should distribute such moneys and present quarterly accounts to the church. It may be that the expression "deserving poor", a still more striking phrase in its local form of "*pauvres honteux*", then became current.

In 1588, the year of the Armada, all previous ordinances relating to the poor were renewed. There is one interesting addition, however. It reads:

"Poor old people, who have neither the means to live or work, are to be subsidised, each in his own parish, from the alms of the church, and is forbidden to beg, unless specially licensed to do so by the Royal Court."

An ordinance of 1592 is an indirect reminder to godparents of their duties. Poor children are to be taken by their nearest relatives or their godparents and put out to service. The ordinance, however, is more an admonition than a command.

In 1597 and 1611 the Royal Court contented itself with a codification of all the ordinances relating to the poor from the dawn of the new religious and social order.

In 1622 begging by children on Midsummer Eve and New Year's Day was strictly forbidden, and in 1625 weddings and funerals were added to the occasions on which this ban was placed. The distribution of largesse at these two feasts and on these occasions was a survival of "Popish" custom, and it was for this reason that the practice was frowned upon.

The Parliamentary Civil War of the 17th century left a terrible legacy of poverty and destitution. The Royal Court was alarmed at its extent, and for the first time treated it as a crime. In the town two officers were appointed to apprehend vagabonds and put them in the stocks. In every parish in the island stocks were set up in the churchyard.

The 18th century had reached its third decade before a parochial poor rate was raised. The rate was an unpopular one, against which

29

appeals were constantly being made. In one way only could the Royal Court deal with these obstructive tactics. It ruled that no appeal against an assessment could be heard until the rate had been paid.

Ten years later saw the building of the Town Hospital and the recognition of poverty as a chronic disease of society. But herding the poor together and making them work also produced its crop of problems. Inmates of the Town Hospital showed a disposition to sell to anyone outside not only the products of their work, but even some of the things with which they were supplied. The Royal Court in 1746, by ordinance, forbade commercial transactions of any kind with inmates of the hospital. There is every reason to believe that the currency used was liquor, for in 1793 the ordinance of 1746 was re-enacted with the addition of a ban on the supply of liquor to any inmate of either the Town or Country Hospital.

There is no record of the existence of a guild of any kind in St Peter Port during mediaeval times. That is undoubtedly why, unlike many old and historic English towns, the island possesses no almshouses. The Victoria Homes, modestly tucked away in Park Lane, behind the mills and factories on the south side of Park Street, provide shelter for some 17 aged people. Their foundation, as their name indicates, does not go back beyond the beginning of the present century.

Apart from the endowments of the Town and Country Hospitals, a few charitable funds exist, none of them of great age, with perhaps one exception. This is the de la Court Fund, founded by John de la Court, a *Jurat* of the Royal Court, in 1588.

This fund has grown tremendously since that date by continuous donations and bequests. A full list of these appears on the walls of the spiral staircase leading up to the Royal Court chamber.

The fund, administered by the Royal Court, was originally used to assist fishermen who had lost boats and tackle in stormy weather, and relief was also granted to shipwrecked sailors.

A similar fund, also administered by the Royal Court and re-corded on its walls, is the Sir William Collings Fund, founded in 1849. It is used

"for the benefit of the necessitous poor natives of this island, or naturalised inhabitants, and also of strangers who shall have resided in the island for seven years, who, through any accident whatever, or from any unseen cause, may need relief."

The Victoria Fund, created to commemorate the Diamond Jubilee of Her Majesty Queen Victoria in 1897, "is applied to relieve all such deserving cases as are not provided for by the de la Court and Sir William Collings Funds."

The Priaulx Charity Fund, a bequest of John Priaulx of Hauteville in 1829, must be devoted to one purpose and none other, otherwise the capital is forfeited to any of the descendants of the testator's brothers. That purpose is to provide surgical appliances for poor men suffering from hernia "who do not belong to any of the hospitals of the island". It is administered jointly by the Royal Court and the Town Constables.

THE NEW TOWN. A few features of interest, hitherto unmentioned, leap into view as the Weigh-bridge is reached from the White Rock. The heights to the west, a plateau of grassy fields less than 150 years ago, is now almost entirely covered with buildings. Prosperous shopkeepers of the late 18th century developed it as a residential area and dubbed it New Town. A residential area it has remained.

Access to it from the heart of the old town—from Market Street and the Commercial Arcade—is by long and steep flights of steps on the flank of Mont Gibel. The narrow, steep, and tortuous road of Vauvert encircles it on the south. From the High Street it is reached by the steep gradients of Smith Street and St James's Street (la Profonde Rue). Indeed, the only good approach is the relatively gentle slope of the Avenue of St Julien, opened as recently as the seventies of last century.

The prison, the Methodist church of St Paul built on the site of what was once the town house of the first Lord de Saumarez and which is now the offices of the States Insurance Authority, and the Anglican church of St James the less, seem to form a barrier between the old town and the new.

On rising ground above St James's stands Elizabeth College. Behind it, to the right, is Upland Road, with the Grange Club on the left. Upland Road runs through what was formerly the cemetery of the mediaeval Friary, which has given place to Elizabeth College. Much of this cemetery has now disappeared. On it was built the old fire-station when that service, now run by the States, was the responsibility of the town parish alone. Another part of the cemetery has been swallowed up by Guernsey's largest cinema, the Odeon.

Upland Road debouches in Candie Road, on one side of which is the Town Cemetery, some of the monuments and mausoleums in which recall Père Lachaise. Here, too, is the entrance to Candie Gardens, with its statues of Queen Victoria and Victor Hugo, its green lawns, its tree-lined avenues, and its monstrous and unsightly glass concert pavilion. The tiny garden in the deep depression at

31

the back is a spot of sheer delight. There are at all times of the year gay flower-beds, and specimens of the flora of the entire world appear to have foregathered. No other garden in the island is so sheltered. Against a southern wall grows a lemon-tree, upon which fruit ripens not every year, but nearly every year.

The fine old house above the Victoria Statue is the Priaulx Library. A legacy to the island, made by the late Osmond Priaulx, it contains not only an unsurpassed reference library, but possesses an enviable collection of very rare books and documents.

No great distance away, opposite the Town Arsenal, is the Victoria Tower. This is a square, castellated tower of red granite, 100 feet high, built on a mound. As a landmark it replaces an ancient windmill. The tower was built in 1848 to commemorate the visit of Queen Victoria in 1846. The well-kept grass borders surrounding the tower are always of a particularly vivid green.

The events of the 19th century are enshrined in this area. Doyle Road, near by, named after the famous and popular Lieutenant-Governor, leads to the Grange. At the top of the Grange is Queen's Road, once la Petite Marche. At its far end is Prince Albert's Road, once la Pierre Percée, leading into Charrotterie. The summit of this steep and winding road is also that of Mont Durand, a residential area at its upper end, a jumble of rather squalid dwellings at its lower.

And all roads end in the misnamed Vallée de la Misère, in the heart of the town, in St Peter Port.

THE TOWN ARSENAL. Across the road from the Victoria Tower stands the Town Arsenal, now the Fire-station, but previously the main depôt for the Guernsey militia.

The history of the Royal Guernsey militia goes back at least 600 years. In 1337, after the beginning of the Hundred Years' War with France, Edward III issued a mandate ordering an "armed array" of all the inhabitants.

This armed array actually went into action on their own soil in 1373. Owen, a banished Welsh prince, invaded the island.

This invasion is renowned in local prose and poetry as *La Descente des Aragousais*. There are three more or less reliable contemporary accounts, as well as a long ballad. A reference to the event also occurs in Holinshed's *Chronicles*.

One spring morning, just before break of day, an invading army, supplied by Charles V of France and led by Owen or Evan of Wales, landed in Vazon Bay. No sooner was this force discovered than an engagement began. But the Guernseymen, of whom there is said to have been 800, were outnumbered, and retreated upon the town. On the plateau upon which Elizabeth College and the streets opposite now stand—le Mont de St Pierre Port—the fight was resumed. This is perhaps why until about a century ago the locality was known as "La Bataille". Half of the defending force and 101 of the invaders were left dead upon the field.

Owen, however, was unable to enter the town, behind the gates of which the Guernseymen retreated. Meanwhile, a force of 80 Englishmen arrived. The Frenchmen thereupon made for the seashore, marched along the beach under the east wall, and attempted to force an entrance into the town somewhere near the church. They were repulsed by the newly arrived English force with heavy losses.

Meanwhile the Governor, Edmund Rose, retired to Castle Cornet, or to the Vale Castle, according to differing accounts, with the remnants of his little army. Owen laid siege to the castle, but, unable to gain any advantage, he soon returned to his ships and sailed away.

This was the third attack made on the island during the reign of Edward III. Between the 14th and 16th centuries Guernsey was from time to time attacked by the French and by bands of pirates, but the local militia-men were always prepared to turn out in defence of their homes.

The oldest existing ordinance relating to the Guernsey militia is dated 1546. It orders all male inhabitants, on their allegiance, to obey their captains. Captains of the various parishes are required to see that the *haquebuttes, ars et trousses* are in good order, *les boulvars* (earthworks) properly constructed, and munitions always ready. Another ordinance of three years later enacts that "the Bailiff should have the survey over all the town parish and should cause bulwarks to be erected wherever required". He was also authorised "to inspect every townsman's *haquebutte*, and to furnish one, with all its appurtenances, to such as had none, fining each defaulter four sols and one denier per day". The same authority was vested in the captains of the country parishes, and they were given the further power of requisitioning horses and vehicles for the transport of cannon and munitions.

Between the years 1625 and 1630, Sir Peter Osborne, the Lieutenant-Governor, issued the following militia orders:

"Orders to be observed by the Captaynes and severall companies: That upon the sighte of any fleete, horses with saddle to be sent to the Towne from each parish.

"That the ordnance in all places throughout the Island be sufficiently mounted and viewed by the Captaynes.

"That there be good draught ropes and tackling for all the ordnance, to remove them upon occasion.

"That there be a sufficient store of drumes, and these serviceable and fitt.

"That all Captaynes and Lieutenants carry partizans, and every Sergeant a halbert.

"That beacons be made ready, and fired upon all occasions of alarme.

"That everyone repayre speedily with his armes to the place of rendezvous upon the alarme being given, and presume not to depart from his cullers without his Captayne's order and leave."

After the Civil War the militia consisted of 13 companies, nine drawn from the country and four from the town. These were formed into one body and commanded by the Lieutenant-Governor.

Early in the 18th century the companies appear to have been embodied into three regiments, each commanded by a colonel.

Before 1755 the coast batteries were manned by men selected from the infantry regiments, but in July of that year two companies of artillery were formed, which later were increased to four. These were troubled times, days of war and rumours of war, and the militia was drilled every Sunday and on fête days and holidays. Sunday parades were abolished in 1798, under pressure from a virile Methodist movement, whose passive resistance could not be overcome by abuse or imprisonment or threats of banishment.

In 1780 the artillery companies were embodied as a regiment of field artillery and a fourth regiment of infantry was formed. During the same year the Royal Court passed an ordinance compelling militia-men to provide themselves with military uniforms. The *douzaines* of the town and country parishes vigorously protested. They pointed out that the Guernsey militia was entirely different from the English militia, for the latter was paid and clothed by Government, and subject to martial law,

" . . . whereas the Militia of this Island are volunteers, being simply a citizen Militia; which receives no pay, recognises no power save the civil power, but who, after the example of their forefathers, are ready to fight against every enemy who may assail their persons or properties."

The ordinance was neither repealed nor enforced, but in 1782 the British Government undertook to supply all necessary clothing and equipment.

At the beginning of the 19th century the militia numbered 3,158 of all ranks, besides 450 boys who were regularly drilled. Apart from the Guernsey Light Dragoons, a troop of mounted orderlies, four field brigades of artillery, and the "battery department" or coast artillery, the force was organised on a regional basis. There was the 1st East (Town) Regiment, which became light infantry in 1833, the 2nd North Regiment, known as "le Regiment Vert", from its green facings, the 3rd South Regiment or "Regiment Bleu", and the 4th West Regiment or "Regiment Noir". All these regiments became light infantry between 1802 and 1804.

Between 1800 and 1820 there were also several independent corps on the establishment of the island militia: the "Fermain Battery Corps", the "Marine Corps", and the "Pioneer Corps". By 1820 these corps had all been disbanded and absorbed into the militia.

For some time after the end of the Napoleonic Wars in 1815 a rifle company was attached to each infantry regiment. In 1830 an aide-de-camp to the sovereign was appointed for the Guernsey militia, and in 1831 the proud title of Royal Guernsey Militia was conferred upon it.

In 1839 militia-men were exempted from active duty in time of peace at the age of 45 and transferred to the reserve.

No further changes took place until 1873, when, at the instance of the War office, the Royal Guernsey Militia was reorganised. The establishment was fixed at one artillery and three infantry regiments and the rifle companies were abolished. An adjutant and permanent staff from the Regular Army were appointed to each regiment, their pay being met by the British Government. The States undertook to provide quarters for the staffs and storage for guns, arms, and clothes in the town and country arsenals.

Twenty-five years later another reorganisation took place. The new militia was organised very much on the lines of the new Territorial Force in England, save that service was compulsory. Every able-bodied man between 17 and 35, except those exempted by law, was liable for service with the colours for five embodied trainings, after which he passed into the first reserve until 45, and then into the second reserve until 60. Recruiting was undertaken by the authorities, who annually drew up lists of all liable to serve. Only a sufficient number of recruits to fill vacancies was taken each year, and men called upon might either volunteer or submit to a ballot. There were always more volunteers than vacancies.

The militia was now embodied during training, and officers and men were subject to the Army Act when embodied and when in

35

uniform. Each unit was trained for 11 days and recruits for 21 days. Training began early in August, recruits being called up first, and lasted till about the middle of October. A special encampment for this training was built at les Beaucamps in the Castel parish. This was soon popularly known as "the huts".

Officers and men were paid while undergoing training. The cost to the States of the new militia was now £4,000 per annum. This included pay and allowances, rations, contingent expenses, and the maintenance of the brigade band.

The new system became very popular and the men were contented. The efficiency of the system and of the men themselves was put to the supreme test between the years 1914 and 1918. The Royal Guernsey Militia emerged from that test with its past unsullied and its glory enhanced.

The outbreak of the First World War led to a complete break with tradition. It saw the formation of a double company, for overseas service, which attracted so many volunteers that the ballot had to be introduced. This double company was attached to the Royal Irish Regiment.

Later, the island, abandoning its charter rights in this respect, adopted conscription on the same lines as the mother country. A service battalion was formed, which was kept up to strength. This battalion distinguished itself and suffered heavy losses at Cambrai.

With the return of peace, conscription was abolished and the militia re-established on its pre-war footing.

The outbreak of the Second World War led to the almost immediate re-enactment by the States of the Conscription Law. This law, unfortunately, had not yet received the royal assent when the island was occupied. Thousands of young Guernseymen, however, who evacuated, voluntarily joined the services.

In the early fifties it was seriously debated whether to reform the militia, but the final decision was against it, largely on the grounds of expense. Today this ancient force only remains as a memory in the minds of the older islanders, helped by the visible reminders in the Militia Museum in Castle Cornet.

THE HARBOUR of St Peter Port, of which all Guernseymen are justly proud, was just built a century ago. It was in the year 1830 that the idea of harbour improvements and extensions was first mooted.

At that date the harbour consisted of two piers, running roughly parallel with one another, both extending more or less in an easterly direction, the southern one from the Town Church and the northern one from the North Pier Steps. The South Pier curved round to the north, and at its extremity was a lighthouse, which first displayed its beams on February 28, 1832. Long before the existence of the lighthouse there was a round house there, probably used as a guard house. Its great age is evident from the fact that an ordinance passed by the Chief Pleas of April 1624 enacted "that the small house at the end of the pier shall be rendered secure at the public expense".

The South Pier is, of course, the present Albert Pier. Its age is doubtful, but from an order of King Edward I, dated March 2, 1275, we learn that:

"Whereas Richard Rose and certain burgesses of Guernsey had represented to the king that certain enemies and rebels of the French king had burnt and destroyed the town, and also broken up a quay which protected St Peter Port against the incursion of the sea, and whereas the said town and quay cannot be repaired without great cost we grant, etc."

The old structure which had been destroyed may have been some kind of mole or breakwater, built of large loose boulders, rather like the miniature breakwater of Divette.

According to the order of King Edward I, the cost of building, or rebuilding, the South Pier, was to be met by a duty of 12 sous *tournois* on all ships, and six sous *tournois* on all boats, arriving in the island. These harbour dues were to be levied for a period of three years. In practice, however, they became fixed and perpetual.

Although the order of Edward I was directed to the Bailiff and the inhabitants of the island, it was executed, in part only, by the Governor, Otho de Grandison. The duties were levied, but were not applied to the building of the pier. This state of affairs prevailed until 1570, when royal commissioners granted permission to the Bailiff and *Jurats* to take and receive on all foreign merchandise brought into the island at any time when war appeared imminent (*en aucun temps suspect de guerre*) a reasonable toll or custom for defraying the expense of erecting and maintaining a pier, repairing the bulwarks, and providing ammunition. To prevent abuse they were ordered to produce annually before the Lieutenant-Governor accounts of their receipts and disbursements. Once again these duties, though raised, were misapplied, until, by an order dated August 25, 1580, the Bailiff and *Jurats* received directions to utilise the money levied in this way, together with other contributions which they were allowed to raise, "by the consent of the

37

generality", upon the richer sort of inhabitants, for the building of the harbour.

From that time the work continued with little interruption until the South Pier was completed. Nevertheless, there must still have been misapplication of the funds, for an Order in Council of 1660 insists that the Court should make proper application of the duties. The construction of the North Pier was ordered by the Michaelmas Chief Pleas of 1684, but the work was not actually begun until the latter end of the reign of Queen Anne, probably about 1703.

The quays were built from 1775 to 1779. The arch over Cow Lane (Rue des Vaches), which has long disappeared, was built in 1783. The tide then ran up this quaint alley. Here cattle for slaughter were landed, hence the name Cow Lane.

Before the quays were built the sea not only ran up to the houses, but also between them, through the lanes and steps leading to the High Street.

A charge was levied on persons whose houses bordered the quays to meet the expense of their construction, and seven who refused to pay their proportion of the cost were brought to reason by being prohibited to have any access to the quays by doors leading from their dwellings.

The entrance of the old harbour, like that of the new today, faced east. The gales most commonly feared came from the south-east. Well outside the old harbour, completely surrounded by the sea at high water, was Castle Cornet, a guardian of no mean strength in those days. Between the Castle and the harbour lay the roadstead. In it were two dangerous rocks, la Vermière and the White Rock, and in 1784, when the war with France made Guernsey an important military and naval base, the States authorised the demolition of these rocks, provided no greater sum than £10 was spent for this purpose. La Vermière may have been destroyed. It has at least been forgotten. The complete destruction of the White Rock was achieved only as part of the work of building the new harbour. Its memory, however, has lingered to this day and bids fair to linger well into the future.

Beyond the North Pier a rough causeway near the present Weighbridge led to Glategny, and where St Julien's Avenue now is were shipbuilding yards. Beyond the South Pier, at Havelet and les Terres, the houses came down to the beach, and here, too, were more shipbuilding yards.

"In place of a miserable harbour, containing an area of about four English acres, we have now one of the best harbours in the

"La Gran'mere du Chimquiere" outside St Martin's Church

The statue menhir in Castel churchyard

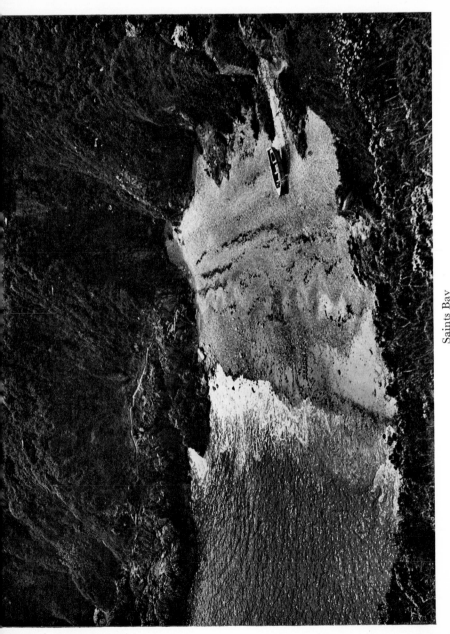

Saints Bay

Moulin Huet Bay, from the Peastacks on Jerbourg Point

Petit Bot Bay

Channel, enclosing a space of eighty acres, with deep water berthage, we have wide esplanades, forming a good harbour frontage, we have healthy and accessible marine promenades, and we have the sewerage of the town conveyed far seaward into deep water."

This is what Miss Henrietta Tupper said in 1876 about the Town Harbour, when she issued a revised edition of her father's *History of Guernsey*, first published in 1854, when he was in his 59th year.

The Old Harbour, as it existed in the first decade of the 19th century, can certainly be described as "miserable". The quay was narrow, rough, and cobbled. The two arms, respectively known as the North and South Piers, were of lower level than they are today and constructed of huge boulders and stones fitted roughly together. All the streams and drains of the town entered into the basin thus formed, and at low tide, especially during hot weather, the stench that arose rendered the houses in the High Street almost uninhabitable.

The beach, or *galet*, from the South Pier to Havelet, known as the Galet Heaume, and that from the North Pier to the bottom of what is now St Julien's Avenue, were little more than dumping-places for all sorts of rubbish.

There was, in fact, some kind of controlled tipping even in those days. Upright granite pillars were erected some distance down the beach, approximately at the half-tide mark, and it was enacted that no rubbish be deposited above the line of these stones. Some of these pillars are still to be seen in Bellegrève Bay.

The first move for a new harbour was made in 1830, when 187 merchants, shipowners, and other business men of the town sent a petition to the then Bailiff, Daniel de Lisle Brock. The petition was drawn up in general terms. All that was asked for was some improvement in the harbour. The efforts of these men were, however, fruitless, and it was not until 1851 that a definite decision was taken by the States.

No decision of the States has ever been greeted with such a wave of popular enthusiasm. The *Comet*, a local English-language newspaper then in being, said:

"The bells of the parish church were set ringing by order of the municipal authorities, and throughout the remainder of the day continued to peal out the welcome tidings. Flags were hoisted on board the ships in port, and most of the principal establishments, with several private buildings, were similarly arrayed in honour of the event. Joy beamed in every countenance, and the exulting populace congratulated each other on the triumph which had terminated a struggle of twenty years duration."

39

All the fences, however, had not yet been taken. There were contracts to be drawn up and signed. Then the original contractors found themselves unable to fulfil their obligations, and the contract was re-assigned to Messrs le Gros and de la Mare. At last, on August 24, 1853, the foundation stone of the harbour was laid by the Bailiff, in the presence of the States.

This ceremony, one of much pomp and rejoicing, was judged of sufficient importance to be placed on permanent record by an artist. Not only did he depict the scene in general, but scores of the participants were easily recognisable in his picture, for he went to the trouble of painting separate portraits of each. Prints of this historic work of art are fairly common in Guernsey homes, and one example, with a key, is to be found in the Guille-Allès Library.

The foundation stone was laid where the Castle breakwater joins the mainland, near the slipway (*dévaloir*) into Havelet Bay, behind the States Abattoir.

The temporary landing-place was first used on October 11, 1858, and for the first time passengers from England were able to walk ashore over a gangway instead of being landed in open boats, a method as uncomfortable and hazardous as it was slow and vexatious. At the same time the new Castle breakwater was beginning to emerge above the waves. Its growth was slow, as the foundation could be laid only when the dead low water of spring tides left the passage uncovered. By the following March, however, the foundation was complete throughout the whole length, and work on the upper part could proceed rapidly.

In April of 1859 the Bailiff, Sir Stafford Carey, reported to the States that during the past seven years the total revenue from the harbour had been £40,000. Expenditure on the harbour had been £104,000. Of £80,000 borrowed, £74,782 had so far been applied to harbour works. The States, by a large majority, thereupon voted £1,000 to complete the south-east corner of the old harbour. They further authorised the raising of a loan of £2,000 to complete the works already in progress. A few weeks later the wall connecting Castle Cornet with the mainland was finished.

On October 25, 1859, a terrible north-easterly gale swept the island. At Portland, Holyhead, and other places it caused appalling damage. In Guernsey the harbour works suffered not at all. Vessels in the old harbour lay in perfect security in the shelter now afforded by the new south arm. In the teeth of the gale the Weymouth packet ran alongside the new temporary landing-stage and disembarked her passengers with ease and safety.

It is an ill wind that blows no one any good, and the gale served

40

to give the builders of the new harbour confidence in their work. Nevertheless there were some who shook their heads and prophesied gloomily that no such good fortune would attend a gale from the south-east. A memorable tempest from that quarter—that of October 12, 1836—had been most disastrous. The sea was now curling round Castle Cornet and causing much motion in the pool and the intended wet dock. In one direction alone lay safety. The breakwater must be extended to the Tremies.

The final word lay with the States and, on June 1, 1860, that body voted moneys for building the Castle breakwater, the promenade at the Terres, the "Massif" on St Julien's rock, the construction of the wall north-east of the Castle emplacement as far as low-water mark, together with the preparation of materials for a future landing-place and the reconstruction of the old south pier-head.

In January 1862, it was decided that before a permanent southern landing-place could be constructed, the old harbour would have to be protected from the north. In May of that year the States authorised the construction of St Julien's pier as far as the extremity of the White Rock.

Throughout the summer and autumn of 1862 work proceeded energetically. A fine promenade was laid out from the bottom of Havelet to just below Clarence Battery. In two places the road was carried through tunnels. One, situated near the public bathing-place, later fell in, and now exists only as a cutting. The material excavated was used as filling for both the Castle and the St Julien's breakwaters.

The Horse-shoe bathing-place was a child of the Harbour Committee. Built between two ridges of rocks, up and down the slopes of which the water had full play, it was an ideal site both for swimmers and for would-be swimmers. The Committee also envisaged a picturesque and pleasant walk, running at the base of the cliffs, through a plantation of trees, shrubs, and flowers, revealing at frequent intervals a seascape of unparalleled beauty, with the Castle in the foreground, Herm and Jethou beyond and, miles away, across a vast stretch of blue ocean, the outline of Alderney.

Such was the dream of the Committee. Its realisation was not disappointing, for in pre-war days the Vallette Gardens compared not unfavourably with the Invalids' Walk at Bournemouth. The German occupation left many jagged scars on this beauty spot. But time, Nature, and human toil have already done much to efface these.

The second tunnel still exists. It has been tidied up and now houses an Aquarium, an enterprising private venture.

41

In 1864 the Southampton packets began landing and embarking their passengers at the White Rock landing-stage at all states of the tide. In 1867 the lighthouse on the Castle breakwater, of dressed local granite, shone for the first time.

In the following years the States refused to proceed with the plan for the building of a floating dock, and the unfinished wall to the north-west of the Castle remains to this day as a monument to those refusals.

In 1885, the Guernsey Cycling Club, a working-men's organisation which had until then confined its activities to club rides in the country, developed an ambition to add racing to these. Looking round for a suitable track, their glance fell upon the neglected and uneven area of the Castle emplacement.

The Harbour Committee lent a benevolent ear to these knights on wheels. The Castle emplacement was placed at their disposal, provided no expense fell upon the Committee. Cycling Club funds were in inverse ratio to enthusiasm. For weeks a gang of members used their modest leisure hours in levelling and tidying the area destined for their track, and the first local cycle sports were held, with official support and patronage.

One year later, however, a letter appeared in a *Billet d'État* which was to end for ever this laudable effort of the working man. It was written by the Bailiff, Sir Edgar MacCulloch whose literary eloquence was irresistible. The States voted the £200. The model yacht pond was built, and the Castle emplacement became the Mecca of model-yacht enthusiasts, old and young.

In 1889 a small wharf was constructed to the west of the three main berths for the benefit of local shipping, and the *Courier* made use of this for many years.

During the same year the entrance to the White Rock Pier, which was rather narrow, was widened by straightening out the wall of the Careening Hard. Two years later, in 1891, the ugly wooden hut which had done duty as a weigh-bridge since 1861 was replaced by a neat little structure in granite, adorned with a clock-tower.

In 1899 the construction of the wharf on the western or town side of St Julien's emplacement was undertaken. As this was, and is, used by ships trading between the island and London, it became known as the London berth.

As a passenger station, apart from any other consideration, the White Rock needed a good water supply. As there were no public pumps there, a reservoir had been constructed at the bottom of Havelot, and water conveyed in pipes to the White Rock. In 1889 all these pipes were relaid.

The upper walk of the White Rock, from the spur to the angle by the slipway, was emptied in 1889. This not only took a great deal of weight off the outer walls, but also provided storage for goods, for coal used in the furnaces of the steam cranes, and for harbour equipment.

The year 1891 saw the landing at the end of the Albert Pier, once used as a wharf by the packets, completely rehabilitated. No. 1 landing at the White Rock was provided with offices, a waiting-room, and a restaurant, at a cost of £2,000.

At the Terres, now becoming a favourite walk, a railing was erected in the upper walk, as the outcome of a serious accident, from the bottom of Havelet to a spot where the first tunnel, which had fallen in, had been. Here a landslide from the cliffs above is visible, and the place was known as the Creux de la Morte Femme, or Dead Woman's Hole. The tale that a woman was buried by the avalanche of earth may therefore well be true.

During this same year 1891 the wall was built along Vallette Bay as far as Clarence Battery.

Between 1893 and 1897, the year of the Diamond Jubilee, the trade of the island grew by leaps and bounds. The growing industry, just attaining its adolescence, was using comparatively vast quantities of coal, timber, glass, cement, bricks, and flower-pots. The importation of these capital goods led to a congestion of shipping in the old harbour.

On June 21, 1893, the States resolved to lengthen the north pier in an easterly direction by 220 feet on the southern or old harbour side and by 160 feet on the outer or Careening Hard side.

This improvement did not, however, prove adequate to solve the problem of the congestion of shipping in the harbour, and in the middle of 1895 the States dredged the Albert Dock area. Henceforth, timber ships—and a week seldom passed when one was not to be seen in the harbour—unloaded their then commonplace cargoes on that quay which is now the island's main bus-stand.

Meanwhile the ladies' bathing-place at la Vallette was reconditioned at a cost of £900, at the instance of the Town *douzaine*. This body, however, undertook to reimburse the States, to the extent of half the cost, plus three per cent, from the revenue of the pool.

The year 1896 also saw the lengthening, by 60 feet, of No. 1 landing at the White Rock.

The only subsequent major addition to the harbour is the New Jetty, which was completed in 1927.

As a piece of engineering, it bears no relation to the existing

43

harbour. It is a vast platform of steel and concrete, built almost parallel to the eastern face of the St Julien's emplacement. It extends far out into the Pool, the roadstead of pre-harbour days.

Immediately preceding, and during the German Occupation, the Harbour was the setting for dramatic events. The decision to demilitarise the Channel Islands was made on June 18, and the following ten days were days of nightmare for Guernsey.

The first indication of this impending tragedy was the departure of all service personnel for England and the shipment of all arms and munitions of war. This was followed almost immediately by the evacuation of school-children. The planning of this was most praiseworthy. There were, of course, inevitable hitches and delays, but by June 21 more than 5,000 children, accompanied by their teachers and a goodly number of mothers, had been transported to England.

Free passages were then offered to men of military age, and some 800 took advantage of this offer. Others, who had registered, on instructions, with the parish constables, as willing evacuees, were promised passages to England and were told that ships would be available.

It was impossible to issue precise information as to when the evacuation of the general public would begin, and this led to scenes which can only be described as panic. Crowds waited day and night in the neighbourhood of the Weigh-bridge from the morning of June 18. A barrier had been erected here across the pier, and they were denied passage through it.

The panic reached its peak, and began to die down as soon as the children had gone and ships became available for general evacuation. The White Rock then witnessed strange scenes. Very little luggage was allowed, and many left without money. People who arrived at the Jetty in their own cars either abandoned these or sold them at ridiculous prices. Many perambulators were left behind. It was a case of *sauve qui peut*.

Out of the population of 43,000, 23,000 left the islands. The effect of this on Guernsey's economy can well be imagined!

Yet during the week following the general evacuation the normal service of cargo-boats was resumed, and the growers, trying perhaps to recoup their losses during the week of interruption, shipped 300,000 baskets of tomatoes to England.

Indeed, this feverish export of produce was still in progress when disaster came. It was on Friday, June 28, that a concentrated air attack was made on the island. The mail-packet and two cargo-boats were lying in the harbour, and a double queue of produce lorries extended from the jetty to the Weigh-bridge. It was a fine summer evening and, apart from dockers and others whose business kept them in the neighbourhood of the ships, a considerable crowd thronged the upper walk of the White Rock.

Compared with the raids, suffered by England, Germany, and the Occupied Countries during the next four years, this appears relatively unimportant. The lorries, perhaps identified by the raiders as a military convoy, suffered most, and the casualties among the drivers were heavy. Apart from this, the material damage to the harbour was small. The sheds at the Cambridge berth were gutted.

The mail packet, the *Isle of Sark*, kept up a steady fire from her one anti-aircraft gun throughout the raid. She escaped damage, as did also the two cargo-boats. The tide was, fortunately, low at the time, and many people took shelter from the machine-gun bullets beneath the top deck of the jetty.

Twenty-eight people were killed outright and 33 seriously injured. A granite tablet let into the wall of the upper walk records the names of the killed.

This was the first and only enemy raid on the island. The occupation began two days later, on Sunday, June 30.

In 1944, after the Allied landings in Normandy, Guernsey was virtually isolated. There had been dearth before. Now there was famine.

The Christmas of that year must have seemed a hollow mockery. For weeks there had been rumours of help through the international Red Cross organisation, and day after day anxious glances had been cast southwards—not towards the Little Russel, for that passage was mined—in the hope of seeing the expected ship.

Then, on December 27, a ship was seen approaching the island. She cast anchor outside the harbour, and those who had defied German orders to surrender field-glasses and telescopes could discern a large Red Cross painted on her flanks.

It was the *Vega*, and never did any ship receive such a welcome as she. Had the approaches to the harbour not been closely guarded, the inhabitants would have thronged the White Rock to greet her. As it was, she was watched with joy and eagerness from every permissible point of vantage. To the inhabitants her cargo spelt life.

Altogether, the *Vega* paid four visits to Guernsey. Her second visit was on February 6, 1945, and her third exactly a calendar month later. When she paid her last visit, on April 5, it was obvious to all that the end of the war was in sight.

45

The *Vega* meant life. The *Bulldog*, a destroyer which stood off the south of the island on May 8, meant liberty. The terms of surrender were handed to a German officer on that day, but as he had no power to sign, and also as he stated that the capitulation of Germany did not officially take effect until one minute after midnight, the presence of the *Bulldog* in territorial waters might be regarded as a hostile act. The commander of the Liberation force therefore agreed to withdraw temporarily.

Very early the next day the surrender of Guernsey by the Germans was signed on the quarter-deck of H.M.S. *Bulldog*.

Never was there such an anti-climax. "Later in the morning," says Ralph Durand, in his *Guernsey under German Rule*,

"the Island, which the Germans had made one of the most impregnable fortresses in the world, which still held a garrison of thousands of soldiers and had a reserve of 16,000 tons of ammunition, was occupied by an advance party of one British officer and 25 men."

Later in the day another force of 200 men arrived and disembarked at the new jetty, and by May 12, the Liberation force numbered 3,000.

THE CHURCH. Ecclesia Sancti Petri de Portu, familiarly known as the Town Church, has the undisputed reputation of being the finest ecclesiastical building in the Channel Islands.

Until considerably less than a century ago it was hemmed in, and its architectural beauties concealed, by narrow streets and squalid houses. The rebuilding of Fountain Street, the erection of the Market Halls, and the laying out of Market Hill, exposed the west façade to view. Other disfiguring and crowded buildings on the south side in Church Hill and the east side facing the sea did not disappear until the first decade of the present century.

The date of consecration of the church of St Peter Port is often given as 1312. This is on the authority of a document known as *La Dédicace des Eglises*, which gives a date of consecration for every pre-Reformation parish church in the Island. *La Dédicace des Eglises* is a very obvious forgery. Apart from anything else, its description of consecration ceremonies are distinctly post-Reformation and out of keeping with mediaeval ritual.

There is little doubt that the first Town Church was made of wood, and that it was from this modest structure that the present building grew. The earliest authentic document in which the church is mentioned is a deed dated 1048, in which William the

Conqueror, then Duke of Normandy, gave it to the Abbot of Marmoutier. Previously, Duke Robert had given St Andrew, St Martin, St Mary of Torteval, St Sampson, and Holy Trinity of the Forest to the Abbey of Mont St Michel. This proves that all these churches were already established at that period. This bequest was subsequently confirmed by King Henry I.

The next documentary reference to the church is the most interesting one.

For 280 years after the loss of Normandy by King John the island experienced successive attacks from the French. These were repelled again and again, but Guernsey did not escape unscathed, and on several occasions the island was occupied. In 1483 traders and other inhabitants of the island complained to Pope Sixtus IV of being molested by pirates and others. There had already developed a mutual arrangement by which, on payment of certain sums, the commanders of both forces could grant safe-conducts to enemy partisans. The protest to the Pope, however, suggests that this had become, in modern parlance, a racket.

Pope Sixtus IV acceded to the petition presented him and issued a Bull forbidding anyone to molest anyone else, either during peace or war, in the Channel Islands, their harbours and the surrounding seas, "as far as the sight of man goes or the eye of man reaches", under pain of excommunication. This valuable declaration of neutrality was ordered to be posted on the cathedrals of Canterbury, London, Salisbury, Nantes, St Pol de Leon, Treguier, and the church of St Peter Port.

The Greffe still treasures a copy of a letter of Charles VIII, King of France, under the seal of the Bailiwick, authorising the publication of this Bull of Sixtus IV, and similar letters of Francis, Duke of Britanny, Guy, Count of Laval, and Louis de Bourbon, Admiral of France.

It is interesting to note here, too, that this valuable recognition of insular neutrality was incorporated in the island's charters. It still appears in that of Queen Elizabeth, long after Papal supremacy had been repudiated.

The privilege did not lapse until the reign of William III, when privateering became a popular and lucrative calling in the island.

A document found in the 19th century, Le Livre Noir de Coutances, states that the Abbot of Marmoutier was entitled to four-fifths of the tithe of the church, the rector receiving the remaining one-fifth and the fees for masses, funerals, and so on. The income of the rector was then 80 livres *tournois*, the abbot receiving 32 livres *tournois*.

47

Records of the earlier endowments are lost. The documents now existing in the Greffe date from 1429. Up to the time of the Reformation constant additions were being made, principally in the form of *rentes*. These were vested in the hands of the churchwardens for the maintenance of divine worship and the repairs of the church. The fund so accumulated was called the *trésor*, a name which exists to this day. In the year 1512 there were no fewer than 116 small *rentes* due by different persons to the church, while between 1492 and 1512 40 new bequests were made. Many of these, being designated superstitious by the Crown, were forfeited at the Reformation and appropriated by the Governor.

Of approximate dates, only a few can be given. The present chancel was built in the 12th century, the portion east of this in the latter part of the 13th century, the long south chapel in 1462, probably about the time when the custom of having sermons preached in church became common.

The spire was restored in 1721, the bells recast and rehung in 1736, and the clock erected in 1781.

The present interior arrangement of the church is as recent as 1886.

In that year, the restoration, during the rectorship of the Rev. C. E. Lee, admitted not only sunshine into that venerable building, but light also into the dark places of its history.

Before that date it was filled with huge pews facing in every direction. One of them, a three-decker, raised its form at the entrance of the south transept, thus giving the casual visitor the very pardonable impression that no such transept existed.

A whole congregation might easily have been concealed in these pews, invisible to the eye of a stranger. That stranger, too, might not enter any of these pews, for they were not "free".

The church also reeked with damp and with the foul odours of decaying oak, leaky gas-pipes, and, it must be admitted, the slowly dissolving relics of humanity.

The restoration did much to undermine the authority of existing guides and guide-books. For example, the much-vaunted cupola of the pulpit and its long-admired crockets of oak were discovered to be nothing but plaster-of-Paris. Its inlaid woods, too, were but a gigantic fraud of painted deal and canvas.

Beginning at the west door—that facing the Market Halls—the fine 15th century linen pattern on its outside panels should be noted.

Within, a broad flight of stone steps leads down to the floor of the nave. There is a handsome rail of oak, and painted standards of wrought iron on either side. Far ahead is the altar, with nothing to impede the view of the eastern window above it.

The rough flagstones, often covered with pools of water, have been replaced by a floor of oak blocks laid in herring-bone pattern all over the church. These blocks are laid on a foundation of concrete, effectually sealing the tombs of the thousands who have been buried in the church.

In the nave many pillars were hidden under thick layers of plaster. Some of these, constituting the oldest part of the building, were found to be of Guernsey granite, the only local granite in the church. The Caen stone, here and there, is perhaps a relic of the church once known to the followers of Duke William before the Conquest.

The arches of local stone, however, are probably 13th century, and may have been placed there in the reign of Henry III.

These early arches, with their imposts 2 feet from the ground, are the most peculiar feature of the church.

In the 13th century the church probably consisted of a nave and two aisles of equal length. The tower and new chancel were built in the 14th century. Two bays of the nave were left, and the ashlar of the tower was made to meet the old rubble-work on the west side of the second pair of arches. It must be noted, however, that the stones at the top of the western arch are new.

When the staircase was built to reach the gallery in this aisle, the designer cut away the apex of this arch to give headway to his stair. A few more new stones will also be found in the nave, in the archway near the tower. These show where the beams lay which supported the organ loft before 1895.

In the south aisle is an old blocked-up doorway. Here was once the only entrance to the staircase which leads to the roof and the tower.

In the south transept, near the corner of the wall which meets the south wall of the nave, was a pulpit, the base of which stretched across diagonally quite half-way to the south-east of the great piers of the tower. Between one pier and the first of the light flamboyant columns were the pews reserved for the governor and the Royal Court. The latter had a long table or desk drawn down the middle. Behind this pew was that of the *douzaine*.

It has been said that the church is not cruciform but hammer-shaped. The south transept was added in 1466. The one bay of the north transept was rebuilt at the same time. That these extensions are not of equal length is due to the fact that the churchyard lay to the south, while to the north the High Street ran almost to the north wall.

Until 1886 the bases of columns were hidden by pews. In some

49

places mouldings were mutilated to suit the convenience of 19th century carpentry. In the Crypte des Gros Piliers of the Abbey Church of Mont St Michel the mouldings at the base of the columns and those of the arches supporting Guillaume d'Estouteville's splendid choir are the same as those of the Town Church and, as they are of contemporary date, may well have been built by the same architect.

Behind the plaster at the right-hand side of the old pulpit is a doorway opening into the little turret staircase. The purpose of this is unknown. It has been conjectured that there was a pulpit there, but the height is too great, and the newelled stair would have made an awkward entrance to the pulpit. Perhaps there was a minstrels' gallery, as at Exeter, but if so no tradition of it remains. The arch of the doorway is like that at the bottom of the staircase, and it may be that it was a means by which the ringer or others in the tower were able to see what was going on inside the church, and be thus enabled to toll the bell at the elevation of the Host. This, however, is pure theory.

The great south window was lengthened long before the 1886 renovation, and its sill, which was formerly as high as that of the de Lisle window close by, was lowered to give light under the then-existent gallery, which darkened all this side of the church.

At the end of the lean-to aisle adjoining, an aumbry was discovered, its piscina being a little way along the east wall of this aisle. Anyone standing by the aumbry and looking up can see a label on the wall plate with the words:

L'an MCCCCLXVI (1466) fut faicte.

The present roof of the south chancel aisle breaks into the tip of the graceful arches, sadly spoiling their effect. Nevertheless, one of the loveliest views of the church is obtainable from this spot. If the north door be faced, a glimpse is caught in turn of all the different arcades which confer so much variety upon the building. On the right is a piscina, and beneath the window there formerly stood an altar, in front of which were tombs of worthies long forgotten.

In the south aisle of the choir another piscina will be found against the east wall. The north aisle houses the organ, which conceals much that is interesting. This includes two windows, the handsomest piscina in the church, a stone bracket, and what may have been an older piscina, or possibly, a cresset stands against the eastern pillar.

Here once stood the font, and a doorway pierced the east wall. Here was also the *consistoire*, and a gallery above, overlooking the chancel, was named after the de Sausmarez. This aisle is the aisle of tombs, for in 1825 the monumental slabs were gathered here. Then in recent years part of it was adapted as a Lady Chapel, in memory of Sir Isaac Brock, a great Guernseyman whose victory and death on the Queenston Heights near Niagara in 1812 saved Canada from annexation by the United States.

The clear space under the tower gives a remarkable effect. The dimensions of the church can be clearly seen. The lengths from north to south and from east to west are identical—91 feet—so that if the transept could be pushed a little northward, the church would be a perfect Greek cross, with arms of equal length.

The windows at the end of both aisles have obviously been lengthened. When their sills were as high as those of the windows over the west door, there was a short buttress on the north and a little niche on the south.

The choir and its aisles, as well as the transepts, had waggon-roofs of wood. The nave and its aisle are vaulted with stone. The dark stain on the north side shows where the stone roof was broken into when the porch and the chamber overhead were built.

The font, gift of the widow and children of Havilland Carey, is modern (1886), and was the third to be placed in the church in the 19th century alone. The Puritans of the 16th and 17th centuries waged ruthless war against the ancient fonts in Guernsey churches. A fragment of a 15th century font still remains in the Town Church. It is the octagonal shaft which supported the bowl, and is of perpendicular style.

The pulpit is the gift of Major and Mrs Charles le Mesurier Carey, in memory of Henry Tupper of the Côtils. Its principal material is Caen stone. The base supports seven columns, the central one being an octagonal shaft of polished marble. The six smaller ones are of fine grey Purbeck. The steps are of Portland stone, and the interior is lined with oak panelling.

The panels of the pulpit represent:

1 The Good Shepherd. (*Pasce oves meas.*)

2 St Peter, holding the keys in his right hand and a model of the church in his left.

3 St Martin of Tours. This saint and town of which he is patron are closely associated with Guernsey. In Alderney there was probably a chapel at one time bearing his name.

4 St Sampson of Dol. He has a bearded face and delicate features.

5 St Magloire.

It should be noted that the pavement of the choir is different from that of the nave. In most churches of any size the choir is raised above the level of the nave. In this church this is not the case, even the sanctuary being only one step higher. To interfere with the original levels would have destroyed the proportions of the arcades, hence the difference in floor patterns.

The chancel of the church is divided, like the nave, into two bays by a fine pillar on either side. The arches are well-shaped, and surmounted by walls of dressed stone. These arches are pointed and have keystones at their apex, a peculiarly French feature. In 1825 the walls were plastered over. The capitals and bases of the pillars had been cut through in earlier times to admit the ends of screens which formerly enclosed the chancel. The walnut screens on either side of the sanctuary were given some years ago by the heirs of the late John Allaire.

The church of St Peter Port can lay some claim to be a cathedral, for, from time immemorial, the Dean has been inducted with the possession of a stall in the church, even when he was incumbent of another parish.

The Ecclesiastical Court of this island was formerly held in the Town Church, and chairs for the dean and rectors existed within living memory.

The people of Guernsey are very proud of the church of St Peter Port, and well they may be. Of it Ansted says:

"It is far superior in design and execution, as well as in historical interest, to any old building within the compass of the Channel Islands, and might well bear comparison with many in England or the Low Countries."

In 1914 the last of the old houses built against the church, on the southern and eastern sides, were pulled down. Not only did this completely open out the church on every side, but the approach to the harbour from Fountain Street was much improved.

Except for the destruction of some very fine, but not ancient, glass, the church suffered little during the Second World War. Thanks to the generosity of the public, this damage has already been made good.

The plane referred to in the following extract from Ralph Durand's book, *Guernsey under German Rule*, was American. He says:

"On June 19th (1944) early in the morning, a single plane dropped an exceptionally heavy bomb in the Old Harbour. . . .

The Town Church was so badly damaged that it could not be used for divine service until the following March."

Of the same incident, Mrs Cortvriend in *Isolated Island* says:

"Nearly all the windows (of the town), including those of the Town Church . . . were blown out by the concussion . . . Very little structural damage was done."

THE CONSTABLES' OFFICE. Walking under the old arch from the High Street into Lefebure Street, one sees on the right the Constables' Office. This fine 18th century building was formerly the Town House of the Le Marchant family, built on land which had come into the possession of that family in the late 14th or early 15th century; its garden sloped back up the hill to the site of the Royal Court House. In 1899 the house was bought by the constables of St Peter Port as their permanent office and Mansion House for £3,500, a very proper acquisition as before that date the constables had to transact the clerical part of their business in their own homes.

The parochial administration of the Parishes of the Channel Islands is unique, dating back many centuries; very probably there was some form of it extant even before the times of the Dukes of Normandy. In Guernsey there are small variations between the administration of the Town Parish and the nine country parishes, but the general organisation is the same.

The senior executive officer of the parish is the constable, *le connétable*, assisted by the second constable, who learns his duties in the first year of office. The first reference to constable in official records occurs in 1570, when the Royal Court insisted that they must see that the Court Ordinances were carried out; but their existence dates back to the Middle Ages and it is known that they, with the Bailiff, *Jurats*, and rectors, formed the embryo States of that time.

In 1581 they were authorised to search for stolen property in suspected premises. They were to do this, however, only in company of two men of means.

These police functions were further strengthened in 1661. This date marks the end of the Parliamentary civil wars, which, like all wars, was followed by a wave of crime. Thefts of sheep, chickens, and other things occurred daily. Victims of such depredations were recommended by the Royal Court to apply to their local constables, who were fully authorised to make domiciliary searches as in 1581.

Whatever the prestige associated with the constableship, the office was always assumed with reluctance. Capable constables were often kept in office for an inordinately long period. In 1778 a *requête* from all the parishes was presented to the Royal Court praying for a legal limit to the period of office. The Court was sympathetic. Although the term of office was not to exceed three years, it need not be more than one year. After one year a new election was permissible on the demand of a meeting of the *chefs de famille*. That decision remains to this day.

It was in 1801 that one constable from each parish was expected to attend the Court of Chief Pleas. This was felt to be necessary in the interests of public welfare and to facilitate the promulgation and execution of laws and ordinances. This custom still persists. Defaulting constables are usually admonished, but they may be fined £10 *tournois*. Although liable to remain until the end of the session, they are nowadays usually excused as soon as they have made their reports.

An Order in Council, dated 1846, refers to the constableship as "a laborious and responsible office . . . compulsory upon all qualified persons".

That is perhaps why the Reform (Guernsey) Law, 1948, while abolishing the property and sex qualification, as with all other public offices, still makes the acceptance of office obligatory on anyone duly nominated, seconded, and elected as parish constable. The Order of 1846 also makes mention of the duties of that office. They were fourfold; to preside over meetings of the *douzaine*, to keep the parish books, to act as parish treasurer and to have entire charge of the police.

The end of the First World War saw the establishment of an island police force under the control of a committee of the States. This removed a most laborious burden from the shoulders of the constables, but their other particular duties remain, along with the generally accepted obligation to act as a sort of parish Ombudsman.

Constables collect the parochial rate, after the total amount for the year has been sanctioned by a summoned meeting of ratepayers and sanctioned also by the Royal Court on the application of the constables. The latter part of this procedure is known as applying for the *remède*. Any and every ratepayer is entitled to appear before the Royal Court when this application is made and raise an objection, despite the sanction already granted by a ratepayers' meeting, and the Royal Court may delete any item which in its opinion conflicts with the law of parochial taxation. When once the *remède* is granted, the rate is finally fixed and cannot be altered.

Strictly speaking, the words "rate" and "assessment" are mis-
nomers. "Parochial taxation" and "*cadastre*" are the true terms,
and "rate" and "assessment" are but clumsy equivalents of these
terms. Parish rates are nowadays paid on the rateable value of real
property, (exclusive of *rentes*), but assessable property in the island
varies considerably from assessable property in England. The
register of properties for rating purposes is known as the *cadastre*.
This is kept, in duplicate, by the individual parishes and by the
Cadastre Department of the States.

To the States, as the central government, the *cadastre* is as important and useful as it is to the parish constables. As a record of
the annual value of real property it constitutes a useful check on
income-tax returns, and it is also the basis on which the tax on
rateable (formerly rental) values is raised.

In 1840 constables had to see that hedges were kept trimmed;
that all roads (except main roads) were kept in repair by those
whose property bordered them; that walls, ditches, and banks were
kept in good order; that proprietors of land below road level
maintained the supporting walls; that soapy water was not allowed
to run in the waterways; that surface drains (servitudes) were kept
open; that pumps, wells, and fountains were looked after, and that
roads were kept clean by proprietors. A register of those under
police supervision in their respective parishes had also to be kept.
In town the constables were expected to keep all pavements clean,
as well as drains and grills. They were empowered to remove
door-scrapers over which the unwary might stumble to their
injury, as well as the stones (*heurteurs*) placed to protect the corners
of walls from injury by passing carts. They only could number
houses.

Some of these duties have now been taken over by States Departments, but the constables still have much to keep an eye on, including the modern needs of street-lighting, and refuse-collection, and
the collection of gun, cycle, and dog taxes. They have, too, to
liaise with officers of the Parish church over the ecclesiastical
affairs of the parish which deal with the church building, churchyard, rectory, land, and some of the church accounts. For in the
Channel Islands the actual church is the concern of the whole
parish, whether they are members of the Anglican Church or not.
For the church's material upkeep money is raised through the
Occupier's rate, as for general parish funds, and this money is
handled by the People's Warden, in a separate account from the
Trésor, or Parish Church Endowment, handled by the Rector's
Warden.

c

Another liaison duty of the constables is with the Procureurs des Pauvres, elected parish officials, who from 1725 onwards took over the duties of poor relief from the churchwardens. Although the States, through the Public Assistance Board, assumed responsibility for Poor Law administration in the 1920's, the Procureurs still give help in particular cases and attend their office weekly to give much-needed advice as well.

A further duty of the constables is to convene the meetings of the Douzaine, or Parish Council, over which the senior constable presides while the junior keeps the Minutes. Until 1846 the Douzeniers were elected for life, but now they are elected for a term of six years. The most important is the Dean, the one with the longest unbroken period of service on the Douzaine, who reads the prayer at the opening and close of the Douzaine meetings and presides over meetings of Parish ratepayers and electors.

Along with the constable, the Douzaine's particular duties include inspection of hedges bordering the public roads, granting of "bornements" or alignments for new walls or fences, reporting on applications for liquor licences, inspecting streams which feed the reservoir and other public water supplies, and checking on the maintenance of pumps, troughs, and other parish property. In general the Douzaine are the watch-dogs for the good name and appearance of the parish.

Their influence too extends beyond the parish in two spheres. Since 1846 they have been empowered to send one of their number as Douzaine representative to the States; thus the voice of the Parish is heard in States Meetings, and the Billet d'Etat, the business for the next States Meeting, is an important item on the Agenda of the Douzaine Meeting each month. Secondly a number of them, under the Reform Law of 1948, attend the States of Election, the body which chooses the senior members of the States, the Conseillers.

ELIZABETH COLLEGE. *A Guide to the Island of Guernsey*, printed and published in 1826 by a certain J. T. Cochrane of Market Street, contains a frontispiece of a panoramic view of St Peter Port as seen, probably, from the Pool. Two prominent background features of today are missing. One is the Victoria Tower, but the windmill, complete with sails, which it replaced, stands out prominently. The other missing feature is Elizabeth College, although it is reasonable to assume that the walls of that building were already rising when this old guide-book was printed.

Indeed, the guide-book devotes a page and a half to Elizabeth

College. Full lists of the directors and staff are given. The staff, including the principal, numbers six. Classics are dominated by Oxford, and it is noteworthy that both principal and vice-principal have attained the Fellowship of their College, St John's. The third master is also an Oxford man, again of the same College. He was possibly a young man, for he has, so far, only attained the academic rank of Bachelor. Mathematics are in the hands of a gentleman from Geneva, French in those of a graduate of the University of Paris, and writing and arithmetic are left to a certain Mr Tyers from Christ's Hospital, London.

These details are interesting only because the foundation stone of the new (and present) College was laid on October 19, 1826, by His Excellency, Sir John Colborne, a name perpetuated in Colborne Road and in Colborne Place at the Mount Row end of Queen's Road. Members of the States, masters and students of the College, and detachments of the militia also attended the ceremony.

It was indeed an historic occasion. The *Sarnian Journal*, a now defunct newspaper which had then been in existence less than 12 months, published the following report:

"After the ceremony, the boys of Elizabeth College were regaled in a most splendid manner under marquees erected upon the lawn in front of Government House, and in the evening, Lady Colborne gave a grand ball and supper. The Royal Court and other gentlemen dined together at Rosetti's, where a sumptuous dinner had been prepared for them. The Douzaines from the country parishes dined together at Cole's Hotel. Wine and biscuits were distributed as refreshments to the troops after the procession upon the New Ground: and the workmen who laboured at the new College were presented with a good solid dinner and a hogshead of wine, by the Royal Court."

The history of Elizabeth College as a public school of which the island is justly proud virtually begins from that date. Although founded as a college by Queen Elizabeth in 1563, its history from that year until 1826 is a sordid one of indifference on the part of the inhabitants and duplicity and dishonesty on the part of some in authority. The *Guide-book* hints at this. It says:

"This College was endowed by Queen Elizabeth, and flourished for many years, until abuses crept in one upon another, and shook the fabric to its centre. In 1824, His Excellency, Sir John Colborne, aided by the Bailiff, the Dean, and the principal families in the island, instituted an enquiry, the result of which was a determina-

57

tion to reorganise the establishment. After the Bailiff had laid his plan before the States of this island, an application was made to His Majesty's Honourable Privy Council to confirm a tax or impôt of one shilling per gallon on spirits, voted by the States to build a new College, and place the whole on a solid foundation. The Lords of His Majesty's Council acceded to the proposals from his Excellency Sir John Colborne and the States and the site for a new College was adopted. This building is proceeding rapidly under the inspection of John Wilson, Esq, architect. In this establishment, a boy may have a classical education, attended by all the professors above mentioned, for about 12 pounds per annum."

Although Saravia, the able Flemish refugee who was appointed the first Headmaster, did his best until he left the island in disgust in 1569, it is not true to say that the College "flourished for many years" between 1563 and 1826. Its history during those centuries was that of many schools in England of similar origin. The intentions of their founders were never carried out, their lands were stolen and their endowments misappropriated.

The Industrial Revolution created a demand for education—an education of a classical and cultural, as well as utilitarian, kind—for the sons of its leaders. They looked to the old Public Schools and, where these had fallen into decay, spiritually as well as physically, they called for their revival and their re-establishment.

Such a leader of the Industrial Revolution in Guernsey was George le Boutillier. He was a Jerseyman to the finger-tips, yet his contribution to the material prosperity of Guernsey during the 19th century was such as to merit him some tangible memorial. Apart from the history books, however, he is almost forgotten.

In 1804, when he was only 21 years of age, he established a drapery business in Guernsey, and almost immediately began to take a prominent part in local politics. It was perhaps concern for his family, consisting of four sons and three daughters, which turned his attention to the question of education.

In 1799, five years previous to le Boutillier's establishment in the island, Elizabeth College had only one pupil. The reason for this scandalous state of affairs, le Boutillier felt, might be traced to the history and finance of the College, which he began to investigate. His efforts met with little encouragement from the authorities. In 1821, however, when Sir John Colborne became Lieutenant-Governor, le Boutillier laid before him a complete plan for the reorganisation of the College. Sir John was most sympathetic. He appealed to the Dean, as Visitor of the College, but finding the latter moved slowly, he ordered, in 1825, a public enquiry, the result of which was a new charter under which the present organisation of the old Grammar School of Elizabeth was set up.

When the school was reopened in 1826, with 40 scholars, the first two names on the register were those of the sons of the Lieutenant-Governor. Numbers three, four, and five, however, were those of the sons of le Boutillier, a recognition, though a small one, of what the College owed to him.

Remembering that, apart from his other great achievements, it was he who first introduced gas into the island, it is not surprising that the *Gazette* gives him the epitaph that could be given to that small but eminent number of contemporary industrial and commercial giants:

". . . a man of novel ideas, one of those ardent spirits who conceive and inaugurate vast undertakings, a master mind that left its mark on every place it passed through".

The *Elizabeth College Register* is more restrained. It calls him

". . . one of the greatest benefactors that ever came to this island".

Of the old Friary whose lands, buildings, and, to some degree, income were bestowed upon the island of Guernsey in 1563 by Queen Elizabeth for the establishment of a Grammar School, very little is known. The order of Franciscan Friars was founded by St Francis of Assisi in 1208. Of the Cordeliers—a name given to the Friars because of the girdle of cord which they wore—Tupper remarks:

"The order of Cordeliers appears to have been firmly established in Alderney, Herm and Guernsey."

It may well be, then, that the site of Elizabeth College was occupied by a monastic order as early as the 13th century.

Sir John Colborne's "enquiry" of 1826 established that the Virgin Queen assigned and conceded for the use of the said school for ever

"the Temple or Church formerly belonging to the minor or mendicant friars, together with the burying ground to the northward, 26 Guernsey perches; and the ground with the neighbouring edifices, and which was formerly encompassed with a cloister to the southward, from the entrance of the great gate tending from the east to west, up to the end of the temple; and the adjoining 30 perches contiguous to the temple, according to the limits of the old walls, lines and boundaries".

59

The western part of the temple was assigned for the reception of the scholars,

"the Choir itself, that is to say, the eastern part together with the edifices and ground aforesaid, were appropriated to the use of the future master and his successors, for the erection of a commodious dwelling, and to form orchards and little gardens".

For water, the Master was allowed the use of the neighbouring common fountain, still in existence in the form of a pump, at the bottom of College Street.

The income conceded was 80 quarters of wheat rent

"out of the receipts of our Lady the Queen in the said Island of Guernsey".

It was from these details, perhaps, that Major Carey Curtis was able to produce the excellent plan which appears in the *Transactions of the Société Guernesiaise* for 1926. This plan shows that the area of land now held by the College is little more than half the original grant.

This plan shows the boundaries of the College grounds to have been the Rue des Frères to the north, the Grange to the south, College Street to the east, and Upland Road to the west. The plan does not include the old Cimetière des Frères, north of the Rue des Frères and west of Candie Road, although this is mentioned in the original gift.

What is certain is that in 1629, when the island was visited by a plague, the Cimetière des Frères was in possession of a certain Thomas Blanche, who was using it as a garden. His title must have been rather shaky, for the Royal Court passed an ordinance by the terms of which victims of the plague were to be buried in the old cemetery. In 1662, however, Thomas Blanche—perhaps an immediate descendant—and John de Quetteville bought this land, but the details of the transaction are somewhat obscure.

Some six perches, forming the corner of the Rue des Frères and College Street, belonged to the College in 1663. But in 1793 this plot appears to have come into the possession of the Lieutenant-Governor, who built stables upon it because of its convenient situation in regard to Government House.

Slightly higher up College Street was the old Great Gateway of the College. A portion of the archway still remains, but the rest was demolished in 1865 when St Julian's Avenue was constructed. It was here, perhaps, that the original church of the Cordeliers stood. The building was used as the first and original College, and it was here that the States held their meetings during the troubled Parliamentary régime, safe from the cannon-balls being hurled at the old Court House in the Plaiderie from Castle Cornet by the sturdy Royalist Governor, Sir Peter Osborne.

The ramshackle buildings which formerly ran parallel with College Street, and served as livery stables, a music-hall and a theatre, have been demolished or transformed in recent years; on their site has arisen a fine set of classrooms and music rooms, known as the Winchester Block, while across a grass courtyard, entered through iron gates in memory of Henry Milnes, stand the main Science and Biology Laboratories. To the south of these is the new swimming pool of standard length built through the efforts of the Old Elizabethans and presented to the College.

Immediately up the street from this site, originally "le Jardin des Frères", stands the Ozanne Laboratory, now in the process of transformation into a four-storey granite building, with Maths rooms on the two central floors, a creative art centre above, and the bottom floor for engineering and other projects.

A plot to the west of this, extending to Upland Road and comprising nearly a *vergée*, was also originally College property. But in 1816 it, too, had passed into the possession of the churchwardens of St Peter Port.

North of this plot, and bounded by Upland Road and the Rue des Frères, is another area of 38 perches which was originally College property. In 1793, however, it had passed into the possession of the heirs of Osmond de Beauvoir.

It is evident that the institution was liberally endowed. How, then, did so considerable a portion of its lands, in the course of three centuries, become alienated? Only one explanation is possible. It was due to the fact that neither the foundress nor the States of the island, who accepted the gift, appointed trustees for its protection.

Why did the States in particular, and the inhabitants of the island in general, for so many centuries exhibit such indifference towards the munificent gift of Queen Elizabeth? It may safely be said that, although the ruling class was to become uncompromising Calvinists later, their attitude in the 16th century towards the reformed religion was, if not antagonistic, at least lukewarm. The gift of Elizabeth College in exchange for a Franciscan establishment which was one of the institutions of the island may not, in their eyes, have amounted to as much as a Roland for an Oliver. The Queen was giving them back what she had taken, not from the Franciscans—for they had not yet learned to regard such orders as being foreign—but from them. They knew, and perhaps liked, the

61

Cordeliers. But they could only despise and hate, maybe, the Franciscan turned Calvinist.

The last Master, prior to the "Enquiry into the present state and condition of Elizabeth College" (1824), which led to the establishment of the new and present régime, was the Rev Nicholas Carey. He was also Dean.

Indeed, for a number of years the school seems to have been regarded as a Church benefice, and the Dean, of his own authority, sequestered the revenues into the hands of the town churchwardens. Commenting on this, the members of the commission of enquiry reported that they had failed to find any principle upon which this practice could be founded. So far from being a Church benefice, Elizabeth College appeared to be a lay establishment and

". . . the Master of it, by the institution and foundation, is not even required to be a clergyman".

Nicholas Carey, appointed in 1795, was not easily ejected in 1824. Eventually, by arrangement with the States, he abandoned his rights to the enjoyment of the buildings, land, and *rentes* of the College, in consideration of an annual pension of £60.

A temporary school building, situated near the College, was obtained. It consisted of two rooms, well ventilated and well lighted, and here, on October 11, 1824, 40 boys were enrolled by the newly appointed Principal, the Rev Charles William Stocker.

His period of office was not a long one. It ended a month or two before the completion of the new buildings. His portrait, however, may still be seen in the Directors' Room, and the College accounts of 1829 include the interesting item: "Mr Stocker's Portrait and Frame, £18 10s.".

During his short period of office Dr Stocker appears to have established a reputation for unmerciful flogging. In this respect, particularly in those times, he was not unique. André Maurois, in his immortal book on Shelley, *Ariel*, says:

"In the year 1809 George III appointed as Headmaster of Eton, Dr Keats, a terrible little man who considered the flogging-block a necessary station on the road to perfection, and who ended a sermon on the Sixth Beatitude by saying, 'Now, boys, be pure in heart! For if not, I'll flog you until you are.'

"The county gentlemen and merchant princes who put their sons under his care were not displeased by such a specimen of pious ferocity, nor could they think lightly of the man who had birched half the ministers, bishops, generals, and dukes in the Kingdom.

"In those days the severest discipline found favour with the best people."

The new school building was handed over to Stocker's successor, Dr Proctor, by the Bailiff on August 20, 1829.

From the sea-front, Elizabeth College forms part of the skyline, and familiarity with its outline has bred tolerance. Time has dealt kindly with its stucco facing and mellowed its colour. Nevertheless, it is, and remains, an architectural nightmare. Built in imitation of a late Tudor style, it has no more pretension to beauty than some of the earlier nonconformist chapels.

H. D. Inglis, in his book *The Channel Islands* (1835), says:

"Elizabeth College is not only a noble institution, but an attractive object. The building itself is decidedly handsome; its architecture is mixed; as a whole, regular, . . . and yet with a monastic air about it."

The architectural taste of Inglis, however, may be measured by a further quotation from his book.

"The 'lions' of St Peter Port are its handsome fish market (now the vegetable market), its hospital or refuge for the destitute, and Elizabeth College. To these may be added the parish church."

The order of preference is noteworthy and needs no further comment. Ansted, however, writing about 1860, says:

"The present structure, unfortunately harmonising in its utter tastelessness with other modern buildings in the Islands, was erected at a great cost, and presents a bald, plastered, unmeaning face, too prominent to be overlooked!"

Tupper is no less scathing. He says:

"In the year 1826, the present huge structure bearing that name, so disproportionate to the limited extent and requirements of the island, was commenced, and in very bad taste, as, in place of the building being covered over with cement, it should have been made smaller, and faced with the fine blue Guernsey granite, cut for the purpose. The style should, moreover, have been Elizabethan, in compliment to the foundress!"

The growth in numbers of the College was unforeseen by both Tupper and Duncan. The latter says:

"The erection of the present College was commenced in 1826; but it is much to be regretted that it was built on a scale of magnitude so little commensurate with the wants and means of the island, as its maintenance is now a great drain on the insular revenue."

Both Duncan and Tupper, however, wrote more than a century ago. Were they alive today they might still criticise the architectural style of Elizabeth College, but they would not criticise its size.

The record of Elizabeth College as an educational institution since 1824 is one of which Guernsey may well be proud. Thousands have passed through its portals, and the roll of fame is a very long one. The Church, the fighting services, the Bar, the scholastic profession, literature and science, all owe much to our Guernsey Public School.

THE PRISON. Certain lords of manors, by the terms of their feudal tenure, were obliged to keep prisoners in safe custody. It is possible, therefore, that there were prisons in the island before the erection of Castle Cornet. What is certain, however, is that as far back as the reign of King John, the Royal Court was empowered to commit prisoners to Castle Cornet in criminal cases; and as, with the lapse of time, the Castle grew more spacious, a prison for civil offences was also kept there.

The gaoler, who bore the title of *Portier du Château*, was paid 12 *deniers* per day from Crown revenue. He also received a small amount of salt and wine, earthenware and canvas from strangers.

The executioner, who bore the high-sounding title of *l'executeur des hautes œuvres*, carried out his functions within the Castle, and the result of his work was plainly visible from the old south pier and the Galet Heaume, now the South Esplanade. A view of *la justice du roi* was regarded in those days as a useful object lesson and a possible deterrent.

But Castle Cornet as a prison had grave disadvantages for its mainland. These had been felt as far back as the reign of James I, when the inhabitants of the town of St Peter Port had seized the opportunity of the visit of some Royal Commissioners to petition for a prison on the island in lieu of that at Castle Cornet. The reply of the Commissioners had been uncompromising. From time immemorial a prison had been kept at Castle Cornet, they said, and without some special and particular warrant from His Majesty or from the Lords of the Council, they might not by law cause any new prison to be erected.

That was in 1607. Thereafter half-hearted attempts were made again and again, without result, for neither the Crown nor the island seemed prepared to meet the cost of erecting a new prison.

The boat used to transport troops to and from the Castle was also used to carry prisoners both to incarceration and to trial. The disadvantages of this arrangement are obvious. In boisterous weather prisoners did not arrive for trial, although the Court was sitting—a source of grievance to both parties. The committal of a prisoner to custody was also subject to delay by unfavourable weather. To meet this difficulty, the military guard-house at one of the two piers of the old harbour was used as a temporary prison by arrangement with the Lieutenant-Governor and the military. But this arrangement did not work well, and there were frequent disputes between the civil and military authorities. The placing together of prisoners of both sexes was open to grave objection. There was opportunity, too, for escape. The gaoler, it appeared, was domiciled in the island and not in the Castle, and weather sometimes prevented him from giving those attentions to the prisoners which common humanity demanded. Counsel for prisoners found it difficult and hazardous to visit their clients for consultation, as did also those clergy desiring to give spiritual consolation to those about to suffer the supreme penalty.

The conveyance to and fro of criminals and debtors must, it was felt, have a deleterious effect on the military efficiency of the Castle. And we were at war with France.

All these arguments were set forth in a petition from the States to His Majesty in Council in the year 1799. The cost of the new prison they contemplated building was to be met by them out of a general tax of sixpence per quarter of wheat rent, although they were careful to state that this must not be regarded as a precedent. When completed, the new prison, like the old, would be His Majesty's Prison, and the payment of its staff and cost of upkeep would be the responsibility of the Crown.

The royal assent was received in 1803. A small committee was appointed to find a site and to make the necessary arrangements for its purchase if it were not already States property. The committee chose a site on the Galet Heaume, the beach extending from the South Pier (now the Albert Pier) towards Havelet. Twenty perches of land were to be enclosed, just above high-water mark. The fact that a 20-foot road and slipway for pedestrians and carts and horses existed along and between the military guard-house, the cemetery and the site chosen, suggests that it was to be in the immediate neighbourhood of the present Picquet House, not built, however, until 1819.

Alas! the committee had made a grave miscalculation. A meeting of the *chefs-de-famille* of the town declared "that the land to the east of the Galet Heaume Quay and the Cemetery is most certainly the property of either the parish or the Church and that neither will cede the said land for the building of a public prison".

The States did not argue. They annulled their previous decision, with, of course, no prejudice to any right they might have to the Galet Heaume, and authorised the choosing of a new site.

That same year, 1807, another site was found. It was behind the Royal Court, and formed part of the Le Marchant estate, upon which the Royal Court had already been built, and of the Lefebvre estate. Both these names are preserved in two streets of the town, but neither in the immediate vicinity of the prison. St James's Street, where one façade is so much in evidence, is officially la Profonde Rue.

Here the prison was erected, between 1811 and 1815, at a cost of £11,000. It was not built in expectation of a high percentage of criminality. It was to accommodate 19 prisoners in separate cells, two for women, five for debtors, eight for felons, and four lock-up cells for the use of the constables. At the request of the States, the prison was officially handed over to the Crown by the Royal Court in 1815.

Mrs Fry, the Quakeress prison reformer of early Victorian days, never visited Guernsey prison in person. It did, however, receive the attention of one of her disciples, Mr Bisset Hawkins, within 15 years of its establishment. The report he submitted was in strict conformity with those passed on English prisons. At the moment extensions are planned, but the prison remains in essentials what it was 150 years ago.

CASTLE CORNET. There is nothing which lends more character to the harbour and town of St Peter Port than the ancient fortress of Castle Cornet.

It was founded in the first decade of the 13th century. It did service as a fortress until 1945, when, with the remainder of the Channel Islands, it was surrendered to British forces by the defeated troops of the Third Reich.

References to the shipping of munitions and materials for the building of fortifications occur as early as 1206.

Work on a large scale probably began during the governorship of Geoffrey de Lucy (1224–6). He is recorded as having spent £66 19s. 1d. on work in "the king's castle of Guernsey".

Documents of the period 1242–50 give some indication of the

66

evolution of the Castle. The repair of the western wall, the roofing with lead of two old towers and six new ones, the building of a barbican near the well, the construction of galleys and of storage for these as well as the repair of old ones, are recorded as having cost £175 3s. 8d.

There is no evidence that the Castle was taken during the disastrous French raid of 1295. It was, however, captured by the French, together with Guernsey and the smaller islands, in 1338. Guernsey was re-occupied in 1340, but only after a siege lasting five more years was the Castle recaptured.

In 1356–7 it was again in the hands of the French for a few months.

During the reign of Queen Elizabeth, it was considerably extended, strengthened, and brought up to date, especially during the governorship of Sir Thomas Leighton.

During the Parliamentary Civil War, the Castle, defended by the royalist Governor Sir Peter Osborne, held out for nine years against the island, which was strongly parliamentarian, and was the last royalist stronghold to surrender (December 15, 1651).

An accidental explosion in 1672 destroyed the 13th century keep and other buildings of the Middle Ages. From that date the governors ceased to reside in the Castle.

Throughout the late 17th and early 18th centuries extensive reconstruction was carried out. As the chief defence of Guernsey, however, it was superseded by Fort George, built at the very end of the 18th century.

As a fortress, however, it was not abandoned. It must also be added that it did service as the island prison until 1811.

In 1949 it was handed over to the States of Guernsey and scheduled by that body as an ancient monument.

As a result, it is receiving more and more attention from the historian and the student of military architecture. The latter will find its history extremely well documented. There are building accounts as early as the 13th century, and these are plentiful and detailed for the 14th, 16th, and 17th centuries and, of course, later.

Records of the composition of the garrison and its relations with the islanders are also common. Plans and sketches date from the late 16th century.

During the Middle Ages, before the governments of Jersey and Guernsey were separated, Castle Cornet may probably have done duty as the principal seat of government of the Channel Islands as a whole.

In the 16th and 17th centuries it was generally regarded as the chief stronghold in the Channel Islands. Most certainly its position, relative to the island and the roadstead, contributed largely to the commercial prosperity of Guernsey and the rise of its capital, St Peter Port.

Picturesque and romantic in its history, and commanded by a succession of distinguished men, of whom biographical details are decidedly not lacking, Castle Cornet stands out as one of the most interesting old castles of the British Isles.

The Great Gate of the Castle, facing seawards, and not towards the town, constitutes its only entrance. This gate is approached from the Castle Breakwater, to which it is connected by a small bridge. A relic of the ancient drawbridge may still be discerned in the vestiges of a stone platform, upon which the drawbridge rested.

The remains of the ancient paved causeway leading to the town may still be seen to the left of the Great Gate. Supplies were brought along this track to the Castle in carts from the town, but at low spring tides only.

Outside the gate is the old shelter for the sentry. Over the Great Gate itself are the arms of Elizabeth, weathered to almost the same extent as those over the gateway of Elizabeth College in Upland Road.

Within, the gateway takes a leftward right-angled bend, and the slots for a portcullis just inside indicate that, whereas the original Elizabethan gateway faced the town, the entrance was later extended and deflected so as to face seawards.

The main gate gives access to the outer bailey.

Here, in the Main Guard Room, are now a number of rooms set out by the States Ancient Monuments Committee as part of the Castle Museum. These rooms contain Ship models and prints, charts of local wrecks, and salvage equipment, historical naval relics, paintings and portraits of island scenes and personalities, relics of the German occupation, from a Nazi flag to a cat's whisker radio, and the latest addition, the Bremner Bequest of delightful paintings of the island in the 19th century by Peter Le Lievre, a skilled local artist.

Nearby in this courtyard is another guardroom where old maps, prints and photographs are set out. On the Castle Wall behind are set four plaques from the Delancey Monument to Admiral James, 1st Baron de Saumarez of Cape St Vincent and the Nile.

On the left, up a small flight of steps, is the Saluting Battery, where six old guns point dramatically out over the Harbour. From here until the First World War the noon and 9.30 p.m. guns were fired.

To the right of this battery, facing seawards, down one short flight of steps, up another and then to the left, is the path to the oldest part of the Castle. This is the Barbican or look-out. The machicolations, supported by corbels, indicate a date not later than the 14th century. Close to the Barbican is a delightful corner, a garden of flowers and shrubs, marking the spot where General John Lambert, Cromwell's deputy, grew the flowers he loved when he spent years in the Castle as a prisoner after the restoration of Charles II.

From the Barbican one reaches the Inner Bailey, now gay with shrubs, neat lawns, and beds of flowers. Gayest of all is the garden in front of the Sutler's house, an old building of 1594, where the present Keeper of the Castle has his home. Close by is the Hospital, dated 1746, which is now another part of the Museum. In its lower floor is the Spenser Collection, relics of the Militias of Guernsey, Sark, and Alderney. Tunics, medals, buttons, and badges, and the Arms of outstanding Colonels of the militia Regiments. On the first floor is a room of great interest, allotted solely to the Guernsey Militia. Here are the uniforms of the different branches of the militia, the Regimental silver, the flags, and the staves of the Drum-Majors. Around the walls are hung the Arms of the Governors and Lieutenant-Governors of the Bailiwick from 1177 to the present day. Two poignant exhibits are a photograph of the donkey which was the mascot of the 1st Bn. The Royal Guernsey Light Infantry in the First World War, and the medal presented to His Excellency General Sir Charles Coleman to commemorate the 900th anniversary of 1066.

Up a flight of steps nearby is the Armoury, where a fine collection of arms and armour, from coats of mail to Bren guns, is displayed. Mr A. O. Hamon, an expert in this field, has been the chief organiser of this display.

Hard by stands the most historic structure of the Castle, the Carey Tower. Mentioned under this name in 1374, when it was scheduled for repairs, it is today in practically the same condition as it was then, save for the uppermost of the three storeys of which it was then composed, which was demolished in the explosion of 1672. This storey was rebuilt, but its height was greatly reduced. The corbels carrying the same design of machicolation as seen on the Barbican were fortunately reproduced, but the pointed roof disappeared.

The Carey Tower was the place of imprisonment of the three *Jurats* during the Parliamentary Civil War. They were James de Havilland, Peter Carey, and Peter de Beauvoir. The last mentioned was also known as "des Granges", from his estate at the town end of the Rohais, where the well-known arch, named the Ivy Gate, still bears upon its keystone the arms of de Beauvoir.

The manner of their capture reflects small credit on an otherwise gallant soldier, the Governor, Sir Peter Osborne, and the story of their escape ranks among the most romantic and classical of prison evasions. The royal writ for their execution arrived little more than half an hour before they stumbled up the steps of the town pier. The congregation of the Town Church was just emerging from Evensong, and all rushed to congratulate them on their providential deliverance.

Turning his back upon the Carey Tower, the visitor should now retrace his steps and ascend a flight of steps penetrating the Barbican. At the top is a square building which until 1811 served as the island prison.

At the beginning of the flight is seen a slit for another portcullis. The gloomy gallery stretching before the visitor is known as the Prisoners' Walk.

Its lower end marks perhaps the entrance to the old Castle, before it was extended during the reign of Queen Elizabeth.

High up on the wall of the Barbican, not far from, and to the right of this entrance, is a skew arch, which tradition designates as the place of public execution by the rope. Certain it is that before the building of the outer bailey "the justice of the King" would be plainly visible from the town.

From the Prisoners' Walk, after passing through several archways, the visitor reaches an open space.

This is the ancient citadel. Here once stood a huge round tower, some 40 feet high, used as an ammunition store. Near by was the governor's residence. It was not a large building, but it included a chapel and a banqueting hall.

Two days before the dawn of 1673 this round tower, the Keep or Donjon, was struck by lightning. The Governor, Lord Hatton, who was in residence, had a miraculous escape from the ensuing explosion. The Dowager Lady Hatton was killed, as was also the wife of the Governor. His infant children, although occupying the same room as their mother, survived the disaster.

The keep, chapel, and governor's residence were never rebuilt. The site of the round tower was for many years used as a signal station. The German occupation left it in a sad state of ruin, but it is cleaned up now, beds of flowers grow where they can, and it is interesting to see how the Germans adapted the 18th century underground chambers for the use of their own troops. From its

L'Ancresse Bay

Fermain Bay

Sausmarez Manor

Fort Grey, Rocquaine Bay

The ruins of the chapel

LIHOU ISLAND

The rock pool known as Venus's Bath

Portelet Harbour

Torteval Church

summit the flag flies each day, and a panoramic view can be had of Guernsey from north to south and of all the other islands and the surrounding seas.

FORT GEORGE. What a contrast today is the site of Fort George. Built from 1780 onwards, it consisted of the Citadel itself, the supplementary Fort Irwin, the outer bastion walls, entered at different points but with the main entrance at the Barrier Gate, the Kent, Adolphus, and Charlotte Batteries and the outlying Clarence Battery on the promontory by Havelet Bay. In the recent past there were also barrack-rooms, married quarters, store-rooms, a guard-house, and other buildings.

The Citadel itself, which was used by the Germans, was virtually destroyed by Allied bombing in 1944 before the Allied landings in Normandy. After the war the Fort George site was sold by the War Office to the States of Guernsey, and they in their turn sold much of the site to an English development company. Now on the plateau among the rising houses can be found little except the Citadel itself, the outer bastion walls, and the Barrier Gate. Outside the area the Soldiers' Cemetery, with its section for German dead, and the Forces War Memorial on the bank above, neatly tended, remind islander and visitor of the many centuries through which English garrisons helped in the defence of the islands.

The other reminder is the lingering memory in the minds of older islanders of La Grande Mourtre.

Long before the building of Fort George, English troops had been quartered both in Guernsey and Alderney. In fact, the adherence of Guernsey to the cause of Parliament during the Civil War of the 17th century was due in part to the fact that the Stuarts had defaulted on their payments of billeting charges.

Apart from their military value, garrison troops in those days served a useful purpose as porters on the quay.

But with the building of Fort George, Guernsey became definitely a garrison town, and there was no break with this tradition until 1940, when, in face of an occupation menace, the British Government withdrew all military establishments and equipment and declared the whole of the Channel Islands to be an open town.

Throughout the 19th and part of the 20th centuries the presence of a regular battalion in the island was regarded as an important economic asset. So much so, that when the States showed signs of apathy or indifference at various times to War Office advice on the re-organisation or modernisation of the local militia, the reaction of

71

the Government was invariably to threaten the withdrawal of the
regular garrison.

It must be remembered, too, that until the outbreak of the First
World War, the Regular Army was a professional army, and that
its officers were drawn almost exclusively from one class. It is not
untrue to say that the officers of regiments stationed here, together
with the Lieutenant-Governor and his staff, strengthened and leav-
ened local society.

Fort George itself could not house a battalion at full strength, but
Alderney, with its many forts, barracks at Jerbourg and Icart, and
forts at Houmet, Richmond, Lancresse, and other places, provided
ample accommodation. A company of the Royal Garrison Artillery
was always stationed at Castle Cornet.

Many crack regiments have been quartered in Guernsey, the
most famous being perhaps the Gordon Highlanders.

At the beginning of the present century, when St James's Church
was the garrison church, Sunday morning parade provided a
weekly pageant for the people of St Peter Port. What could please
the eye more than the colourful dress uniforms of the marching
troops, or the ear more than the strains of the regimental band?
The Summer Evening Bands Committee, a sub-committee of the
local Chamber of Commerce, found in this military band a useful
and popular source of entertainment, of which it made good use for
promenade concerts in the kiosk in Candie Gardens. In this
connection it must not be forgotten that in those days the radio
and the cinema were yet unknown.

The presence of a regular garrison inevitably raised questions of
policing. Even as recently as the beginning of the present century,
St Peter Port was policed by some half-dozen uniformed men, paid
out of parish rates and styled, because they were deputies of the
parish constables, assistant constables. Although these were not
without jurisdiction over men of the garrison, the military did their
own policing, and on Saturday nights, when shops remained open
until 10 and public-houses until 11, a picquet patrolled the town
and dealt with the military side of the all too frequent brawls which
arose between soldiers and disorderly elements of the civilian
population.

As early as 1819 a picquet house, including a cell, was built on
the sea-front facing the Albert Pier. This building, a fairly substantial one, has now become the offices of a local 'bus company.
Many a soldier, menaced by a raging civilian mob, must have
thanked Providence for the solid protection of that cell.

On one day, and on one day only during the year, were regular soldiers and local militia-men ever seen together. That was on the Queen's Birthday, May 24, the day of the Grande Mourtre. Early in the morning, pedestrians, equestrians, vehicles of all shapes and sizes, and militia-men in full-dress uniform crowded the roads. The various regiments paraded for roll call at the various arsenals and then marched in fours to the Fort.

Wheeled traffic made its way to the Fort through the Barrier Gate, the easterly terminus of Colborne Road. Within this gate was the guard house, with the sentry walking up and down. Of traffic control there was none, nor, apparently, was any needed. Turning sharply to the left, vans, gigs, and pony-traps threaded their way across a narrow drawbridge into the grassy amphitheatre known as Belvedere Field.

Fully three-quarters of this, from Belvedere House upwards, was roped off, and a few fatigue-men shepherded the vehicles behind these ropes. A zero hour was fixed, after which no further traffic was allowed to enter. Certain portions of this space were of course reserved for privileged visitors, such as the Bailiff and members of the Royal Court.

Soon the high bank overlooking the town was one tightly packed mass of people. It was a good-humoured crowd, flinging loud greetings at one another in local French and making those cynical, though unmalicious, witticisms which lose their point and their wit when translated into English.

The regular troops are already drawn up on the parade-ground. There is a stir in the crowd. Through the narrow opening beyond the drawbridge a flash of scarlet is seen. The militia is coming, the Town Regiment, the South, the North, and the West. And here is the company of field artillery, and last, but not least, the Elizabeth College Officers' Training Corps. As each unit swings past, someone in the ranks is greeted by a member of the crowd. The troops pass on, and soon are drawn up, like their professional comrades-in-arms, on the parade-ground.

Now there is expectancy among the crowd. Staccato orders ring out from the parade-ground. The massed bands of regulars and militia are called to attention. The band-master's baton is raised. It is lowered, and immediately the strains of the National Anthem crash out and the Union Jack is broken at the top of the flagstaff. Across the drawbridge a small body of mounted men advance down the field. They are headed by the Lieutenant-Governor, in plumed hat and uniform no less resplendent than that of his staff. He is greeted with cheers, which he acknowledges with a slight inclination of the head to right and left.

He rides on to the parade-field. There is a short colloquy between him and the officers assembled there. Then, to the sound of slow music, he moves up and down the serried ranks. The inspection concluded, the ceremony of the trooping of the colour is carried out, the popular feature of which appears always to be the synchronised slow stepping of the horses. This purely British military custom is usually left to the regular troops. On one occasion, however, when the regular garrison consisted almost entirely of raw recruits, it was the proud privilege of the Royal Guernsey Militia to troop the colour.

One more ceremony remains: the march past, with the Lieutenant-Governor taking the salute. Its end is well timed, for at noon precisely a gun booms out from Castle Cornet. It is followed by 20 more, for this is the royal salute which marks the end of *la Grande Mourtre*.

St Martin's Parish, the southerly neighbour of St Peter Port, is the first of the High Parishes, on the higher ground of which the centre, south, and west of the island is composed. It centres on the old hamlet round the Parish church and the Grande Rue which runs along nearby. A good deal of the Parish is residential, but there are farms and the glass-houses of growing properties scattered through it. There is much of interest to see and explore, from the ancient Gran'mere image at the entrance to St Martin's churchyard to the States Horticultural Experimental Station in Burnt Lane.

LE HAVRE DE BLANCHELANDE, SAINTS. One of the prettiest walks in St Martin's on a fine summer day is perhaps that to the Fishermen's Harbour at Saints. The occupation saw the disappearance of the gate at the end of the road leading to the bay, and motorists are now tempted to descend the slope flanked on the left by the steep cliffs of Bon Port and on the right by terraced *côtils*, despite the wet patches due to innumerable springs. Bearing right, a road, still of sufficient width to take light motor traffic, seems to be cut, like a shelf, out of the side of the cliffs. In one place the road passes through a cutting, made within living memory, to bypass a landslide. The road then slopes downward until it reaches rocks, covered by the sea at every tide.

There, before the War, stood a column of granite, a worthy relic of the stonemason's art, which bore the name Lefebvre. For their own purposes, the occupying forces overthrew this and tumbled it into the sea. It is worthy of recovery and re-erection, for thereby hangs an interesting tale.

It is fairly evident that this part of Saints Bay has been a fisher-men's harbour for centuries. At the end of the year 1866 a petition, signed by 41 fishermen, was sent to the Bailiff, Sir Stafford Carey. Among the signatories appear the names of Martin, Mauger, Mansell, Robert, and de Mouilpied. All these are names associated with St Martin's, and with this particular district of St Martin's. Indeed, tradition has it that Saints Bay received its name from the fact that an exiled Archbishop of Rouen named Mauger landed there, with the lady for whose love he had denied his vows and sought exile in Guernsey.

The petition set forth the urgent need of a breakwater at Saints for the protection of boats. Nothing had been expended on this anchorage since 1836. The number of boats had vastly increased since that time. There were now about 50 of them. The advantages of a prosperous fishing industry were urged, backed by the argument that greater numbers would not fail to take up the fisherman's useful calling if suitable protection were afforded to their boats.

Following the presentation of the States engineer's report the Bailiff received a letter from the Lord of the Manor of Blanchelande, Captain Lefebvre, whose ancestors had held the fief since 1563. Up to that date it belonged to the Crown, and was then ceded to Nicholas Careye.

Captain Lefebvre desired to co-operate in this important work and to associate his family with the undertaking. Not only did he offer to contribute £500 towards the cost, but he expressed his willingness to grant facilities to the builders to quarry stone to the extent of his seignorial rights, provided, of course, that the quarrying caused no damage to adjoining St Martin's property. This proviso is interesting, for it recalls that the seigneur of Blanchelande, some 25 years before, had narrowly averted a law-suit for damages threatened by the St Martin's authorities. He had leased certain mineral rights at le Mont Durand to the Blanchelande Mining Corporation, and it was alleged that the mining operations for silver had drained local wells.

A second report from the States engineer submitted a more ambitious plan, which was approved, the cost to be met out of the revenue of St Sampson's Harbour.

The scheme was practically completed by the end of November 1868. Then came disaster. On December 12 a north-easterly gale of unprecedented fury burst upon harbour works "not yet consolidated", and, to make things worse, this occurred on top of the spring tide, which on this occasion was observed to be abnormally high.

75

The gale was a staggering blow to the hopes of the Saints fisher-men. They do not appear to have recovered from it for nearly 10 years, for it was not until 1877 that they made a renewed attempt to secure a harbour for themselves.

Meanwhile, however, a scheme of a far more ambitious nature—the construction of a harbour at Portelet (Rocquaine)—had reached the States. This had the effect of making that body post-pone consideration of the Blanchelande scheme until the supervisor had prepared a plan and estimate for the Portelet project.

When the States met they were confronted by a convincing *requête* from the western parishes, signed by no fewer than 90 pilots, fishermen, sailors, and boatmen, supported by the rectors, con-stables, and *douzeniers* of Torteval and St Pierre-du-Bois. The contents of this and the other relevant documents printed in the Billet give an impression of some rivalry between the west and south coasts of the island, with the partisans of the Saints scheme fighting a losing battle. These admit that although some 50 boats were kept at Saints prior to 1868, that number was now reduced to about 20. But they attributed this reduction to the lack of natural protec-tion. Fishermen were discouraged and would not risk their boats. A fishery renaissance could be safely prophesied, provided a harbour were built. The cost of this would be trifling. It could be met from 18 months' revenue of St Sampson's harbour.

The States eventually decided to do nothing. They did, however, at the same session, vote a credit of £105 for the construction of a little stone jetty at Perelle Bay.

Once again Blanchelande Harbour fell into historical obscurity.

But in 1909 the States, taking pity on the fishermen, who had no convenient dry landing-place, erected a quay, some 50 feet long, at a cost of £750 and at the same time the Lefebvre Memorial, which was in danger of being washed away, was moved to a safer place.

Of the three openings in the natural rampart of the island, extending from Pleinmont on the west to les Terres Point on the east, Saints Bay is the only one situated exclusively in the parish of St Martin.

Access to the bay is obtained by an opening through a granite bulwark, of comparatively little length in relation to those of Fer-main and Petit Bot. On the left-hand side of the opening, facing the sea, there is no wall at all. On the right, what little is left of the stone bulwark is crumbling and overgrown with vegetation.

For many years the stream flowing down the valley was led by a channel over the top of the wall to cascade on the beach below.

The wall is now broken down to beach level. This may be due to neglect over the past century or to the action of the occupying forces from 1940 to 1945, who dammed the stream higher up the valley and made use of it to drive a dynamo for the generation of electricity. Similar measures were adopted by them at Fermain and at Petit Bot.

The slipway, or *dévaloir*, leading down to the beach, partially destroyed during the occupation, and now restored, is flanked on one side by natural rock and on the other by the masonry of the bulwark. A casual glance at the natural rock face will discover, in perpendicular alignment, two iron staples, the upper one of which still retains its ring.

It is obvious therefore that chains were stretched across the opening as an additional measure of defence. Indeed, in September 1803, when fears of a French invasion had attained fever heat, the Lieutenant-Governor demanded the placing of *"une Bombe et Chaine"* at the bays of Fermain, Saints, and Petit Bot. If by this is meant some kind of boom to impede the entrance of shipping, the subsequent withdrawal of the demand by Sir John Doyle becomes understandable. He was no doubt persuaded that the day-and-night vigil of militia-men, the chain barrier across the top of the slipway, the barrier and trench on the left, at least two gun-platforms on the right above what is now the fishermen's harbour and, later, the Martello tower, nestling in the hillside above, on the right, provided adequate precautions against a surprise attack from the sea.

The inhabitants of "la Contrée de Saints" had, in any case, already made great sacrifices in the cause of insular defence. A boom across the bay would have seriously interfered with both fishing and vraicking. The destruction of the cliff paths must have interfered to a large extent with the pasturage of sheep on the common, as well as with the cutting of furze for fuel for the oven and of bracken as bedding for the cattle.

The steep and wide (by Guernsey standards) road leading inland from Saints Bay dates, in its present dimensions, from Napoleonic times. Less than half a century ago it was little more than a muddy track, but modern road-building technique has, happily, rendered it negotiable at all times without destroying its old-world charm.

On the right the cliff rises steeply, but on the left is a depression, to which the road forms a ledge, in which the stream has been canalised.

The somewhat inelegant stone hut on the landward side of the bulwark marks the end of one of Guernsey's overseas telephone cables.

A couple of hundred yards or so up the steep path from the bay is a turning to the left leading to the fishermen's harbour. There has probably been a track here from time immemorial. In its present state, however, the road must date from the building of the Martello tower in the first decade of the 19th century. When the ill-fated harbour of Blanchelande was under construction in the sixties, a period when Guernseymen had become very harbour minded, the road was further improved.

The road upward, from this turning as far as the gate—removed during the occupation—is flanked on the left by a loose stone wall, which forms the boundary of private property, and on the right by precipitous cliffs. This land on the left, now neglected and over-grown, still bears signs of previous cultivation. There are traces of terraces, referred to locally, according to their character, either as *"côtils"* or *"pendants"*. Here crops of potatoes, and later of flowering bulbs, were grown as recently as the beginning of this century. But that was in the days when labour was cheap and plentiful. Modern machinery has rendered the cultivation of these tiny fertile plots an uneconomic proposition.

The previously mentioned barrier or gate marked the limit of the common in this direction. The boundaries of the common consist of a loose stone wall running along the crest of the cliff on both sides of the valley. Here and there the wall is pierced by a gate giving access to a lane. These walls are the property of those whose fields border the common, and the keeping of them in repair is the responsibility of these landowners, a responsibility of which they were in the past frequently reminded by the parish constables. Where these walls were destroyed by the occupying forces, however, they have not been re-erected, and no official action appears to have been taken. The gates, too, which are the property of the constables in their representative capacity, have not been replaced.

This is understandable, for the purpose of these walls and gates has long since passed away. Flocks of sheep once roamed the cliff common, and it was important that these animals should not stray. Within living memory, the cliff commons of St Martin's have pastured no sheep. Sheep roamed Lancresse Common at the beginning of the present century, but golf and the cheapness of New Zealand mutton drove them away, while the motor car abolished the common gates. The few goats which graze on the cliff are, like the local cattle, tethered.

The meandering valley road goes steeply upwards until it reaches the old farm-house now known as La Barbarie, but formerly as l'Abbaye, as being the site of Blanchelande Priory.

Before this point is reached, however, there is a turning to the left, leading to the Icart Road. A branch lane in this turning, to the left, is known as La Ruette du Navet. This lane emerges in the Icart Road opposite Rose Farm, and ran on probably via la Marette, a track for fishermen and vraicqueurs from Saints Bay to the village of La Villette. In this *ruette* are two old wells or fountains which, like all such old wells, are public property. Although "holy" and credited with power to heal the *maladie de la fontaine* (eczema), a coldly scientific Board of Health has boldly labelled them "Unfit for Drinking".

No other parish in the island is so rich in public fountains as St Martin's. On the road upwards from Saints Bay, some 50 yards below and opposite la Barbarie, is a fountain and an *abreuvoir*. The *abreuvoir* is an oblong, shallow trough through which the water overflowing from the well runs unceasingly. It is used as a drinking-place for cattle.

It is possible, however, that in the past many of these troughs were utilised as places for washing clothes. This primitive method of laundering is not yet obsolete in France, and at the beginning of this century, when the stream flowing from Colborne Road valley widened out in front of the group of houses forming the angle between the Ruettes Brayes and Prince Albert Road, women were frequently seen washing clothes here in the primitive French style.

MONT DURAND. On January 17, 1843, the *chefs de famille* of St Martin's, an assembly exclusively male, met in the parish church at 11 o'clock in the morning. Neither place nor time was unusual. Parochial meetings of this kind were common and frequent. The attendance, which numbered between 30 and 40, may possibly have constituted some 70 per cent of the tax-paying community of those days.

It was an indignation meeting, but it was orderly and business-like. It knew what it wanted, and it was prepared to take every necessary step to that end and to foot the bill. Its decisions, after deliberation, amply testify to this.

The working of the silver mine at le Mont Durand had led to the drying up of the wells, fountains, and drinking-troughs in the immediate neighbourhood. It had had still more widespread effects. The spring of La Bouvée fountain had become seriously depleted, while wells in the neighbourhood of Les Courtes Falaises were reported to be running dry.

79

Aggrieved parties had already taken action. On January 4, about a fortnight previously, the Royal Court had been approached with a request for an order for the closing of the mine. The outcome had been unsatisfactory. True, the Court had made an order for the discontinuance of the exploitation of the mine. But the order was not final or permanent. The ban was to last but one month, and during that period plaintiffs and their associates were advised to collect every fact which might tell in their favour and every penny which might bolster up the justice, equity, and legality of their grievance.

Bettering these instructions, these litigants persuaded their fellow *chefs de famille* to do everything possible to put a stop to the working of the mine.

Particularising over the word *everything*, they authorised the constables and *douzeniers* to ask for the intervention of other parishes and of the States. Should no sympathy be forthcoming from these sources, the parish was to act alone and sue the mining company for damages. The funds to meet the expense incurred were to be raised by parochial taxation.

These decisions were drastic and unusual. The *douzaine* might have temporised by ordering a *vue de justice, en corps*. It might even have delegated the matter to the appropriate canton and awaited its report. As it did neither of these things, let us constitute ourselves a canton and view the site. We shall meet at the Croix Bertrand where Sausmarez Road links up with Les Camps and Jerbourg Road. Going from there, through the lanes and past an old farmhouse, we shall reach a point where the cliff-path to the right leads to Moulin Huet, the left to Jerbourg. Before us is a shallow depression, down which flows a muddy stream. It ends in a waterfall, over a crumbling precipice.

But we are intrepid climbers. Fortunately we have chosen a day when the tides are springing and an hour when the tide is at its lowest ebb. We follow a path to the right. A promontory of jagged granite rocks, crowned with sparse vegetation, lies before us. Scrambling down, making use of every furze-bush, every turf, every ledge, and every cranny, we eventually reach a beach of slippery boulders. It has been a perilous climb, but we console ourselves with the reflection that climbing back, though more arduous, will probably be less dangerous.

We look for a cave. Yes, there it is in that eroded cliff face, which is the end of that shallow valley we saw above. The stream is precipitated over the cavern entrance and drenches us as we pass through it. The floor is ankle deep in water. A swift stream of reddish hue has channelled the floor. Gropingly we move forward. One of us strikes a match. Momentarily it makes the darkness visible. Another produces a candle from an inside pocket. He strikes a match to light it, but a drop of water from the roof extinguishes the match's flame and reluctantly he returns the candle to his pocket. Someone with more foresight has brought an electric torch. We stand still while he flashes it all round, but it reveals very little save the rain-like drip of water from sides and roof. How far in does the cave extend? We fear to penetrate farther. Our voices echo eerily when we shout. Still we entertain no doubts. This is *the* gallery of the silver-mine.

Is it natural or is it artificial? A little of both. Nature began the work. First it tilted the strata, like the pages of a loosely opened book standing on edge. Then it allowed the strata to fall apart, creating a vein or fissure, through which water penetrated, carrying with it the soft clay which lies beneath our feet and which the spring tides periodically wash away from the cavern's mouth.

Was there ever any silver here? If there were, we should find traces in this clay. A chemist member of our party stows away a few pinches in a match-box. "I shall test this when I get home," he says.

But, as a canton, we have done our task. Let us go back and report to our *douzaine* and to our *chefs de famille*.

The *chefs de famille*, however, desired neither a *vue de justice* nor a cantonal inspection. All they wanted was a stoppage of the mining operations. When, on May 3, the constables and *douzaine* reported to them that legal proceedings had already been started, they begged these authorities not be weary in well-doing. They urged the constables to defend the rights of the Saint Martinais to the bitter end, even to the extent of presenting a *requête civile*. *Carte blanche* was given them to take any measures they might consider suitable.

It would appear uncharitable to impute timidity or lack of faith in their cause to the constables and *douzaine*, until we reach October of the same year. Then we find two interesting letters placed before another meeting of the *chefs de famille*. One is from the Secretary of the Blanchelande Mining Corporation, as the Company was termed, a Mr W. Payne Georges, and the other from the Lord of the Manor of Blanchelande, Mr George Lefebvre.

The former writes:

"Gentlemen,
Altho' I am perfectly satisfied of my right to work the mines of Blanchelande under the lease granted to me by Mr le Febvre, yet

as it is possible that the exercise of that right be injurious to the parish of St Martin and that to obtain a final decision of the question the Parish as well as the other parties would be subjected to a most serious expense, I beg to state that with a view to conciliation and in order to avoid further trouble and litigation, I am willing to abandon all the rights given to me by the above mentioned lease and to pay 15 pounds to the Parish authorities, once paid, towards filling up the Mont Durand mine, provided the Parish of St Martin block up the said mine and withdraw its action against the late company for the pretended damage occasioned by the working of the said mine.

You will please to understand that in making this offer I reserve myself entire in all my rights, so that should it not be accepted by you I shall be in all respects in the same position as though the offer had not been made.

I remain, Gentlemen,
Your obedient servant,
W. Payne Georges."

The letter of the Lord of the Manor was no more conciliatory. It read as follows:

"Gentlemen,

Should the proposition which I understand Mr Georges has addressed to you relative to the closing of the Mont Durand mine be acceded to by the Parish of St Martin, I beg to state that I shall willingly restrict myself and heirs not to exercise any right of research for precious metals on the Blanchelande Manor except under sufficient securities given to the satisfaction of the Parish of St Martin.

Geo. le Febvre."

One conclusion can be drawn immediately from both letters. Neither the Company nor the Lord of the Manor entertained any hopes of deriving a penny of profit from the mine. They were only too anxious to rid themselves of a white elephant.

The *chefs de famille*, however, were more concerned with the blocking up of the mine than with the slender financial prospects of the Company. Again appointing the parochial *douzaine* and constables as a sub-committee, they authorised them to discover if it were possible to block the mine, the best method of doing so and the cost.

The sub-committee lost no time in carrying out their mandate. On November 8, 1843, they reported that in their opinion it was practicable to seal up the mine. The doing of this would necessitate the building of two walls, each six feet thick, "with stone, brick, lime, cement and sand, at a distance of about 50 feet from the extremity of the mine (the opening on the shore, apparently) and the other at a distance of about 43 feet from the first", the cost of which was estimated at £45.

The *chefs de famille* decided to come to terms with the Company and the Lord of the Manor, and to have the mine sealed up. They agreed that the cost should be met out of taxation, provided this did not exceed £30.

The decision was, however, not unanimous. There was one protest from one *chef de famille*, and this was considered of sufficient importance to be placed on record. It is interesting in that it throws a dim ray of light on facts hidden or lost in legal archives or offices.

He said that £15 was nothing compared with the damage done to private wells and public drinking-troughs and that future damage of the same kind was incalculable. While reserving his own rights, he begged to observe that the parish had asked for £5,000 damages. This protest is most certainly a *cri de cœur*.

All reference to the silver mine at le Mont Durand disappears from official records, but it may be added that the same Company made a trial lateral boring at La Fosse, a tiny creek on the St Martin's side of Petit Bot. The tunnel still exists, and may be easily explored. This working, fortunately, led to no political complications, but, like the Mont Durand venture, it yielded no profits.

MOULIN HUET AND WATER LANE. "Every visitor to Guernsey", says Ansted, "is taken to Moulin Huet, and few parts of the island are more crowded with exquisite morsels of rock scenery."

The name Moulin Huet, however, applies only to the seaward end of the valley, and not to the cove, whose ancient and now almost forgotten name is Vier Port. Huet is one of the very few Celtic words found in the Channel Islands.

The site of the mill bearing this name is now occupied by a group of houses set down deeply in the valley, near the spot where the road divides into two footpaths, the one on the left leading to the Courtes Falaises and that on the right descending to the bay.

The marshy area, overgrown with alder and blackthorn, immediately opposite the end of the steep slope of the Water Lane, is the site of the original mill-dam. Part of the wall exists, and anyone prepared to risk wetting his feet will find in this wall the remains of one of the old sluices.

The old mill-pond must have been of considerable size and power,

83

for it received all the water coming down both the Moulin Huet valley from la Fosse as well as that coming from the Water Lane.

The valley is particularly rich in surface wells, all of great antiquity. The first will be found in a tiny private lane, leading to a fine old farm-house now known as Fay Dell, just below the Bella Luce Hotel. There is another, still in use, a few yards from the pillar-box at le Rocquet. A few more yards farther, below the road leading to Blanchelande Convent, are two more.

To these wells must be added those springs which during the early months of the year work so vigorously that they may be seen gushing from the road surface. This natural phenomenon has given rise to a widespread theory, not devoid of scientific support, that the water supply of the island has its origin in the Alps.

This approach to Moulin Huet—one of many—gives a glimpse, especially at the foot of the hill, of unspoiled beauty. There is only one jarring note. On the crest of the cliffs rising steeply on the right is a large building, reminiscent of a shredded-wheat factory. This is the High School of Blanchelande Convent. It is noteworthy, however, that this same building, viewed from the Icart Road, conveys a distinctly conventual impression.

In an attempt at afforestation, the water-meadows on the left have been acquired by the States and planted with alders and willows.

From a track on the right, flights of rough stone steps, at intervals, will conduct the rambler to the cliff path above, just outside the boundary wall of the common. Viewed from the other side of the valley, however, these flights of steps will be observed intersecting a whole series of what is perhaps the finest set of cliff terraces in the island.

Less than half a century ago these *côtils*, then private property, produced crops of daffodils and pheasant-eye narcissus, and to this day a few of the latter may still be found blooming in spring. These terraces are now public property.

The Water Lane is very steep at its lower end, and this steepness is reflected in the depth of the channel through which the water flows. One-third of the way up, the lane becomes almost level, and the flow of the water in the channel, which occupies half the width of the lane, is calm and unhurried. The footpath allows passage in single file only.

English influences are in all probability responsible for the name of this ancient trackway. Its true name, which must now be known to very few, is la Ruette des Olivets.

The lane ends at what must be the best-known wishing-well in Guernsey. Here the water is so limpid and clear that the rocky sides and bottom, uncontaminated by vegetable growth, stand out clearly and distinctly, creating an illusion of shallowness. The trough which takes its overflow, whose verges not so many years ago were fouled by cattle brought here for watering, is now little used, an indication of grave insular economic change, which advocates of self-sufficiency will find somewhat disquieting.

The wishing-well is the centre of a village of rather greater size than la Fosse. It is known as la Ville Amphrey. There is a group of old farm-houses in a lane to the left of the wishing-well, but these have suffered less from modernisation than those of la Fosse. Another fountain and trough, so hidden and secluded that its location is discovered only with difficulty, indicates that Guernseymen of centuries ago were as mindful of the importance of water supply as they are today.

The village of Ville Amphrey, like all Guernsey villages, has been encompassed and submerged in the flood of modern building. It was a farming community which perhaps cultivated the open fields of les Camps extending beyond the wishing-well. Here now is a colony of council or, more correctly, States houses, and it is to this colony, rather than to the old village, that the name of Ville Amphrey is now applied.

Another very narrow lane to the left of the wishing-well, known as la Ruette Fainel, leads to le Vallon, the seat of the Carey family until recent years. Both the house and its setting are extremely picturesque.

At le Vallon end of the Ruette Fainel are a pump and a granite trough. These are parish property, and explain the existence of a public right of way which, apparently encroaching on a private estate, might deter many a stranger from exploring it.

The crest of the Careys, one of the leading Guernsey families, carved in granite over one of the entrance archways, displays three Tudor roses. During the 16th century William Carey of Somerset married a sister of Anne Boleyn, the ill-fated mother of Queen Elizabeth, and it is from this collateral connection with the Royal family that the device was presumably adopted.

PETIT PORT. The path above Moulin Huet which skirts the boundary of le Vallon estate, leads to the Courtes Falaises. It opens up charming vistas every few yards. At one point it is on the very edge of a crumbling chasm; at another a tiny plot of land, bearing every sign of cultivation in the past, can be seen.

The gate which once stood at its narrowest point disappeared during the Occupation. To the left of this gate is a towering pinnacle of granite, covered with copper-hued lichen, familiarly known as the Cuckoo Rock. Above this the path widens out, and at its highest point is deflected to the left by the shallow valley, overgrown with trees, appropriately known as the Courtes Falaises.

The seat at this corner—Carey's seat—which disappeared as a result of the war, has now been replaced.

The rambler, aiming to reach Petit Port, Jerbourg, or the Peastacks, all of which are here in sight, has a bewildering choice of roads before him. He may continue along the road upwards until he reaches le Vallon. On the way, where once a gate stood, he will be struck by the sight of a patch of wild rhubarb, which for size and rankness must be unrivalled in the island.

Above the gate, on the right, is another wishing-well, clear and cool, the spring of which is inexhaustible even in the longest drought. Its overflow fills a trough for cattle, but the cleanliness of its immediate surroundings gives evidence of its lack of use.

From le Vallon the wayfarer can join the straight Jerbourg Road, another creation of Doyle's for military purposes. This road runs parallel to the south coast.

But the goat-path on the cliffs themselves is far from difficult, and yields an uninterrupted vista of rocks and sea.

The descent to Petit Port is by flights of seemingly unending steps, green and slimy in a few places from the seeping water of a sluggish spring. At the very bottom of the steps there was formerly a typical Guernsey fountain, from which picnic parties used to fill their kettles. But this has been destroyed by a fall of rock.

At low water Petit Port has the finest stretch of sand in St Martin's. The steps by which the bay is reached, and which render it comparatively easy of access, replace a dangerous, winding, crumbling path of the early days of the century, known, aptly, as the Corkscrew. Another path somewhat of this nature, but allowing access only at half or low tide, may be found on the right, but it is dangerous and little used.

On the night of July 14–15, 1940, scarcely a month after the occupation of the Channel Islands by the enemy, these steps at Petit Port were scaled by a small party of British Commandos.

Hubert Nicolle, a Guernseyman serving with the Hampshire Regiment, had already made a successful lone landing and got away to report. This was to be followed up by a four-point Commando landing, at Moye Point, at Petit Bot, at a point farther west on the South coast, and at Vazon Bay. The only actual landing was made at Petit Port by a force under the command of Lt.-Colonel Durnford Slater. After climbing up the steps, they found an empty machine-gun post and an empty Jerbourg barracks. As it was then time to return to the waiting boats, they built a road block on the Jerbourg Road and returned down the steps to the beach. The rough seas forced those in charge of the boats to send in a dinghy to collect the men and their arms. After a few trips this sank, and three men who could not swim had to be left to be rounded up by the Germans. Though Slater himself later dismissed the raid as a "ridiculous, almost comic, failure", it was a useful experience for those taking part, and it caused uneasiness among the German garrison, and great excitement and many rumours among the "occupied" island population.

There are some remarkable features of Petit Port which cannot fail to interest the geologist. On the Jerbourg side is a gigantic perpendicular cliff-face of granite, cleft from top to bottom by a crack, also perpendicular, visible for a considerable distance from the Moulin Huet side. The Cannon Rock, again on the left-hand side facing the sea, is a remarkable formation. It is a more or less circular mass of granite, with a flattened, conical-shaped crown overgrown with grass. This mass is attached to the main cliff by a grassy isthmus a few yards in breadth.

The Cannon Rock is fairly easily approachable from the land. At low tide it can be reached from the beach. It will then be seen that a natural tunnel pierces this isthmus. For untold centuries the sea has been widening this tunnel, and one day the roof will fall in and the Cannon Rock be separated from the mainland. Like some of its neighbours, the Peastacks, it will then stand isolated and alone.

JERBOURG. The ascent of the steps from Petit Port is hard work. At the top there is a right-of-way past German bunkers to the Jerbourg Road.

An alternative path is a steep goat-track to the right. Almost immediately the wayfarer finds himself on a rectangular level plateau or terrace of fair extent, bearing every indication of artificiality. On its Moulin Huet flank is a low bank, which would provide ample cover for recumbent warriors. The remaining faces appear to have been quarried perpendicularly from the surface of the cliff. A small force of men could easily bivouac here in comparative safety and comfort, concealed from any opposing force approaching from the sea, and, in the days when weapons were less lethal, could have successfully countered a landing via the corkscrew path by the simple expedient of toppling boulders over the parapet.

Here is the Mur de Jerbourg, the first of a mass of defences begun,

D

perhaps, by prehistoric man, improved by the Romans and our mediaeval ancestors, utilised by the implacable enemies of Napoleon and, finally, drowned with concrete and steel by Germans as part of the defences of the Atlantic Wall.

The Château de Jerbourg, reference to which is frequently found in old records, probably never existed. An entrenchment, however, is easily traceable from this plateau above Petit Port, across the Jerbourg Road, and extending down one side of the valley of Divette (the Pine Forest) to sea level at Marble Bay, whose true and significant name is Pied du Mur.

A probable loop in this entrenchment enclosed two *hougues*, or mounds, reminiscent of borough mounds, which, it must be remembered, were not always wholly artificial. One of these was the hillock upon which stands Doyle's Column. The other, on the opposite side of the road, was utilised by the Germans as a gun-site. It is probable, of course, that these two mounds once formed a single elevated mass, through which Doyle cut his military road to his new barracks above Telegraph Bay.

These defences across the Jerbourg isthmus, collectively known as Jerbourg Castle, extending almost from Bec du Nez to Petit Port, were definitely committed to the charge of Matthew de Sausmarez by Edward III in 1330. "Men of the commonalty of the said island", the document states, "shall be received there with their goods and chattels." In short, in the event of invasion these defences constituted the last ditch.

It is interesting to note that to this day the Seigneur of Sausmarez retains, among many other titles, that of Châtelain of Jerbourg. This title received royal confirmation as recently as 1921, when His Majesty King George V visited the site. There Sir Havilland de Sausmarez, Bailiff and Seigneur of Sausmarez, as third cup-bearer of the King, "whensoever he should visit the island", provided the cup and handed His Majesty his tea, the King having graciously so modernised and commuted this ancient service.

A laconic remark by Tupper on the ancient Jerbourg defences is also not without interest. He says:

"The promontory of Jerbourg, so strong by nature, would have been the better site (for Fort George) had it not been too distant from the town, Castle Cornet and the roadstead."

On the side of the road opposite Doyle's Column is a car park. This marks the beginning of a lane and cliff path, skirting the western face of the Jerbourg peninsula, which present features of interest at nearly every step.

At the extremity of the car park is a hummock of earth utilised by the occupying forces as a gun-site. It is now honeycombed with concrete tunnels which emerge some distance ahead in a disused gravel pit. The exterior appearance of the mound, however, has changed very little.

This hummock has, rightly or wrongly, been identified as the site of the keep of Jerbourg Castle. For, as has previously been pointed out, the existence at any time of a castle in the true sense of the word is open to grave doubt.

The path meanders, sometimes in deep depressions hollowed out by water, sometimes between high hedges, and sometimes shoulder deep in gorse and bracken. The great bay which has Icart Point on the one hand and the promontory ending in the Peastacks on the other as its two encircling arms, is in view the whole time. Blackthorn grows in profusion, whitening the scene in spring with its blossom and bearing a heavy crop of sloes in late summer and autumn.

A small field on the left, unusually level, and surrounded by a stone wall, may easily escape observation. It was at one time the drill-ground for the troops quartered at Jerbourg Barracks.

The Peastacks comprise three main rock masses, named respectively le Petit Aiguillon, le Gros Aiguillon, and l'Aiguillon d'Andrelot.

L'Aiguillon d'Andrelot bears a superficial resemblance to "an aged man enveloped in the gown and cowl of a monk". That is why it has been called le Petit Bonhomme Andriou. According to Sir Edgar MacCulloch, in his *Guernsey Folklore*, fishermen and pilots were wont, when passing these rocks, to remove their hats, to offer a libation of wine or cider, or to cast a biscuit or some old garment into the sea.

Peastacks is a fair translation of *Tas de Pois d'Amont*, apart from the omission of the last word in the French. But this omitted word is important, for the corresponding chain of rocks off Pleinmont bears the name *Tas de Pois d'Aval*. Following Métivier, MacCulloch says that "Amont (meaning *en haut*) is the Guernsey word for east, Aval, meaning *en bas*, their word for west". Both seem to have missed the fact that *mont* (mount) and *val* (valley) may equally well stand for upper and lower.

The road from the Peastacks to Jerbourg Barracks, though a private one, is considerably more than a path. Below it nestles Telegraph Bay, where the cable connecting Jersey with Guernsey ends. The eastern coast of the island has now been reached, and the northern arm of the bay, a group of rocks jutting well out into the sea, is St Martin's Point.

The descent to this point down a long flight of steps is at first rather steep. Later the gradient is gentle and there are comparatively large areas of springy turf which, in the 16th century, must have provided a comfortable foothold to the crowd which witnessed the execution of a pirate named Richard Higgins. The record of his sentence may still be seen at the Greffe.

In 1565, Tupper and Duncan both agree, the Royal Navy was most efficient. Despite this, however, piracy was common in the Channel. Richard Higgins, captain of the *John* of Sandwich, was an unlucky man. His ship was wrecked on the coast of Guernsey, and the pinnace in which he and part of his crew escaped drowning was captured.

These men confessed their guilt, and were imprisoned in Castle Cornet until the Queen's pleasure should be known.

This was not expressed until the following year, and was of a most singular character. It stated that the men arrested "were deceived by representations made to them that the object of their voyage was purely commercial".

Who had made these representations? Was it the local authorities? Her Majesty's will was no less amazing. Taking into consideration that these men had been some time in custody, the Governor was ordered to choose two or three of the "Most culpable and fittest for example" and execute them out of hand. The remainder were to be set at liberty, with orders to repair to London and sue for pardon.

The wishes of Elizabeth were respected sparingly by the Governor, Queen's commissioners, and Royal Court. Richard Higgins alone was selected for execution, and one November day a pinioned Higgins, escorted by the Sheriff and attendant *bordiers*, proceeded to St Martin's Point, near the full sea mark, and there, by the same officers, was hanged and strangled till he was dead.

In the neighbourhood of the rock, where once stood the gallows upon which the body of Richard Higgins hung for an indefinite period as an object lesson to his fellow pirates, now stands a lighthouse. From it in foggy weather a wailing note is heard, in which the imaginative might well detect the spectral voice of Higgins. This lighthouse is reached by a short bridge of reinforced concrete, which spans a rocky chasm. Its crossing, however, should be attempted only on a fine day, for in stormy weather the waves dash over it with considerable force.

Jerbourg Barracks, immediately above St Martin's Point, passed out of the ownership of the War Office after the First World War. In the early days of the present century, when the island was never without a regular garrison, the barracks were used as married quarters.

At the far end of the barrack yard is a mound thrown up by the Germans, upon which they erected a powerful range-finder. And all round are gun-sites, trenches, and strong points.

The barracks mark the end of the military road constructed by Sir John Doyle. Here stood an old farm-house, which has been reconstructed to form a modern hotel.

CALAIS AND THE PINE FOREST. From the *hougue* upon which Doyle's Column once stood, the road back towards St Martin's slopes gently for some 30 or 40 yards, until it reaches a turning on the right. Beginning as a short, straight descent, this lane turns abruptly, first to the left and then to the right, running past a farm-yard peopled by ducks, geese, and chickens, and there is a genuine old Guernsey farm-house as a background. This is the Bouvée Farm.

During the summer months, Boy Scouts, camped in the fields behind, are very much in evidence.

The Bouvée Lane, as this road is called, continues as a hedge-bordered track for a few yards farther. The road then becomes, for a considerable distance, a footworn track across unfenced fields. Then the hedges reappear and the track continues as a narrow defile, overshadowed by trees and bushes impenetrable to sunlight, until it debouches at Calais, just above the St Martin's side of Fermain Bay.

Before the War these fields were fenced. The occupation forces threw down not only the hedges bordering the lane, but also those dividing the various fields. The outcome is, by Guernsey standards, a vast open area of pasture-land.

The purpose of the Germans in removing these boundaries is not clear. Today the area has the aspect of an aerodrome of moderate size and, noting also that Doyle's Column was removed, the guess may be hazarded that this open space was intended for use as an emergency landing-place for aircraft.

On the landward side the Germans established a rather elaborately arranged cemetery, where, among others, the victims of the raid on Fort George, on the eve of the Allied landings on the Normandy beaches, were buried. This land has now been returned to its owner and the bodies buried there have been removed to the Foulon Cemetery.

In transforming this group of tiny fields into one large open space, the Germans restored this area to its condition in the 16th century. It was then a *bouvée*, defined by Métivier as "as much land as an ox can plough in one year". And although in Guernsey a *bouvée* is calculated to be 20 *vergées*, or rather more than eight acres, this *bouvée* comprises a considerably greater area.

A notice-board at the Jerbourg end of the Bouvée Lane says: "To the Pine Forest". The Pine Forest is the climax of a "grassy and ferny hollow, below the Doyle Column at Jerbourg". The track to that grassy and ferny hollow may easily be missed. At the bottom of the first slope of the Bouvée Lane, where the road turns first left and then right towards the Bouvée Farm, there is a modern house on the right. An unsightly concrete platform followed by a flight of concrete steps will be seen next to the gable of this house. These steps lead not only to a quaint marshy dell, with the ubiquitous well and *douit*, but also to a deep track, soon opening out into a narrow valley, very damp and boggy. This is the path to Divette.

In spring this lovely glen is a veritable treasure-house for the field botanist. Despite the lush vegetation, the archaeologist, too, will not fail to mark the deep vallum which crosses the path at one spot. But Divette has never received systematic examination from any archaeologist. Aerial photography, if undertaken at any time, might reveal buried foundations and unknown earthworks which would solve the enigma of Jerbourg Castle.

Only an occasional glimpse of the sea is obtained from this path. Towards its end the vegetation gives place to pines, under which a thick carpet of pine-needles effectively spells death to any other form of plant life.

Beneath these pines an almost level strip of land extends to the crumbling verge of the shore, where in Napoleonic days a shallow trench was dug and a parapet, facing the sea, thrown up.

To the right of the path is a finely cut granite pillar, announcing that this pleasant spot, once private property, was given in perpetuity by its owner, Sir Havilland de Sausmarez, to the States and people of Guernsey, a few years before the Second World War.

The descent to shore level is short, steep, muddy, and slippery, but not dangerous. It ends on a breakwater of huge boulders, loosely thrown together, of unknown age and origin, and connecting a rocky mass with the gravelly and crumbling cliff face. On its right is a beach of small sea-worn rocks and shallow pools, and on the left a sandy creek forming an excellent miniature bathing-place at all states of the tide.

The bay to the left, easily reached from Divette at low tide, or by climbing the rocks fringing the shore at any other time, is Pied du

Mur, though commonly known as Marble Bay. The origin of this name is obscure. It may perhaps be ascribed to the existence of a vein of quartz which, streaked with rusty red, has the appearance of white marble. The largest outcrop of this type of mineral will be found above Petit Port, and the boulder, bearing the Pied du Diable or Devil's Footprint at Jerbourg, is of the same kind.

Here, too, is a fine cavern called the Marble Cave, its entrance fringed with the fern known as *Asplenium marinum*. It boasts a chimney, much like the Pot in Sark, but of inferior proportions. The top of the chimney is much overgrown with brambles, resembling in this respect the Creux in Herm.

There are several points at this spot where the cliff face may be scaled. All involve a scramble and demand caution and a good head. Once the grass verge is attained, the Bouvée Lane may easily be reached by cutting across a field.

If the cliff path be followed, however, Bec du Nez will soon come into view, and the descent to the fishermen's landing-place, though steep, is neither difficult nor dangerous. Indeed, the remains of the road originally made to the gun platform still exist, as does also the old vaulted ammunition store.

These fortifications, like so many others, date back to 1803. The then Lord of the Manor, Matthew de Sausmarez, was willing to grant, freely, the land required and access thereto, and in addition to this, permission to quarry the stone needed in the immediate vicinity.

But he attached certain conditions to his offer. There was at Jerbourg a tower or watch-house, used by the militia, built in 1780. He demanded the use of the two bottom storeys of this building, for what purpose is not clear, as well as of the attic of the watch-house at Bec du Nez. The roof of this he undertook to keep in repair. He insisted, however, that access to the land at Bec du Nez should be restricted to those connected with watch-house or battery.

The States rejected this offer. But Matthew de Sausmarez was a persistent man. By 1807 he had won the support of the local Commander-in-Chief, Peter Heron, who wished to establish a signal station at Jerbourg. Peter Heron commanded the respect of the States, and on his advice the tower was withdrawn from militia use and handed over to the seigneur of Sausmarez. Precisely where this tower or watch-house stood is uncertain. It may perhaps have been pulled down when Jerbourg Barracks were built.

It was this same Matthew who, in 1798, insisted on his right to be transported to Jersey by his tenants. His right was not disputed. He was conveyed thither and landed at the nearest, but not most convenient, point in this island. Here, however, the tenants claimed that their responsibility ended, and Matthew was compelled to make his own arrangements for the return journey. History does not record whether the tenants claimed or received the dinner which was their due for this service.

The Bec du Nez landing, upon which small sums of public money have been spent for centuries, is in good order, and a few boats are kept there. It is, however, nowadays used far more by owners of pleasure-boats than by fishermen seeking to wrest a livelihood from the deep.

The observer among the boats at Bec du Nez is looking across the wide stretch of Fermain Bay. To the left he sees the mouth of the valley, closed by the longest of all Guernsey bulwarks. Near the centre a slipway disappears from view through an opening in the wall. And above the wall the top of a Martello tower is exposed.

At the opposite side of the bay, at a spot seldom left dry by the tide, is a flight of steps, to which are moored one or two boats. Here the water, particularly at high tide, is very deep, and the place therefore finds favour with devotees of diving. Though not easily approachable from the land, these steps have from time immemorial been kept in good repair. Nowadays they are known as the Moorings, which is a perfect translation of their old name les Amarrages.

FERMAIN. Although there are good cliff paths to Fermain Bay from both its northern and southern flanks, the best approach is down the valley from the Fort Road. This lane descends steeply in an almost straight line on the southern edge of the valley, until it reaches the Châlet Hotel. There it makes a hairpin bend across the base of the valley, and then continues as a winding track until it reaches the bay.

The stream which runs down the valley forms the boundary between St Martin's and St Peter Port, and the bay is shared by both parishes. In the early days of the century one side of the bay was allotted to ladies and the other to gentlemen for bathing purposes, but this rule no longer applies.

Fermain Bay Lane is officially known as la Ruette des Orgeries, or the lane of the barley fields. Here perhaps was the source of the raw material for the brewery which existed on the South Esplanade, then called the Galet Heaume, as far back as the days of the Stuarts.

Traces of cultivation in the distant past are far more common on the north or St Peter Port side of the valley than on the steeper St Martin's side. From a point near the back entrance of La Favorita Hotel a footpath runs above the road. From this the old terraces or *côtils*, now covered with trees, are still distinctly visible.

Nowadays the valley is relatively well wooded, and its beauty has not been marred by indiscriminate building. At the top, near the Fort Road, is a quaint house of no great age, built in the style of le Vallon and probably designed by the same architect. It is known as Feremina.

At the bottom of the first slope is the Châlet, erected as a private dwelling at the beginning of the century. Its then owner, a man of considerable mechanical genius, made use of the stream to run a dynamo, housed in a picturesque kind of summer-house some distance down the valley. The Châlet was probably the first private dwelling in the island in which electricity was used for lighting. A much enlarged Châlet now does duty as a hotel.

During the occupation, the Germans also established a water-driven dynamo for the generation of electricity. But this was placed much lower down, almost at beach level.

The long bulwark across the mouth of the bay cuts off part of the beach. The result is a steep bank of pebbles at high-water mark, which has the effect of making bathing at high tide by non-swimmers somewhat dangerous.

Fermain has always been regarded as one of the weak spots in island defence. The bay provides good and sheltered anchorage, out of reach of the guns of Castle Cornet, and landing from boats may be easily effected on the beach. Indeed, in summer visitors are transported between the bay and St Peter Port by a regular service of motor-boats.

It was here during the days of the Commonwealth that Captain Bowden of the *Bramble* cast anchor and sent a boat ashore to pick up the three Parliamentary Commissioners, whom he subsequently and treacherously handed over to the tender mercies of that sturdy royalist, Sir Peter Osborne, in Castle Cornet.

At the end of the 18th century, too, a press-gang party landed here, penetrated as far as the Hubits and forcibly carried off three young St Martinais. This was a flagrant breach of the insular charters, and when the Royal Court protested, two of the men were sent back. The third was probably either at sea, or he may perhaps have found the life of the navy so congenial that he elected to remain in it.

It is not surprising, then, that Fermain boasts numerous batteries, some of them of very large size, a number of watch-houses and ammunition sheds, and a Martello tower, built for the most part during the last decade of the 18th and the first of the 19th centuries.

The picnic-house, on the north side, is an old watch-house. It has served its present peaceful purpose for considerably more than half a century, until recently in the hands of two or three generations of the same family.

Typical Napoleonic defences crown the bluff to the north, which overlooks Castle Cornet and the town of St Peter Port. Here there is an ammunition shed, a small gun platform, and the famous Pepper Pot. The last-named served a double purpose. It was an extremely strong sentry-box, designed to shelter its occupant in all weathers and, white-washed on the outside, it did and does duty as a sailing-mark.

The most important village for which Fermain forms an outlet to the sea is les Hubits, a rambling aggregation of farms in a series of depressions sited to the west of the Fort Road. Almost at its extremity stands the Tree Top's Hotel, once the seat of the Jeremies, a family which for generations distinguished itself in the arts and professions and played a leading part in the public life of the island.

Not far from the hotel is a small marshy area known as the Mare Mado. Mado is probably Madoc, the name of a Welsh prince who, when Guernsey was captured and occupied by the French in 1338, was probably the leader of the enemy forces. An underground movement in St Martin's parish, with a membership of 87, attacked the French at this spot. The Guernseymen were defeated, and retreated on Petit Port, where they embarked for Jersey. They found refuge at St Ouen's. Among them were John de la Marche, captain of the parish—that is, chief officer of the militia—Peter de Sausmarez, James Guille, Peter Bonamy, John de Blanchelande, and Thomas de Vauriouf. It should be noted that all these are old St Martin's names. Further, the occupying force cannot have been a large one, to invite attack from 87 men. Had the other parishes pulled their weight, the invaders might have been expelled.

ICART. There is a broad similarity between the two south-coast inlets, the most easterly of which includes the bays of Moulin Huet and Saints and the most westerly Petit Bot.

The extreme westerly point of the first is Icart. This may be reached by climbing the cliffs from the road leading to Blanchelande Harbour, or by following the road, constructed by Doyle at the beginning of the 19th century, from the Grande Rue, near St Martin's church.

The first part of this road, known as the Route des Coutures, cuts through the Cure, as the glebe land is called, and it is interesting to note that along this road there are several old farm-houses with their gables on the roadside. The Route des Coutures replaced, as a thoroughfare, the Ruette de la Vallée, more commonly known as the School Lane, which linked the village of la Bellieuse, the centre of St Martin's parish, with that of la Fosse.

The Route des Coutures, more commonly known nowadays as Saints Road, ends at a fork, the left-hand prong of which is the road to Saints Bay and the right that to Icart. Throughout its length the latter follows the crest of Saints Bay valley. It possesses a few quaint old cottages and farms, some with charming names. There is la Boissellée, a dwarf, rambling cottage, now tiled, but once thatched, and overgrown with roses. Another old farm bears the name of la Galliotte.

One farm, built in a hollow, has fine old granite chimney-stacks of the kind said to be favoured as resting-places by witches, but much of its charm has been irretrievably ruined by the substitution of corrugated iron for thatch upon its roof. On the lawn in front are the stone troughs of an old cider-press. These are not uncommon in the island. A similar one, filled with earth and planted with gay flowers, will be found on the lawn of the Convent of the Sacred Heart at Blanchelande.

Just beyond the turning known as the Marette Road, which leads to la Villette, a particularly fine view of the Peastacks opens up. Formerly, a house concealed this superb landscape. It was known as la Marcherie, and was owned and used as a country house by Victor Hugo. At the beginning of the present century his descendants were wont to spend the summer there. Later it became a guest-house, but during the occupation the Germans demolished it to the foundations, for the obvious reason that it impeded the view.

Beyond the Marcherie there are few houses, and the fields, particularly on the Petit Bot side, are much favoured in summer as camping sites by Boy Scouts and Youth Clubs.

Before the extremity of the Point is reached, a turning to the left, closed by a gate, leads to the cliffs on the Saints side, and the Martello tower, on the edge of the fishermen's walk, comes into sight. From this spot the cliffs can be followed by a fairly negotiable path right round. In places, indeed, it is possible to descend to sea level. Intrepid climbers, interested in geology, will find at low tide in some of the tiny creeks much to attract their attention. There are one or two caves, all tidal and none of great size. A few potholes may also be found among the rocks. Although these will bear no comparison in size with those of Sark, they are nevertheless interesting, the smoothness of their sides and the symmetrical cauldron-like shape illustrating the slow and persistent action of the forces of Nature.

Whereas at the eastern end of the inlet some of the rocks of the Peastacks are completely cut off by the sea, at the western end we have a rocky mass connected with the mainland by a narrow neck, reminiscent, on a very small scale, of the Coupée in Sark.

The lofty plateau above the Château, from parts of which the bays on both east and west may be viewed, has a considerable area of level ground, on a portion of which a car park has been laid out. From here the whole of the coast from Icart to la Moye may be seen.

The barracks, built by Doyle at the beginning of the 19th century, and which provided the *raison d'être* for the construction of the road, have now completely disappeared, and the old War Department Land, enclosed by the loose stone walls forming the boundaries of the parish commons, passed into private hands a year or two after the end of the First World War.

During the occupation the Germans made good use of Icart Point as part of their Atlantic Wall, mounting several heavy guns and constructing concrete fortifications and an intricate system of trenches.

In places the cliff boundary has disappeared so completely that it is scarcely possible to establish where it stood. The numerous concrete shelters and strong points would yield only to dynamite. But they have for the most part been covered with earth and turfed, so that they are now beginning to resemble nothing so much as the round barrows so common on the South Downs of England.

LA BETTE AND LE JAONNET. There are many spots between the Château d'Icart and the bay de la Bette in the north-eastern corner of the inlet where the cliff may be descended, not with ease, but at least with comparative safety, as far as sea level.

Almost immediately below the site of the wicket gate, which gave access to the common from the car park, there is a formation much resembling the Cannon Rock at Petit Port. Its cone towers up into a pinnacle of bare weather-beaten stone, and its flanks are clothed in thick, short, velvety grass. The sea, however, has not driven a tunnel through it.

Near by is the Creux ès Chiens, whose mouth is several feet above beach level. To enter it, a difficult scramble up a rock-face rendered smooth by the action of the sea is unavoidable, but the result is well worth the effort.

The cave is not large. It penetrates into the cliff side only a short distance, and resembles nothing so much as the beginning of a mine gallery. Its roof, however, which exudes reddish drops of moisture, is richly overgrown with fine, because undisturbed, examples of the fern known as *Asplenium marinum*.

It should here be made clear that even at the lowest of spring tides it is not possible to explore the rocks, coves, and caverns at shore level between Icart and la Moye without continually re-ascending the cliff side. Vigour and enthusiasm are the indispensable characteristics of the explorer of this romantic coast.

La Bette, sited relative to Petit Port, and resembling it in many respects, is very difficult of approach. The path down is almost perpendicular, and its loose gravel surface makes it very dangerous. At dead low tide, however, when it has a considerable area of sandy beach, it can be approached with comparative ease from the next opening, Jaonnet, between the cliff-face and a reef of rocks running parallel to it.

Jaonnet, especially at low tide, is one of the most delightful coves of the island. It forms the seaward end of a valley beginning almost in the Marette Road. But, unlike those of Saints and Petit Bot, its mouth has not been eroded down to sea level, but is bitten off abruptly to form a lofty perpendicular lip.

On a jutting outcrop of granite on its eastern side a set of rude steps was carved in the distant past. These do not descend quite to sea level, and the final descent to the bay is by iron ladder.

Jaonnet at low tide is like the arena of a natural amphitheatre. It is a delightful bathing-place, with a stretch of sand rivalled only by that of Petit Port. There are numerous caves penetrating the rock-face of the frowning cliffs, and on three sides the cove is wrapped in a mantle of gorse and bracken which grows with the utmost luxuriance.

The gorse or furze, Norman-French *jaon*, modern French *genêt*, has given its name to the bay. In the days when dried furze was an important fuel, used in the baking of bread, the possession of a *jaonnière* or brake was highly prized, and such land was not regarded, as today, as marginal land.

The cliffs can be descended again at la Fosse, another shallow valley whose beginning can be traced to la Fallaise, the road leading to Petit Bot on the left-hand flank of the main valley at St Martin's. The descent here is somewhat perilous and there is no beach. There is a mass of rock of varying colours, almost level, but with a rough and jagged surface.

This is a spot favoured by amateur fishermen. It was here, too, that an abortive attempt was made to mine silver, and a horizontal trial boring in the side of the cliff, which can be entered from beach level, is well worth exploring.

The heights between la Fosse, and Petit Bot are known as Mont Hubert. Of late years part of these have been planted with firs, and the effect is very fine.

At one more place before Petit Bot is reached can sea level be attained. This is la Grande Ruette, also favoured by amateur fishermen, who, while not able to reach beach level, can find spots from which they can cast their lines into deep water.

As before, the line of retreat is the line of approach, and no descent is possible into Petit Bot bay from this side save by following the cliff path, either to a point in the valley just above the Martello tower, or by joining the steep and winding slope of the Route de la Fallaise, which, linking up with that from les Pages, leads direct to the bay.

SAUSMAREZ MANOR. Beside Sausmarez Road stands Sausmarez Manor, the most interesting extant family house in Guernsey. The front façade can be seen from the road through the iron gates, which have the family crest of a falcon on each of the outer pillars, and the stretch of lawn leading to the front steps can also be seen. But there are more grounds behind, a fish-pond, tennis court, woodland, and small area of parkland, with often a Guernsey cow or two grazing.

The family are first mentioned in Guernsey history in 1254, when William de Salinelles, the Seigneur of Samares in Jersey, acquired the Fief and Manor in St Martin's. Of the mediaeval manor house a portion can still be seen in the lower courses of a granite outbuilding across a courtyard from the present manor.

In 1557 the fief and manor passed by inheritance to John Andros, son of an Englishman, John Andrews, Lieutenant to the Governor. John Andros built the Tudor house which still stands obliquely at the back of the later dwelling, and there generations of Andros lived until the early days of Sir Edmund Andros, Governor of the Colony of New York, and Lieutenant-Governor and Bailiff of Guernsey. He did not consider the old Tudor house suitable for his position, and planned a finer dwelling. At his death in 1714 his will was found to stipulate that his nephew John must build the new house within a year, and the result was the Queen Anne house, a fine and stately building of grey granite with red granite coigns.

Meanwhile a younger branch of the de Sausmarez family had survived and prospered, relatively, through the dangerous 17th century by wool-trading and privateering. The family capital was also increased in the mid-18th century by the inheritance of the prize-money which Philip de Sausmarez had won as his share from Anson's great voyage round the world. Thus his elder brother John was able to buy back the fief and manor house in 1748 from the Andros family.

John's two sons, Matthew and Thomas, succeeded in turn as Seigneur, and it was Thomas, who had 28 children from two marriages, who built the Regency house on the back of the Queen Anne house, to house them all.

Little remains of the Regency house as in 1873 Thomas's youngest son, General George de Sausmarez, who had bought out his brothers, decided to pull it down and replace it with his Victorian house. This comprised a large dining-room and drawing-room, and an entrance-hall to link it with the Queen Anne house. Some clash of styles was inevitable, particularly as the General had served in the East India Company, but the whole conglomeration of houses makes a fascinating dwelling, full of history and character.

Near the entrance gateway, on Sausmarez Road, is a little building, with the first floor overhanging. This is the Seigneurial Court House of the Fief de Sausmarez. There are a number of fiefs, or manors in Guernsey, some held by the Crown, others by private individuals, and there are other places where these relics of the old feudal courts can still meet, the paved lane by St Saviour's Church, or the churchyard of St Marie de Castel for instance. But when these courts, presided over by the seneschal and with the other officers in attendance, do meet, they are but shadows of their former Norman and mediaeval selves.

THE CHURCH OF ST MARTIN DE LA BELLIEUSE. On a mound, which may, or may not, be artificial, stands the parish church, with a picturesque cluster of old Guernsey farmhouses nearby. The church and the farms are at the original centre of St Martin, with a stream, good arable land around, and an ancient pre-Christian image to remind all passers-by how venerable the site is. This statue-menhir, which now stands as one of the gate-posts at the churchyard entrance, is very ancient, possibly dating back to 2000 B.C. She is a representation of the great Mediterranean Mother Goddess of fertility, and is popularly known today as La Gran' mère du Chimquière, the Old Lady of the Cemetery.

The church is partly Norman, partly flamboyant in style and dates from the 11th to the 13th centuries. Like nearly all Channel Islands' churches, its roof is vaulted, and the present covering of slate is probably less than two centuries old. The church has suffered badly at the hands of restorers. Some of the Norman windows are quite modern, and the stained glass in them is far from artistic. Much of the interior stonework has been spoiled by plaster.

The font, just inside the south door, which is covered by a porch considered to be one of the finest existing examples of flamboyant work in the Channel Islands, was for many years used as a pig-trough. It is a remarkably fine example of cut granite, not improved by restoration. It is unique, in that it is the only pre-Reformation font in the island.

The tablets on the walls are to the memory of Careys and de Vics, Gosselins and Lefebvres, Sausmarez and Andros, all well-known St Martin's families. Under the tower, which divides the south nave from the choir, is buried Amias Andros, Seigneur of Saus-marez. He was appointed Bailiff of Guernsey by Charles I, but did not exercise his office until 1660, when the Stuarts were restored to the throne of England. He was in Castle Cornet, the Royalist stronghold, when the three Guernsey *Jurats*, de Beauvoir, Carey, and de Havilland, were treacherously trapped by Sir Peter Osborne. He was a general, probably the last general, of the Guernsey militia.

THE PRINCESS ELISABETH HOSPITAL. The States had originally intended to build a new mental hospital in the de Putron estate by Fermain. But the site was considered unsuitable, and before the Second World War they bought a new site at the Vauquiédor, in the north-east corner of the parish, in an area of farms and fields. Here the buildings were completed in 1939, but it had scarcely been started as a mental hospital when the Germans arrived to take it over and use it as a general hospital. After the liberation, the States decided also that it should be a general hospital, and after adaptation and conversion it was officially opened by the Princess in 1949.

Its original buildings, standing in pleasant grounds, now have beds for 146 patients, who are attended by a resident nursing staff and by general practitioners who come in. More recently, addi-tional departments have been added: a Pathology department, and a Radio Diagnostic department; and a Nurses Home has been built. The latest innovation, in 1967, has been a Training School for enrolled nurses, established in a new building. This school is designed to recruit mainly from the Channel Islands, but it can take in nurses from elsewhere if there is room. The Hospital authorities work closely with the St John's Ambulance Brigade, which is based in the Rohais. Their ambulances bring in patients

The dolmen known as Le Trepied, near Perelle

The chapel of Ste Apolline

The model church
La Grotte at Vauxb

Sausmarez Park

The gateway to Vale Castle

The German tower on Sausmarez Fort

The harbour at St Sampson's

St Sampson's Church

from all over the island, and their marine ambulance, the *Flying Christine II*, waits at her moorings in the harbour, ready to pick up patients from the other islands.

Not far away, across the fields, is the Corbinerie Estate. This fine Regency house, in a small but attractive park, was left to the States by the Rev. P. T. Mignot, and is now being adapted for use as a training and occupation centre for mentally-handicapped adults.

The Forest Parish lies next to St Martin's along the South coast, and is a parish largely of farmers and growers. It has its centre round the church and Le Bourg, the old cluster of farms, and has inside its borders the most westerly of the south coast bays, Petit Bot, the airport, and the Tektronix factory nearby, the charming little village of Le Variouf and the fine Perron du Roi menhir standing at the Forest Road-Petit Bot junction.

PETIT BOT. This appears frequently in old documents as Tibot, and sometimes as Petit Bosq. The two valleys from the Forest and the St Martin's sides are to this day fairly well-wooded and to these bosky valleys we may perhaps trace the name.

There are three good road approaches. One in each parish follows the base of the valley. On the Forest side this begins at the Bourg, the original main village of that parish. The road is steep and winding, and should the pedestrian deviate to the right, through narrow, tortuous lanes, he will discover, on higher ground, two more old villages, les Houards and le Variouf. The latter is picturesque and largely unspoiled.

On the St Martin's side the valley begins at les Pages, on the outskirts of la Villette. There is at first steep ground on the right. Later this gives way to tiny marshy meadows, and several water-lanes, where hart's-tongue ferns grow rank, wind upward to the main road between St Martin's and the Forest.

It is at the beginning of one of these lanes that the Route de la Fallaise joins this valley road, forming a hair-pin bend. The Route de la Fallaise, beginning as les Croutes, follows the crest of the valley. Where the road begins to descend, just before a sharp turn to the right, where a wicket gate gives access to the cliffs, an old farm-house lies in the hollow. This is the seat of the principal tenant on a Royal fief known as la Velleresse de la Fallaise. It was the duty of this tenant and his fellows to keep watch over the sea for the approach of pirates or enemies of any kind (Fr. *veiller*—to watch).

A fine view of the valley and bay opens up from this road,

particularly of a fine natural rock arch on the Forest side near Portelet.

Much water runs down both these valleys, water which in the past was put to good use. The old wooden water-mill, although completely neglected, was a feature of Petit Bot until the occupation. The old mill house, used as a tavern, and the water-wheel, were both destroyed by the Germans, so that the streams might be used to run a dynamo. The water is now collected at sea-level by the States Water Board and pumped into the reservoir at St Saviour's.

LA MOYE. The cliff walk from Petit Bot to la Moye begins very steeply, and remains so until the bay of Portelet is reached. The descent into this bay, which has many of the features of Jaonnet, is not easy, and should be attempted only when the tide is low.

Between Petit Bot and Portelet there are numerous batteries, and one or two buildings which are relics of defences built during the Napoleonic scare. That this part of the coast was closely guarded is evident from the fact that in 1781 the Royal Court awarded, and the States agreed to pay, to Pierre Allez the sum of 8 guineas for a horse, used by Charles Priaux in patrolling the cliffs.

Henceforward, provided the pedestrian keeps to the crest of the cliffs, the going is good. The path is for the most part a cart-road, leading to a small group of farm-houses called les Fontenelles, from whence a good road leads to a considerable hamlet called les Villets.

The steep cliffs between Portelet and la Moye are known as les Sommeilleuses. In places these cliffs can be scaled, and there are one or two caves which are worthy of inspection.

Eventually the cart-road from les Fontenelles peters out and becomes a narrow goat-track on the edge of the cliff, and in one or two places on the brink of steep precipices which are now guarded by an iron rail. This path ends on a miniature peninsula having once again many of the features of the Château d'Icart or of the Peastacks.

In a cove below, easily reached by a serpentine path, is a fishermen's harbour. Here there is good and safe bathing for those who swim and dive.

Above, a good road, forbidden to motorists and built on the edge of a perpendicular cliff, leads to le Gouffre, an abrupt end of a valley beginning at les Villets.

THE CHURCH. Like almost all the old churches and chapels of Guernsey, the Forest Church is built on the site of earlier pagan worship. Of this, a vestige remains in the upright stone at the end of the wall forming the corner of the main road and the road descending to Petit Bot Bay. That stone, now marked and known as le Perron du Roi, was originally part of a dolmen called le Trépied des Nouettes, and must at one time have stood much nearer the church than it does today.

Another menhir, which stood in the neighbourhood of the church, and known as la Roque des Faies, was unluckily destroyed when road improvements were effected.

A building of some kind, dedicated to Christian worship, existed on this site probably as far back as 1048, when William, Duke of the Normans, bestowed six churches in Guernsey on the Abbey of Marmoutiers. Among these six was that of la Sainte Trinité de la Forêt, and that dedication, in all civil and ecclesiastical documents, remained that of the Forest Church until at least the end of the 16th century.

That spurious document, *La Dédicace des Eglises*, gives its dedication as Sainte Marguerite and the date of its building as 1163. In fact, the church contains much 15th and 16th century work. The east end of the south aisle is probably the most ancient part of the building, and the boulders upon which the corners rest may possibly be parts of an old dolmen.

The north aisle is undoubtedly a much later addition.

The position of the rather elaborate piscina in the sanctuary suggests that the original floor level has been raised.

The tower contains a peal of four bells.

Extensive renovation of the church took place in 1891. It was then that the old high pews were removed in favour of pinewood benches. An organ was also added.

The clock in the steeple, the cost of which was raised by public subscription in the parish, commemorates the Diamond Jubilee of Her Majesty Queen Victoria.

After the Reformation the livings of the Forest and of Torteval were frequently combined.

Of all the Guernsey churches, the Forest was the only one compulsorily closed by the Germans during the Occupation. This took place as early as August 1940, following an R.A.F. raid upon the Airport, which is in close proximity.

The church was regarded as vulnerable in case of further raids. Henceforth the church of St Pierre du Bois became also the parish church of the Forest, and banns of marriage for both parishes were read there.

Not far away from the Church, in a cottage among a cluster of farmhouses known as Les Houards, is housed the "Occupation Museum", a private collection made and exhibited by Richard Heaume.

THE AIRPORT. The linking of the island with England, and with Jersey, by air, which has made such an impact on the life and prosperity of the island, started in 1923. A flying-boat service was started between Southampton and St Peter Port, which operated in a small way for a number of years. But this petered out, and attempts to link up Guernsey with the Portsmouth-Jersey air service of Dragons and Expresses, were not successful.

Meanwhile, there was increasing pressure on the States of Guernsey to remedy this lack of communication, and after considering sites at Lancresse, upper Torteval, L'Erée, and the Vingtaine de l'Epine, the States finally agreed to buy 126 acres at Le Villiaze. As this was good farmland, the decision caused much heart-searching, but in May 1939 the Airport was officially opened by Sir Kingsley-Wood, and the air service steadily expanded.

With the increasing threat from Hitler's Germany, all regular air services were withdrawn on June 15, 1940, and for a short time the Airport was operated by the R.A.F. Then on June 30 the vanguard of the German occupation forces flew in, and the Airport was under their control for almost five years. Its use by them was limited, owing to R.A.F. attacks, and although they enlarged the airport area, they let the drainage system deteriorate, and in the later period of the war made the airport unusable.

After the liberation it took some time to get the Airport back into working order, but by October 1945 civilian flying was re-started with Bristol Wayfarers, Rapides, and Dominies. The number of passengers carried increased steadily, and the success of the project led to Channel Airways coming under the control of BEA.

Changes and improvements continued, but the main problem facing the Airport authorities was the inadequacy of the runways for modern large aircraft. A big and costly scheme of modernisation was thus put in hand from 1958–60, which finally produced a new hard runway of 4,800 feet and more spacious and adequate terminal buildings. Thus the Airport could handle Viscounts and Dart Heralds, and face confidently the possible arrival of larger and larger numbers of passengers. The confidence of those who believed in the value of a modern airport was not misplaced, as passenger arrivals rose to 279,151 in 1963; and, by that date 5,547 short tons of freight were being handled. This freight link was especially important for the flower section of the island's horticultural industry, for by it flowers could be carried quickly and safely to the best markets.

Since the major reconstruction of 1960, other improvements have been carried out. A new arrivals' hall was built in 1963, and in 1967 the east wing of the terminal building was modified, to provide seating for a further 150 waiting passengers, and a bigger buffet and bar. For freight, a hangar was converted to a store, and various works were carried out in the airport area, drainage of a low-lying part known as the Bowl, and construction of hard shoulders on either side of the runway and extension of the aircraft parking apron. It was thus an exciting moment for the staff when the first BAC I.II landed in safety in 1965, and another milestone when the first BEA Vanguard landed on July 18, 1967. But the item of equipment of which the Airport Control are most proud is the Plessey ARI long range radar equipment, the first of its kind for civilian use, which was finally handed over to the Board of Administration on May 27, 1965. This air navigational aid caused world-wide interest, and experts came to see it in action from as far afield as Portugal and Peking.

An exciting by-product of its use has been the close co-operation worked out between the Airport, the Guernsey and Jersey lifeboats, the *Flying Christine* marine ambulance, and the French rescue helicopter from Granville. This has led to the location of a number of missing ships, and the sending of successful medical aid to sick men on cargo boats passing to the north in the main shipping lanes.

A final comment on the Airport's growth and usefulness. In 1967 just over 390,000 passengers were carried, as were some 6,488 short tons of freight, and the number of aircraft movements had risen to 3,456.

The Parish of St Pierre du Bois and the Parish of Torteval cover the south-west corner of the island. Their coastline runs from the Havre de Bon Repos by La Corbiere point, along the south coast westward to the headland of Pleinmont, and then turns to include the big bay of Rocquaine as far as L'Erée and the headland of Fort Saumarez, with Lihou island lying across the causeway. Their internal boundary runs more or less diagonally from this point back south-east to the Havre de Bon Repos. They are parishes mostly of agricultural holdings, with a scattering of tomato and flower glasshouses, and a fishing community operating from Portelet Harbour and Rocquaine Bay.

THE COAST. A glance at the map will show that between the Gouffre and Pleinmont there are no major inlets. The coast is no less bold and picturesque, but it is far less frequented than any other part of the uplands of the island.

From the Gouffre the coast can be followed, but only by making constant detours: for many of the paths are dangerous, and some end on the edge of precipices from which steps must be retraced.

On the main Forest-to-l'Erée road a turning to the left leads to the promontory of Pleinmont. On the left of this road there is an intricate maze of lanes, whose turnings terminate again and again on the cliffs.

On the cliffs themselves old cart-tracks will often be found leading to Napoleonic battery sites, old watch-houses and, sometimes, to small, disused quarries. One such leads to la Corbière, resembling its namesake in Jersey only by its appellation.

From the creek known as Havre de Bon Repos, situated to the west of Corbière, until the site of the old watch-house at Pleinmont is reached, there are comparatively few buildings of any kind to be seen between the high road and the coast. Here indeed is desert land.

Havre de Bon Repos was regarded, both by the adversaries of Napoleon more than a century ago and by the occupying Forces, as a vulnerable spot in the coastline. The former erected a building, known as the Prévôté watch-house. The latter built a formidable tower of concrete and steel.

Still farther to the west is the tiny creek of Creux Mahie, much less visited now than in the early days of the century. Here is the largest cave in the island, with a length of some 200 feet, a breadth varying from 40 to 50 feet, and a height of from 20 to 60 feet. Its floor is broken and uneven, and the vaulted roof is irregular.

The descent to this cave is not too easy, for in places the path is gravelly and crumbling. The entrance is small and not easily seen. A strong light is necessary to explore it, and old clothes should be worn, for the sides of the cave are smoke-begrimed. In the past fishermen guides were wont to illuminate the cave by kindling bundles of dry furze. This gave a wild and beautiful effect to the cavern, but it also deposited a layer of carbon on its walls which time seems powerless to obliterate.

On the west side of the beach at this point there is a *souffleur* which works at half tide.

From the Creux Mahie onwards the path improves. At Les Tielles clouds of sea-birds fill the air with their melancholy wailing. To the east the cliffs sweep to the Corbière, and to the south the French lighthouse standing on Les Roches Douvres can be seen on a clear day. The ruins of the Mont Hérault watch-house were patched up and used by the Germans. A lane from behind it connects with the Torteval Road.

Below and slightly to the west of Mont Hérault is the Baie de la Forge. Like the Creux Mahie, it has a *souffleur*, to which, perhaps, we may trace its name. There is also a shallow cave. The approach to this tiny creek can only be described as perilous.

The Tas de Pois d'Aval, the opposite number to the Tas de Pois d'Amont or Peastacks, marks the curve of the coast to the west. This headland is credited with the same legend as that attached to the Lover's Leap in Alderney.

The Creux ès Fées at Houmet, not to be confused with the dolmen bearing that name at l'Erée, is, except in legend, not nearly so well known as the Creux Mahie.

This cave is much smaller than the Creux Mahie, but its entrance is larger and the exterior far more picturesque. The particles of mica in the granite about the entrance glitter in the sunshine like fairy tinsel. The entrance is 24 feet high and rather more than 11 feet in width, but the doorway is divided by a mass of granite.

The right-hand opening gives admission to a large cave, 48 feet in length, 15 feet wide and varying in height, with a maximum of 12 feet.

The smaller cave on the left is no more than 3 feet wide, and the rocks on either side are coloured with a peculiar marine growth of a blood-red colour.

Within this smaller cave, the legend says, is an opening no larger than an oven, which is the gate to fairyland.

Through the crooked valleys of Torteval and the pleasant glades of St Pierre-du-Bois numerous lanes and roads wind down to Rocquaine. Behind an old and picturesque farm-house, along one of these, a few stones mark the site of the chapel of St Brioc, forsaken long before the Reformation might have laid it low. A fishing village on the Channel coast of Brittany bears the same name.

In a field bordering les Paysans, just below les Islets arsenal, where States houses have now been built, rises, in the middle of a field, an unhewn pillar of granite, some 12 feet in height. This is a menhir known as la Longue Roque. Many legends are attached to it. It was once known as la Palette ès Faies, and until comparatively recently the Guy was burnt at its foot on November 5. This cere-mony may be an unconscious survival of some New Year festival, for the Guy was known as Boud'lo, probably a corruption of Bout de l'an.

Fort Grey, the round white tower with sloping walls, standing on an inconsiderable eminence some few yards from the sea wall and road, and connected with the latter by a narrow causeway, is a fortification which has for centuries been adapted to every military change. It is also known as the Château de Rocquaine, and was, in the past, associated with the unholy revels of the witches; it has a third popular name, the Cup and Saucer.

Rocquaine Bay boasts no other fortification, but on the rising ground behind many an old gun-site may be found, built against Napoleon, and adapted in some instances by the unwelcome invader of the Second World War.

The sandy beach of Rocquaine Bay, immediately opposite the Imperial Hotel, is considerably below road level. It can now be reached in one of two ways—by clambering over the rocks where the high wall ends, or by walking a few score yards in the direction of l'Erée and descending to the beach by the slipway.

Until 1939, however, there was a narrow opening in the wall, revealing a set of corbelled granite steps descending steeply to the beach. The occupation forces destroyed this very fine example of the Guernsey mason's art.

But they destroyed far more than art. These steps, being unsupported at the outer end, emitted a distinct musical note when struck by any metallic object, and, as there were 33 of them, and the note of each had been tested and recorded, they constituted a natural xylophone.

Pleinmont is unquestionably one of Guernsey's beauty spots, and the narrow, meandering road which leads from the hotel to the point is never completely deserted at any season of the year during the hours of daylight.

The sheltered cove of Portelet, only a few yards beyond the hotel, is a children's paradise in summer. At all states of the tide it has what most of the southern bays lack—a good area of fine, firm sand. Its approach, too, by a long, wide and not too steep slipway, is easy.

The slope of the beach is so gradual that the smallest children can paddle in perfect safety, and, although the swimmer may feel aggrieved at the distance he is called upon to walk before reaching water of sufficient depth to swim, he is compensated by the tepid warmth which is a natural corollary of these conditions.

Indeed, this is a fact that must have struck John Ferguson most forcibly, for he makes ingenious use of it in the plot of his local thriller: *Death Comes to Périgord*.

The primitive harbour and breakwater are of no great age, although they probably replaced some harbour works of an earlier date. During the second half of the 19th century there was considerable agitation among the pilots and fishermen of that district

for the construction of a harbour. Many plans were placed before
the States. Committees of investigation were appointed and lengthy
reports were rendered again and again.

There was even a suggestion that a harbour, capable of accommodating ships of considerable size, would result in the development
of the granite trade at Torteval. It is a matter for congratulation
today that the States frowned on the project, for the prospect of
the bracken-clothed promontory scarred with the hideous wounds
of uncontrolled quarrying must send a shiver down the spine of
every Nature-lover.

Nevertheless, Portelet, as its name implies, has developed as a
little port with a definite use, apart from its fishing fleet, its vraicking
carts, and its gatherers of ormers. It is the home port of the keepers
of the lighthouse.

THE HANOIS LIGHTHOUSE. At the top of the beach, beyond the
dwarf wall built to arrest the erosive effects of the highest spring
tides, is a neat granite building which houses the stores and equipment of the Hanois Lighthouse. On its gable, above the door, are
the arms and motto of Trinity House. A flight of steps round the
side and back of the building brings the traveller to the road,
immediately beneath the high, steep bank upon which are built the
solid cottages of the keepers.

These suffered severely during the German occupation. Nearly
every piece of timber which entered into their construction was
removed for fuel. Viewed from the road level, this derelict condition
seemed scarcely appreciable, for roof and walls remained. A close
view, however, showed them to be completely gutted.

Now they have been restored and stand, neat in their white
paint, looking out over the seas which their men guard so labori-
ously.

Many ships have been lost on that reef of rocks to the south-west
of Guernsey known to merchant seamen as the Hanways. Perhaps
the greatest disaster occurred in 1807, when the *Boreas*, a small naval
frigate, was lost with half her complement of 154 men.

Tupper, who gives a long and detailed account of this disaster,
expresses indignation and astonishment that the *Gazette de Guernesey*
of that time made no allusion whatever to the matter. Modern
journalism may not be without its faults, but can anyone imagine
any newspaper of today ignoring a happening so important and so
disastrous?

Wrecks on the coasts of Guernsey were formerly of common
occurrence. Between 1835 and 1862, a period of 27 years, no fewer

than 97 ships were lost or stranded. Between 1862, when the Hanois Lighthouse came into use, and 1875, there were only 14 wrecks.

After repeated applications, in 1858 Trinity House intimated to the States, through the Board of Trade, that it was willing to erect a lighthouse. A condition, however, was attached. Guernsey was to come within the jurisdiction of the Elder Brethren and pay the coasting rate, instead of, as before, the overseas rate.

In accordance with precedent, the States appointed a committee. This committee prepared a form containing the name of every vessel, with her tonnage, which had arrived at, or sailed from, Guernsey in 1858. Two blank columns were left, which Trinity House was asked to fill in. One was to contain the coasting rate and the other the overseas rate for each vessel.

The outcome was unexpected. It showed that in 1858 Guernsey had paid £940 19s. 4d. more in overseas rate than it would have paid in coasting rate.

Trinity House was not slow in appreciating that it stood to lose by imposing the coasting rate on Guernsey. It withdrew its conditions and agreed to build the lighthouse. The foundation stone was laid on August 15, 1860. The light was first kindled on December 8, 1862.

The local dynamic force in the building of the lighthouse was *Jurat* H. Tupper. In recognition of his efforts, the French residents of the island decided to present him with a model of the lighthouse. Unfortunately, he died before it was completed. The model, in granite, 4 feet in height, was presented to his widow and family in 1875.

No view of the lighthouse is obtainable from the terrace of the Hanois Cottages. The view is obscured by a towering pinnacle of granite a few score yards nearer the point, round which winds the coast road, to form a hair-pin bend, the last of a series, with the road descending from the high plateau above.

On this rock there stood for many years a flagstaff, used for signalling purposes between the lighthouse and the land. Here, too, on fine summer days, the women-folk, armed with flags, might often be seen semaphoring messages to their menfolk on the lighthouse. Nowadays the telephone has rendered obsolete this picturesque practice.

At the foot of this rock there has been a certain amount of quarrying, and in the shallow depression so created, the occupation forces built a shelter of considerable strength and blocked the road with a tank-trap. Of the tank-trap traces alone remain, but the shelter is still there.

Throughout the length of the road, between the wall and the sea, there is a strip of land, varying in width from a few feet to a considerable number of yards. For the ocean does not expend its fury on this portion of the coast, and what erosion has taken place, has been due to the action of rain. The lush vegetation with which this strip is covered is an added protection.

The road ends in a natural amphitheatre with a floor of short, springy turf rising gently to the high cliffs above.

The ancient fort, Château Pezeries, attached to the mainland only by a narrow causeway of turf-covered, crumbling gravel, must have done sentinel duty for many centuries. The Napoleonic wars saw guns, of considerable calibre for those days, mounted there, and it was then, too, that the powder magazine, with its vaulted roof, so reminiscent of those of local churches, was built.

From the landward end of the causeway paved slipways are seen going down into the tiny bays on either side. That on the right is comparatively short. That on the left, however, winds across a beach of rough shingle and far out between reefs of rocks, some of which must have been quarried away to make room for its breadth. The labour involved in the construction of these slipways is indisputable evidence of the value which islanders attached to seaweed as a fertiliser.

On the beach the edge of the bay is again protected against sea erosion only by a dwarf wall. Along the edge above is a trench with a parapet towards the sea. This trench now forms a path.

Not many yards ahead, this path is cut at right angles by a gigantic natural wall of rock, pierced in one place by a natural gateway, through which the wind, when in the right quarter, rushes with considerable force. On the left, high up on this wall, some rough masonry, tinted by time to the colour of its surroundings, suggests an elevated platform from which the lighthouse might be viewed.

Approached by a winding and precipitous path, it is found to be a gun-site of considerable area, affording a view not only of the lighthouse, but also of another amphitheatre, almost a replica of the first, again completed with an almost identical wall of rock, at the sea end of which a tiny paved platform suggests a dancing-floor for fairies rather than a site for a toy gun.

The path through the gateway to the second amphitheatre is of solid granite, and, once through, runs for a short distance beneath tall, beetling rocks, within a few feet of the beach. A curving parapet and curving trench follow the edge of the creek, consisting of a mass of rocks. Beyond this, approximately one mile from the shore, rises the tower of the Hanois Lighthouse.

A casual glance seawards gives the impression of a continuous but irregular reef of rocks between Lihou Island and Pleinmont Point. All these bear interesting names. Grouped closely together are the Aiguillons, the Mauve, the Grand Hanois, the Petit Hanois, upon which the lighthouse is built, and the Cat Rock.

LE TABLE DES PIONS. There is one interesting archaeological feature of Pleinmont which can easily be overlooked by the casual visitor. This is the "Table des Pions".

Just within the first amphitheatre, not far from where the road ends, and a few yards only from the crumbling edge of the shore, is a shallow dome of turf, surrounded by a circular trench. The outer circumference of this trench is marked by a number of rough stones of no great size.

Here, centuries ago, in the "age of faith", at four o'clock on a fine June afternoon,

"the pions sat down on a vast green carpet round a circle hollowed in the earth in the form of a round table and there partook of their meal."

This is the apt description given by Syvret, the Jersey historian, in his *Chroniques*.

The "Table des Pions" marks the extreme range of the "Chevauchée de St Michel". This procession or cavalcade, as its name implies, may at one time have been an annual event. It is even possible that it evolved from some pre-Christian ceremony, for some of its rites and customs are very reminiscent of the Roman Saturnalia.

The organisation and accomplishment of the *chevauchée* was the duty, and perhaps the privilege, of the Court of the Fief St Michel. This was a Church fief, and it was perhaps because it was the largest Church fief in the island, besides being a dependency of the important Abbaye de St Michel in Normandy, that this duty was assigned to it.

Of the religious origin of the *chevauchée* there can be no doubt. During the Middle Ages it was carried out under a charter from the Bishop of Coutances, metropolitan of the Channel Islands. It was always held in June, just prior to the Fête-Dieu, or Feast of Corpus Christi. Its object was to see that the highway was clear for the processions of the Blessed Sacrament, processions held for a period of at least one week and organised separately, in all probability, by each parish and each religious establishment.

After the Reformation the custom did not entirely lapse. The

Fief de St Michel, which had escheated to the Crown, was required, once in every three years, to see that the King's Highway was kept open. But the Catholic origin and nature of the ceremony must have been repugnant to a Calvinistic feudal court, and the *chevauchée* gradually fell into desuetude. It was revived during the governorship of General Sir John Doyle in 1813, and was revived again in 1966 to mark the celebration of the 900th anniversary of the connection between Guernsey and the English Crown.

The *chevauchée* of 1813 has been described in detail by many historians. It took place on June 9, and a meeting of the feudal court on May 13 made all the arrangements.

June 9 was a day of brilliant promise, when the court met at the Vale Church at an early hour of the morning. The whole of its personnel was present: the *sénéchal*, the *vavasseurs*, the *prévôts*, the *bordiers*, and the *sergeants*, as well as the Crown officers. All were mounted, carried swords, and were accompanied by one or two valets or *pions*, according to rank.

These valets—young men chosen for their good looks, and 36 in number—were all attired, as had been previously prescribed by the Court, in black caps, with a red ribbon trailing behind, white shirts, white vests braided with red, long white breeches tied at the bottom with red ribbon, and white stockings. Each carried a lance, the end of which was adorned with a red rosette.

A roll call and inspection by the *sénéchal* was followed by an alfresco breakfast, after which the cavalcade moved off. At the entrance of the Braye du Valle the *pions* were temporarily released from their duties and allowed to claim the privilege of kissing any woman they met, no matter what her class, it being understood, however, that only one *pion* kiss the same lady.

The *pions*, the chronicler drily observes, were not deterred from claiming this privilege by *"une giroflée à cinq feuilles"*, a charming and untranslatable popular locution for a slap in the face.

Passing through the Landes du Marché, the Marais, and the Ronde Cheminée, the cavalcade reached the Hougue à la Perre. Here they were joined by the Lieutenant-Governor and his staff, and the band of the regiment of the garrison, suitably attired as rustics.

The Lieutenant-Governor, significantly, went to the tail of the procession. The regimental band took the lead. At 11 o'clock the town was reached.

Outside the west door of the Town Church a round table had been placed, upon which were Guernsey biscuits, cheese, and wine. With these provisions the members of the cavalcade fortified themselves. They also entertained the onlookers with song and dance.

Forming up again, the cavalcade proceeded up the High Street, Berthelot Street, and the Grange. Here the *pions* were once more released. At the Ville au Roi the procession was regaled with fresh milk.

From the Ville au Roi the procession continued its course, by roads and lanes which have either been transformed or do not now exist, to Jerbourg. Here they halted in a furze-brake known to this day as le Feugré. A remote and secluded place, this was an ideal spot for a prolonged rest.

A right-about turn now took the *chevauchée* to the Forest, and another halt was made at the Bourg. It then proceeded to Pleinmont, which was reached at a quarter to three. Here a substantial luncheon was served, the *pions* making use, as before mentioned, of the "Table des Pions".

It must not be forgotten that throughout the progress of the cavalcade the lance-bearer noted any overhanging branches less than $11\frac{1}{2}$ feet high, that being the length of his lance, as well as any projecting roots or large loose stones over which the unwary might trip. Proprietors of land where these irregularities occurred were later mulcted in a fine. Each *prévôt* took it in turn to carry the lance and dealt with his own fief.

The procession returned by way of Rocquaine, the Rouvets, St Saviour's, and the King's Mills. Here the miller brought out wheat and flour for inspection. Continuing the route by Camp du Roi and the Salines, the now tired wayfarers reached the Vale Church by seven o'clock. Here the *greffier* pronounced the blessing and the *chevauchée* came to an end.

The day, however, was not yet over. A dinner, at the expense of His Majesty and attended by the Lieutenant-Governor, was served, apparently out of doors. It was of long duration. They sat down, says the chronicler, in sunshine and rose in moonlight.

L'ERÉE. At its northern end Rocquaine ends in a broad cape of no great elevation, known as l'Erée. Here the sea has little power and the gap in the sea-wall is replaced by sand dunes. Unfortunately, during the occupation the Germans made great inroads into these for the construction of their Atlantic Wall, and precautions have had to be taken to protect a portion of the coast hitherto regarded as safe.

At its westernmost end the cape rises to a hillock, upon which stands the fortress known as Fort Saumerez. This hillock the

Germans honeycombed with tunnels. The tower was heightened considerably and disproportionately to form a look-out, and one or two heavy guns were mounted on the mound. Firing practice was carried out with these upon the few remaining buildings on Lihou Island, and these were promptly reduced to rubble.

The Creux ès Faies, a passage grave of considerable interest near by, was also turned to military use. In the Napoleonic era, however, the soldiers stationed at l'Erée barracks, of which the foundations alone now remain, used it as a convenient hiding-place when they were too drunk to return to barracks. The rubble in it, removed by its first excavator, Lukis, was placed there by the colonel of the regiment to stop this practice.

Despite the legend that the fairies issued from this cavern to dance at le Mont Saint or on the Catioroc, this passage grave was long used as a stable by the country folk. Classified as an ancient monument, it is now the property of the States.

To the east of Fort Saumarez, and encircled by roads, is a large level area representing an abortive attempt made some years before the War to establish an aerodrome. Sand dunes and the coast road north of the Fort separate this tract from the sea. It is marshy in winter, and dry and barren in summer. Near the dunes was constructed, at the beginning of the century, a sizable cistern, into which sea-water was pumped, and in a small building alongside was installed the necessary plant for attempting to extract gold from it. The venture was a short-lived one.

Around this tract is a number of old cottages, some tiled, some slated, but most originally thatched. A few are derelict. L'Erée is reputed to have been a witches' colony and these cottages to be their dwellings.

Some interesting facts emerge from the *Livres de Perchage*, Land Register, of the various fiefs, all dependencies of the great Fief le Comte, which deal with this district. Her Majesty (Queen Victoria) is said to have seized *un camp de terre*, measuring eight perches, *faute d'homage*. The *faute d'homage* is explained later, when we learn that the said "camp" had been submerged by the sea a good many years earlier.

Other fields in the district are also listed as having been submerged by the sea. A phrase often used is:

". . . *lequel pré est entièrement couvert de galet.*"
(. . . which field is entirely covered with shingle).

In spite of this, however, the fields are listed regularly every 20 years. It is a legitimate conclusion that hope was entertained of the recovery of this lost land. But later we are given another example, couched in the following terms:

"... *entièrement pris par la mer et au dehors de la muraille contre la mer.*" (... entirely engulfed by the sea and outside the sea wall).

Whatever hopes may have been entertained by the various groups of 12 good men and true who drew up these lists, it is clear that the sea has made considerable inroads at l'Erée.

LIHOU ISLAND. From the headland of l'Erée, a paved road, rather more than a quarter of a mile long, runs across the beach to the small island of Lihou. This track is open twice a day, at low tide, and visitors to the island should take care to make the return journey in good time, if they are to avoid being marooned for several hours.

This track, whose upkeep is now the responsibility of the local authorities, has apparently been maintained for centuries. It has always been of great importance to gatherers of vraic, who spread their harvest to dry either on the mainland of Guernsey or above high-water mark on Lihou.

Lihou is to the west coast what Castle Cornet is to the east. But the island is very much larger, its greatest length being 600 yards and its greatest breadth 150. Its area is roughly 18 acres.

Lihou possesses some capital rock scenery, and the rocky pools are full of interest to the zoologist.

For some years after the Second World War Lihou was untenanted, and remained a lonely place, haunted by the cries of oyster-catchers and curlew, and with only the remains of the old Benedictine Priory of Notre Dame and the ruins of the farm-house to remind one that men had ever occupied it. But since 1965 it has entered on a new and most exciting phase in its long career. Lt.-Col. P. A. Wootton, the present owner, has made it the base for the "Lihou Youth Project" the aims of which are defined as the three S's—a spiritual outlook on life, a scientific outlook on life, and a sociological responsibility for life. He has rebuilt two granite buildings on the site of the old farm-house as headquarters for the Summer Youth Camps, while the tented camp itself is established on the east side of the island by what is now called "Torrey Canyon Bay". The bay got this name as it was one of the areas worst affected by pollution of oil from the *Torrey Canyon* disaster. One of the main practical objects of the camps is archaeological work on the site of the old Priory, but the members are also encouraged to study meteorology, marine biology, botany, entomology, astronomy, and ornithology.

One particularly interesting line of research which is being followed is that into the habits etc. of the Meadow Brown butterfly of Lihou, a sub-species which differs even from those on nearby Guernsey, and which is not yet affected by insecticides.

The right to dry vraic (seaweed) on Lihou was bitterly contested up to the beginning of the 19th century when the island became private property. Such arguments were natural, for from time immemorial seaweed, vraic or *varech*, has played an important part in the agricultural economy of the Channel Islands. Ploughed deeply into the soil, it is not only a source of valuable fertility, but on the light sandy soils of the west and north it must, apart from this, have had highly beneficient mechanical effects.

Up to the early years of the present century, vraic entered, too, into the domestic economy of the island. Amongst the cottagers along the low-lying shores of the west coast, it was dried, stacked and used as winter fuel.

Vraic produces a dull-red smouldering fire, which can be kept in continuously. The faint acrid smell of its smoke used to be a feature of the west coast. The ash is an assimilable form of fertiliser, rich in potash.

This ash has also been exploited for its valuable chemical constituents, chief among which is iodine.

During the 19th century Guernsey possessed quite a number of small iodine-extraction plants, but these have disappeared before the highly efficient chemicals works of the mother country.

The gathering of vraic has always been a common right—that is, it was never subject, as were so many things, to feudal dues. That it was a cherished right is patent from the many customs and laws which, in the course of centuries, surrounded it.

The first cutting of vraic (*varech scié*) began at the first new, or full moon, after Candlemas (la Chandeleur) and lasted until the middle of March. This crop was devoted exclusively to the manuring of the soil, and repeated ordinances limit it to this use.

The second or summer cutting began just before midsummer (la St Jean) and continued until the end of August. During the first moon of this period, however, the poor, who, it may be assumed, would cut it for fuel, were alone allowed to gather it.

Vraic gathered by this class of society is referred to in the old Ordinances as "*varech à la poche*". The legal definition of "poor" throws perhaps some light on the meaning of this curious phrase. The poor are those not subject to taxation and possessing neither cart nor draught beast.

This class was forbidden to borrow carts and horses. They were restricted to cutting the vraic and carrying it above high spring-tide mark. Even the use of a barrow was forbidden.

Drift sea-weed (*varech venant*) could be gathered all the year round, between sunrise and sunset. Here again a concession was made to the "poor", who were allowed to gather it between sunset and sunrise.

They could, in short, take advantage of a clear moonlight night, provided the vraic so gathered were for their personal use alone.

The gathering of vraic, *scié* or *venant*, on Sundays was absolutely forbidden.

The use of boats for vraicking was severely frowned upon. It was probably felt that this rendered vraicking so easy, comparatively, as to lead to dangerous inroads on a valuable crop which natural growth might not make good.

Poaching by "foreigners" appears to have been rare. A case, however, did occur in 1830. An emergency ordinance of that year refers to "a criminal practice" of recent date on the part of a foreign ship or cutter. Vraic had been cut, loaded and carried away from the Bailiwick—an unforgiveable sin—from the rocks off Herm. The police authorities of those days were given strict instructions to apprehend such criminals, and the Court threatened not only to confiscate their boats, but also to fine heavily each and every member of the crew.

The importance attached to vraic as a fertiliser by the authorities is underlined in this ordinance by the statement that natives, and natives alone, are entitled to cut vraic in the Bailiwick. This is further emphasised in the extract:

". . . considering the importance attached to the preservation of varech, for the cultivation of the lands of the said Isles, and the necessity of seeing that the inhabitants alone have the enjoyment of it . . .".

The stamps issued by H.M. Post Office to commemorate the liberation in 1945 of the Channel Islands from enemy occupation depicted a typical vraicking scene of the early days of this century. Vraicking continues today, but in a more mechanical and commercial way.

THE PARISH CHURCH OF ST PIERRE-DU-BOIS. According to the *Dédicace des Eglises*, the consecration of the church of St Pierre-du-Bois took place on June 29, 1167, by Bartholomew Basset, Bishop of Coutances, by the consent and at the request of Sir Peter Cornet, the Governor, keeper and captain of the forts, places and castles of Guernsey, called the Holy Island.

At the conclusion of the ceremony, Sieur Pierre Brehaut, a prominent St Pierrais, apparently placed the vane on the pinnacle at the command of the bishop.

No record could be more apocryphal. The whole of the church, as it exists today, is the work of the 15th century, although it has been contended that the tower is of earlier date.

The names Forest and St Pierre-du-Bois suggest that these two parishes were once densely wooded. But whereas the Forest Church stands on an eminence, that of St Pierre-du-Bois, though built on a hillside, shows nothing but its square tower above the surrounding country.

Its situation on a hillside, however, has given it a feature peculiar to itself among all the churches of the island. Its floor has a marked upward slope from west to east. The first pillar—that built into and supporting the west wall of the church—measures 10 feet from the moulding of the capital to that of the base. The pillars decrease successively in height, the last measuring 6 feet 3 inches.

The church consists of a nave and two aisles, with a small sanctuary. The flattened shape of the arches forming the arcade on each side of the nave point to a late period of the flamboyant style.

The windows exhibit some interesting features. Two of these in the south wall are small and differ entirely from the others. This has been accounted for on the hypothesis that the windows were prepared out of the island and that two of them were broken in transit. When local workmen were called upon to make good the damage, they were not sufficiently skilled to imitate the tracery of the others.

The ornamental tracery is also absent from two of the windows on the north side.

The rose window is of no great age. It dates, probably, from the beginning of the 19th century.

The living, which, like all Guernsey benefices, is in the patronage of the Crown, was held for more than a century, from 1803, by the local family of Brock. During their incumbencies extensive restorations to the church were carried out.

In 1867, during the rectorship of the Very Rev. Carey Brock, the old square pews and three-decker pulpit disappeared, and the Communion table, which had stood in the middle of the church from Presbyterian times, was moved to the east end.

An unsightly gallery, which blocked the west end, was removed in 1885, and during that same year the old barrelled roof, which had become dilapidated, was replaced.

In 1906 the whole of the seating was renewed in American oak, wood-block floors replaced the flag-stones of the aisles, and new pulpit, clergy desks, choir-stalls, and organ were installed.

It is generally agreed that mediaeval brasses, so common a feature of the village churches of many English counties, are never found in the churches of the Channel Islands. At St Pierre-du-Bois a large flagstone, removed perhaps from the aisle during the renovations of 1906, leans against the north outer wall of the tower. It bears the impressions of several small brasses, but of the brasses themselves or of any inscription no trace remains.

The earliest mention of the parish of St Pierre-du-Bois is found in a charter, dated 1048, by Robert, Duke of Normandy, confirming a gift made by his father of certain parishes in the island to the Benedictine Abbey of Mont St Michel. The Abbey took the great tithe of the church, and it is probable that the original edifice was erected under the guidance of its fraternity. All such early churches must have been built of wood, and it is not unlikely that this one was destroyed in some piratical foray.

A most interesting mural tablet, to the honour of James Perchard, and erected by the inhabitants of St Pierre-du-Bois, will be found against the wall of the north aisle, near the Lady Chapel. How far back the Perchard family dates it is impossible to say. It has been connected by marriage with the families of le Marchant, Sausmarez, le Mesurier, le Serre, and de la Condamine.

Two Perchards, father and son, held the living of St Pierre-du-Bois between 1606 and 1663. Succeeding generations of the family must have forsaken the Church for commerce. The James Perchard of the tablet made a gift of £1,000 sterling to the poor of the parish of St Pierre-du-Bois. This was, for those days, a most munificent gift.

The Donation Board, which covers a large area of one of the walls of the Board Room of the Town Hospital, provides further evidence of the wealth and generosity of the Perchard family. Between the years 1743 and 1783 its members contributed no less than £1,250 to this institution.

A monumental tablet in the Town Church completes the story. It was erected by Peter Perchard to the memory of his wife, who was a daughter of Henry le Mesurier, and to four of their children, all buried in St Mary Abchurch, London. An addendum to the tablet records the death of Peter himself, and gives a few biographical details. He was Sheriff of the City of London in 1793. In

1806 he was elected Lord Mayor. Unfortunately, he survived his mayoralty but ten weeks.

THE PARISH CHURCH OF TORTEVAL. Berry's *History of Guernsey*, published in 1815, contains an illustration of a Torteval church built in the age of faith. It bears a great resemblance to St Martin's, St Saviour's, and several other of the parish churches of the island. The square tower appears more squat than that of St Saviour's, and the steeple less pointed than that of St Martin's. The pinnacles at each corner of the tower, however, are reproductions of those on other parish churches.

This church consisted also of two naves, and the exterior buttresses have a familiar appearance. In the wall of the south nave are two square-headed windows, evidently of post-Reformation date. The east gable windows of both naves are late flamboyant, and the south porch, almost hidden by trees, is as quaint as that of St Saviour's.

For many years the Rector of the Forest officiated also at Torteval, which adjoins his parish. It is obvious, however, that Torteval was sadly neglected, for the old church fell into ruin, and the present building, in which much of the material of the old was incorporated, was erected in its place, and more or less on the same site, in 1818.

The present church is a simple little building, sturdily built of grey granite, with a fine barrel-vault of wood to roof the nave, and a conical spire, unique in Guernsey, rising from its tower-base.

ST PIERRE-DU-BOIS AND TORTEVAL—THE PATOIS. Many of the island speakers of patois come from these parishes, and they are the backbone of L'Assemblaie Guernsiaise, the local patois-speaking society. A local writer of considerable eminence, writing in the year 1883, said of the insular dialects: "the French of the Channel Islands is not a BAD French, it is merely an OLD French".

That these dialects in their spoken form are slowly dying cannot be denied. Fortunately, however, they are enshrined in literature, and in this form, they will survive, and provide abundant and useful material for an inconsiderable, but none the less useful, body of students, research workers in comparative and historical philology.

Meanwhile it should be a matter of deep pride to Channel Islanders in general, and to Jerseymen in particular, that one of the pioneers of English literature (if we except the very early Anglo-Saxon writers) claims Jersey as his birthplace.

His name was Wace, and he appears to have had no other known name. He wrote, as every history text-book asserts, a long narrative poem called "Le Roman de Rou". This was in the 12th century, for

Wace, born at the beginning of that century, died in England in 1184.

He wrote in French, the Norman-French of those days. But English literature claims him, for Norman-French was the official language of England for many generations after the Conquest.

As may be expected from the period in which he lived, Wace was an ecclesiastic. He was educated at Caen, the *alma mater* of many Channel Islanders, and for 19 years was Prebendary of Bayeux. He finished the "Roman de Rou" in 1160.

As Wace and his poems exist only as names for the vast majority of people, it may be useful to quote a passage from the "Roman de Rou".

> *"Tote rien se torne en déclin;*
> *Tout chiet, tout muert, tout vait à fin;*
> *Homs muert, fer use, fust porrist,*
> *Tur font, mur chiet, rose flaistrist,*
> *Cheval tresbusche, drap viesist:*
> *Tout ovre fet od mainz perist."*

In modern French this would read roughly as follows:

> *"Il n'y a rien qui ne se tourne en déclin;*
> *Tout tombe, tout meurt, tout va à fin;*
> *L'homme meurt, le fer use, le bois pourrit,*
> *La tour fond, le mur tombe, la rose flétrit,*
> *Le cheval trébuche, le drap vieillit:*
> *Tout œuvre faite de mains périt."*

To those for whom the local patois is a heritage of childhood, these lines of Wace will strike a familiar chord. To lovers of Lamartine, Hugo, or de Musset they will appeal, not as mere rhyming, but as real poetry.

The "Roman de Rou" is a long epic poem, giving the history of the Norseman Rollo who, after fighting the French for many years, finally embraced Christianity and became a subject of the King of France, Charles the Simple, who bestowed upon him the dukedom of Normandy, of which the Channel Islands formed part.

Rollo's name is immortalised in the famous custom, peculiar to Guernsey and Jersey, known as the *Clameur de Haro* or appeal to Rollo. Curiously enough, however, Wace makes no allusion to it in the "Roman de Rou". There is, however, a story which illustrates how the Duke executed his laws with uncompromising severity and unwavering justice, which makes the attribution of the *Clameur* to Rollo a credible theory. A certain peasant, ploughing in the fields, returned to his cottage at midday, leaving his plough in the furrow. He felt fully assured that, under the rule of Rollo, no one would steal it in his absence. While he was taking his meal, however, his wife went out and removed the share and coulter. Upon his return to the fields the peasant saw he had been robbed, and straightaway repaired to the Duke, to whom he made his complaint. The Duke, in sympathy with the peasant's loss, gave him five sous. Returning home, the peasant told his wife first of the robbery and then of the generosity of Rollo. She was jubilant and, showing him the share and coulter, which she had concealed, pointed out that they were five sous to the good. But the story was soon bruited abroad, and finally reached the ears of Rollo, who summoned the peasant before him. The peasant was asked if he were aware of the thieving habits of his wife, and was obliged to reply that he was. Thereupon Rollo sentenced both to be hanged, the wife for theft and the husband for complicity.

> *"Esgal leis, esgal paines, esgal mal vos atent,*
> *Esgal jugement ont ki emble, e ki cunsent."*

That the *Clameur de Haro* is an invocation to the first Duke of Normandy has been dismissed by some authorities as purely legendary. *Haro* has been explained as a primitive cry of joy or pain, from which the modern "hurrah", as a cry of victory, has been derived. In French *"crier haro sur quelqu'un"* means to protest with indignation at what he has said or done. Shakespeare uses the word in precisely the same sense, but *haro* seems to have disappeared from modern English.

The practice of this ancient custom, however, in either of the larger islands is very far from extinct. In both Guernsey and Jersey it is used as a summary remedy against encroachment on real property. In Guernsey, for example, if a man find his neighbour dismantling a wall which is not the property of the latter, he first calls upon him to desist. If his neighbour refuse, he calls two witnesses, in whose presence he repeats his protest and utters the words: *"Haro, haro, haro, à l'aide mon prince! On me fait tort!"* He and the witnesses then recite the Lord's Prayer in French. The aggressor must then instantly desist, otherwise he is liable to be punished for a breach of the peace and contempt of the King's authority, for the property is under the protection of the King from the moment the *clameur* is raised. The appellant, however, must within 24 hours lodge his protest in writing at the Greffe. He must also pursue his action before the Royal Court. If he fail to do so, the other party, in his turn, may become plaintiff and compel the other to justify his action before the Court. In any case, the Court proceeds to a decision in the affair even though a *vue de justice*—that is, an inspection of the site—may be considered necessary. The decision, when made, is irrevocable, for there is no appeal to the King in Council from a decision on a *Clameur de Haro*. The party against whom the decision is given is mulcted in a fine, for the raising of the *Clameur* without cause and a breach of the peace by encroachment on the property of another are regarded as equally criminal.

The Parish of St Saviour, running north-westerly from the outskirts of the Airport to Perelle Bay, is another rural parish—a parish of farms, and scattered glasshouses, especially in the low-lying coastal strip, and some small residential areas. It centres round the parish church, in the picturesque area named Sous L'Eglise, and contains in its boundaries the island reservoir, the chapel of St Apolline, and the factory of Tektronix (Guernsey) Ltd.

THE COAST AND LE CATIOROC. Between the headland of l'Erée and that of le Crocq, upon which Fort Richmond is built, lies Perelle Bay. At the southern end of this bay is a tiny islet, bearing the name of Capelle Dom Hué. Its name lends colour to the tradition that it was once the site of a hermit's cell. The reputed foundations of this may still be seen, and in the past a few flint weapons have been found there.

On the coast, standing well above the road, and opposite la Capelle, is the Trépied Dolmen of le Catioroc. In an attempt to straighten the road at this point, the Germans drove a deep cutting through the hillside, without interfering, fortunately, with the Trépied. This hillock is the traditional scene of the witches' sabbaths.

Sir Edgar MacCulloch, in his *Guernsey Folklore*, devotes a whole chapter to the subject of witchcraft. John Linwood Pitts, for many years chief librarian of the Guille-Allès Library, also wrote a brochure on the subject, which was published in 1886. Both authorities quote the official records of the Greffe and, as each cites different cases, the two supplement each other in a way distinctly valuable to the student.

The Greffe records cover a period of 71 years—from 1563 to 1634. A superficial inference from these dates would be that the decline of the old, authoritative religion and its replacement by a protestantism of private judgment, a heterogeneous mass of conflicting and contradictory theologies, led the ignorant masses to resort to a primitive, if not a prehistoric, form of voodooism.

But reference to the history of witchcraft generally shows this inference to be false. Executions for witchcraft took place in France in 1275, long before the Reformation. Joan of Arc was burnt as a witch at Rouen in 1431.

Coming to more modern times, serious disturbances on account of witchcraft took place in Massachusetts in 1648–49, and in 1683 dreadful persecutions from the same cause raged in Pennsylvania, the colony founded by the gentle Quaker, William Penn. The Puritans of New England hanged 19 persons for witchcraft in 1692.

It must be noted, however, that until the Reformation the crime of witchcraft came under ecclesiastical jurisdiction. A statute declaring all witchcraft and sorcery to be felony was not passed in England until 1541. This statute was re-affirmed and strengthened by Queen Elizabeth in 1562 and by James I in 1603. The seventy-third Canon of the Established Church, 1603, forbids the clergy to cast out devils.

This Canon may have had the force of law in Guernsey. Apart from this, however, the Royal Court does not appear to have promulgated any penal statutes on the subject. The crime was treated as one against the Common Law of the island.

There can be no doubt whatever that those gatherings at Rocquaine Castle and other places, known as Witches' Sabbaths, did take place. In all probability they were a vestige of an old pagan religion, carried on from force of habit long after their real origin and significance had been forgotten.

The belief in *sorcerots*, witches' spells of a peculiar kind, in powders for use in bewitching others and in the evil eye, mentioned in the depositions, has never completely died out. As recently as 1912 a woman was tried by the Royal Court of Guernsey for witchcraft. There being no law to cover this crime, she was charged under Article 10, subsection 8, of the Police Law of that date, with carrying on the trade of fortune-telling and witchcraft.

Her principal accuser, who was also her dupe as well as principal witness, was a voluble Frenchwoman. The accused had cast a spell upon her, and had said she would die if she (witness) did not pay her a sum of money. She had first regarded the accused as a *quéraude* or white witch, and had enlisted her aid when her cattle died, bewitched, of course, by some person unknown. She had been supplied with a number of powders, for which she had paid various sums, and had been instructed to bury these in the garden at the four points of the compass. These had been dug up by the police and found, on analysis, to be a proprietary baking-powder.

Other witnesses appeared, who left no doubt in the minds of the members of the Court that they (the witnesses) were firmly convinced that the accused was possessed of supernatural and evil powers.

The defence was a rational one. People came to her, accused said, of their own free will for advice. What money they gave her was their own business, and was not asked for. She could not be blamed for their credulity, nor did she think it was immoral to take advantage of it. That kind of thing occurred in other spheres of life, and she had to live.

The Court, not being a 17th century one, was sadly puzzled. The crime almost, but not quite, amounted to obtaining money on false pretences. Regarded as disorderly conduct, it was an offence subject to eight days' imprisonment. The Court inflicted this penalty.

Sorcerots, the lumps of matted wool and feathers found in a pillow or cushion after long use, were referred to in another police-court action a month or two prior to the outbreak of the First World War. A man was accused of neglecting his children. They were in a verminous condition. His defence was that they had been bewitched, and, in proof of this, he referred to matted lumps of wool and feathers which, he asserted, he had found in the pillows they used and which could have been placed there only by a sorcerer.

The Bailiff drily remarked that he knew of no spell of this nature which could not be counteracted by a regular and liberal use of soap and water.

THE RESERVOIR. Above Perelle Bay, at le Mont Saint, a lovely valley has been drowned to form a large reservoir, which should for generations to come solve the problem of water supply for the island. The huge concrete dam is no unpleasing structure, and when artificial lake and sea are brought into line, with the arches of the dam cutting the vista at right angles, the effect produced is one of a large and placid lake. The reservoir is now surrounded by trees and is a most lovely spot, a haunt of birds of all kinds. There is a possibility that this area may be made into a nature reserve, but in the meantime it gives pleasure to all who visit it, and especially to the trout fishermen, whose Club has the right to stock and fish the reservoir.

THE CHAPEL OF ST APOLLINE. In the Middle Ages there were many chapels in the island, St Jacques and St Julien in St Peter Port, Notre Dame de Pulias and St Thomas d'Anneville in St Sampson's, St Magloire in the Vale, St Brioc in St Pierre-du-Bois.

But now that of St Apolline, in St Saviour's, is the only one remaining intact. Like other ancient monuments, it is under the charge of a committee of the States, who purchased it in 1873. A simple rectangular building, with square-headed windows and a vaulted roof of stone, it still bears upon its walls faint traces of frescoes.

Documentary evidence of the foundation of the chapel is preserved at the Greffe. In 1392 one Nicholas Henry was licensed by the Abbey of Mont St Michel to erect a chapel on the manor which he held of the Abbey at Perelle. The chaplain was required to swear fealty to the Prior of the Vale. In 1394 the licence was confirmed by letters patent of King Richard III.

Originally called Notre Dame de la Perelle, we find it referred to, in a document dated 1452, as "Notre Dame de la Perelle, appelleye la Chapelle Ste Appolyne".

ST SAVIOUR'S CHURCH. A long arcade divides the two naves and chancels of which St Saviour's Church consists. Under the square tower, which terminates the northern nave on the west, is the baptistery, and the font in it is a post-Reformation one, removed from the Town Church in 1886, when that church was renovated. The west end of the arcade is probably of 14 century date, but it is continued eastward by arches of a later flamboyant type. A plain chantry on the south side is used as a vestry.

The registers of the church are very interesting. One quaint entry in the accounts of the Trésor reads: "Paid Mr Abraham Lenfesty, according to receipt, one halfpenny". Among the church treasures is the oldest known copy of the *Dédicace des Eglises*, already referred to.

Both tower and spire have interesting histories. The latter was destroyed by lightning during Evensong on Sunday, January 30, 1658. The former was used as an observation and machine-gun post by the Germans during the occupation. It was a good spot for this purpose, commanding an extensive view of l'Erée, Lihou Island, and the barracks at Richmond.

The use of the church for military purposes by the occupying forces established no precedent. As recently as 1826, an alarm gun, a 24-pounder, was mounted in the churchyard.

One inconspicuous monument within the churchyard, a plain slate, now rather worn, commemorates a melancholy incident of 1819, when the *Pitt* cutter, from Jersey to Falmouth, foundered on the rocks between l'Erée and Richmond. Eleven of the victims are buried here.

Near the entrance to the churchyard is a large stone at the end of the wall, on one side of which appears a large cross and on the other a smaller one. This Christianised menhir is a good example of the way in which the early Christian priests used a site which was already sacred for its pagan associations as the centre for their new religion.

A road winds round church and churchyard to the west and south, on the right-hand side of which is a valley, with water-meadows. From the meadow immediately below the church which is part of the curé or glebeland the Germans drove tunnels like large sections of the London underground into the hillside as stores for food and ammunition and hide-outs for men and machines. The entrances to these fantastic works have now been blocked up, and the debris the Germans left in the valley has been hidden by gorse, brambles and grass.

Not far away, in Le Frie Baton area of the parish, are the dilapidated and forgotten remains of the formidable Mirus gun-battery set up by the Germans. There, in huge circular concrete bowls, the four 48 ton 12 inch guns revolved on their rollers, ready to hurl their great shells 37 miles out to sea.

THE FIEF JEAN GAILLARD. The narrow, sloping, cobbled path, fortunately unspoiled, leading up from Sous l'Eglise to the church, terminates in a flight of stone steps, at the top of which is held the Court of the Fief Jean Gaillard. The Gaillards were Gascons, and the earliest mention of them by name in Guernsey is dated 1313. They played an important and, on the whole, honoured part in local history and possessed considerable holdings in St Peter Port. The male line failed at the end of the 15th or beginning of the 16th century, and but for these few stones, the memory of the family would have disappeared.

TEKTRONIX GUERNSEY LTD. In Guernsey there are a number of light industries, ranging from light engineering to coppersmiths and pottery, but one firm stands out in size and importance. It is the factory of Tektronix Guernsey Ltd., now based on the borders of St Saviour's and St Andrew's parishes, but with its original building of 1,600 square feet near the track in St Sampson's. The Company was established in Guernsey in September 1958 as the first overseas base of Tektronix Inc. of Oregon, USA, to manufacture and market their products in the European Common Market and the European Free Trade area. The main product of the factory is the fascinating instrument, the Oscilloscope; its use is explained in the firm's brochure as follows—

"The world of Tektronix is a world of exploding time.

"In it a split second is a commonplace; the infinitesimal is something to divide; each of its fragments something to measure.

"To master his world man must understand and, where, possible, measure its changing face. In the minutest sliver of time incredibly small events occur, billions upon billions. Anyone one of them may change you tomorrow.

"To measure them, and to do so exactly, demands instruments of precision never before called forth. Such an instrument is the laboratory oscilloscope."

Other departments at the factory deal with the Marketing side, which, via Guernsey's airlink with London and elsewhere, carries their products to 20 different countries. As well, customer service and advice is provided by field engineers who follow on after the sale of an instrument.

So successful was the original venture that the Guernsey branch was promoted to be a subsidiary in 1961, and in 1963 the new modern factory in St Saviour's was started, with the Airport just around the corner. The buildings have been further added to recently, and now the total area in use, including the original building in St Sampson's, is approximately 100,000 square feet. In these buildings work a highly-skilled and dedicated staff of about 550 men and women, many of them islanders who have been given the technical training to carry out the meticulous and delicate assembly of the instruments and to test and inspect them before they are despatched overseas, to Europe, East Africa, the near East, Australia, and New Zealand.

Although against the background of the parent company in the USA, with its great works at Beaverton, near Portland, Oregon. and its offshoots in the Netherlands and Japan, the Guernsey subsidiary may appear to be on a comparatively small scale, yet the presence of this highly technical outward-looking firm in the island is a most valuable asset, for financial reasons of course, but also for many others.

The brochure also offers a more prosaic explanation:

"A Tektronix Oscilloscope is a sensitive sophisticated instrument designed to measure electrical phenomena, many of which happen too fast to be seen, or are too slight to be felt, and indeed to measure any action too fine to be gauged by direct means but which can be converted into electrical terms."

The Parish of St Andrew is the only Guernsey parish which does not touch the sea at some point. A long triangle, it runs north-east from the Airport to Footes Lane in the north and to La Brigade Farm in the south, and its borders go with St Peter Port, St Martin, the Forest, St Saviour's, Castel, and the Vale. It is the most agricultural of the parishes, with many farms and old granite farmhouses, though there are some residential areas in the eastern corner. Symbolically perhaps, the parish has the States Dairy just inside its borders, but it centres on the parish church, with its house cluster round it. Two other large buildings of different interest are Les Vauxbelets, and Havilland Hall, the 19th century Palladian country mansion of the De Havilland family, now owned by Count Blucher, and a treasure house of relics and paintings acquired after Waterloo.

BAILIFF'S CROSS. Up the road from Havilland Hall and the Vauquiédor is the crossroads, Bailiff's Cross. Incised in a stone set in the wall there is the cross, which is reputed to commemorate the story of the wicked Bailiff, Gautier de la Salle. The story goes that in the 14th century one of the Lihou monks had been murdered and the King's officers went over to Lihou to investigate. One of them, Ranulph Gautier, slew the murderer, and was forced to flee the island, but later won his pardon from the King and returned. Gautier de la Salle, the Bailiff, ignored the pardon and had him imprisoned and murdered in Castle Cornet. At last in 1320 a Royal Court of Inquiry, among other findings, found him guilty, and he was taken by the traditional route to the hangman's gibbet in St Andrew's. On his last journey the condemned man did penance at this wayside cross.

THE PARISH CHURCH. The church of St Andrew suffered cruelly during the 18th century from would-be renovators. From the arcade, separating the northern from the southern nave, one pillar was removed and a long elliptical arch substituted. This act of vandalism was done to create a clear space in front of the pulpit.

The eastern part of the arcade was thereby weakened, and to remedy this, the easternmost arch was built up. Later a great quantity of rubble was removed from the massive stone roof.

The present century has seen the restoration of the arcade, and all danger of catastrophe has been averted. The altar, too, has been removed from the north to the south chancel.

Like so many other Guernsey churches, St Andrew's is mentioned in the gift of the Duke of Normandy to the Abbey of Marmoutiers. It bears the title of:

Ecclesia Sancti Andreae de Putente Pomeria
(Church of St Andrew of the sloping orchard).

The *Dédicace* gives its date as 1284, but parts of it are older than this and other parts more recent. The building is well supported by buttresses, and the square tower at the west end of the northern nave is solidly built and shows very large and massive granite quoins. It is castellated and surmounted by a squat spire.

Of the church, Mrs Louisa Lane Clarke says:

"It is prettily situated in a valley, and the sheltered churchyard boasts of the earliest violets in the island."

The baptistery is beneath the tower. The font is modern. In this connection it must be remembered that fonts were not in use in the island at the beginning of the 19th century. It was customary for the parish clerk to attend with a small silver ewer, out of which he poured water into the hand of the priest at the time of the baptism.

At St Andrew's and St Saviour's, and perhaps in other parishes, these elegant little ewers still exist.

The old records of the Guernsey Church Council, the Presbyterian Colloque (1600–18), which tried people for improper living, non-attendance at church, wife-beating, and other crimes against morals, are kept at St Andrew's. The Colloque was very powerful, and sometimes challenged the authority of the Royal Court.

Before the renovation, a curious 17th century pulpit existed in the church, in which was a rudely carved panel, representing St George and the Dragon.

Not far from the church, in the direction of St Peter Port, is the Manor House of St Helene. This is a very small fief, with an area of roughly 200 *vergées* or 80 acres, of which the rector of St Andrew's has always been chaplain. To this day the Rector holds a field for which, in pre-Reformation days, he said a mass on the day the fief court was held. After the Reformation he was only required to recite the Lord's Prayer. Nowadays even this service has become nominal, for the fief court seldom, if ever, meets, the feudal dues of *chef-rente*, *champart*, and *poulage* having been remitted in 1896.

LES VAUXBELETS. On the side of a hill overlooking a lovely quiet valley stands Les Vauxbelets. The kernel of this large building is an old 17th century mansion. But from 1904 it was added to and enlarged until the massive pile was finished as it is today. The work was done by French monks of the order of The Brothers of the Christian Schools, an order founded in 1680 by Jean Baptiste de la Salle to give education to boys in a spirit of absolute charity. When all religious schools were proscribed in France, the Brothers and Sisters scattered to carry on their work elsewhere. By 1914 at Les Vauxbelets four Colleges were running, providing for local boys, for French secondary students, for agricultural training, and for teacher training.

Recently Les Vauxbelets has passed through lean years, and very nearly closed down. But now, under the leadership of the Director, the buildings are being restored, and the teaching tradition is being revived with the establishment in one part of the Dayton Primary School, and in the central building of an International Language School.

Below the College, in the valley, is the Farm, with its barns and large cattle byre, and this is now the headquarters of the little band of monks who carry on in the same spirit as the early pioneers.

By the track from the farm to the Bouillon Road is the Little Chapel, visited by thousands. This amazing little building, with its grotto beneath, was the creation in 1923 of Brother Deodat, who had already built and then knocked down again two smaller ones. Patiently he built the shell of the building, and then started on the task of decorating it with small pebbles, broken pieces of pottery and china, and shells.

The Parish of Castel (or Câtel) is the largest in the island, 2,525 acres, and contains considerable contrasts in scenery and buildings. In its uplands inland there are many farms, the big mansions of St George, Haye du Puits, and Saumarez Park, and the lovely valleys of Talbot, Fauxquets, and Moulin de Haut. At a lower level the main road, Les Grands Moulins, winds through the charming village of King's Mills, with the granite walls and the square or arched doorways of old farm-houses. At, or below, sea level bungaloid estates have been constructed on what was previously waste, salt-flat or marshland, and there are scatterings of glass-houses everywhere.

A recent discovery in a field at Le Feugre, inland from Cobo Bay, shows that the bungalows are not the first dwellings to be put up in this area. Here has been found the site of a 10th century long-house, which is to be excavated professionally as opportunity occurs.

Rising high, to the south of Cobo, is the rocky promontory of Le

The old harbour

ALDERNEY

The main street in the town of St Anne

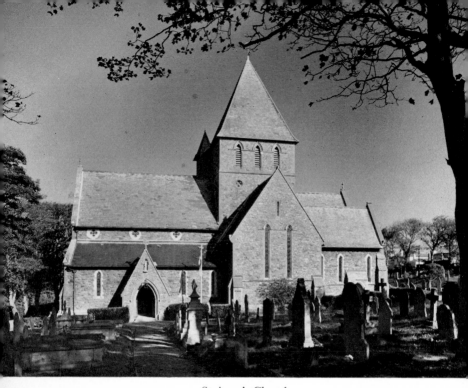

St Anne's Church

ALDERNEY

Telegraph Bay

Creux harbour, Sark

La Coupe, Sark

Guet. The slopes below are covered by a thick forest, and on the rock itself stands the Watch House, one of a number which were built at strategic points round the coast in the 18th century for the local militia to use in their guard against invasion. From this summit there is a panoramic view of the west coast of Guernsey from Pleinmont right round to Herm.

THE COAST. Beyond le Crocq is the wide sweep of Vazon Bay. At low tide the broad stretch of sands lends itself to such sports as motor-car and cycle racing. The foreshore behind it is extremely low and in places very marshy. This area is still known as the Grande Mare.

There can be no doubt that this bay was once the site of an extensive area of wooded country. Bog oak is occasionally laid bare after stormy weather, and peat was dug out of its sands for centuries. Despite its poor quality as fuel, this peat was known as "Gorban", a corruption, it is thought, of "Corban", used in the New Testament to mean "a gift".

The Fief le Comte still has rights of *pesnage* over Vazon Bay— that is, the right to levy a toll for the nuts and acorns eaten by pigs driven into the forest. This indicates that the subsidence, or inundation, of land, which brought Vazon Bay into existence, occurred in historic times.

The promontory which forms the northern horn of Vazon has a 19th century fort upon it, known as Fort Houmet. Until the beginning of the present century it housed a portion of the English garrison. After the First World War, however, it was used as a camp by youth clubs. German concrete additions have not improved it, but though ruinous, its warm red granite walls still give the feeling of quiet strength.

Vazon Bay has played a great part in the history of the Royal Guernsey Militia. Not only have the firm, level sands been used at low tide as a parade-ground, but for many years the bay was a rifle range of considerable length. The firing points were in the neighbourhood of the Martello tower and the butts against the natural wall of rock forming the southern flank of the Houmet promontory.

The next opening, lying between Houmet and Grandes Rocques, and known as Cobo, actually comprises three bays: Albecq, Cobo proper, and Saline. The rocks between Albecq and Cobo are of a pleasing reddish hue, and one, because of its shape, bears the name of the Lion Rock. There is a good deal of red granite in this neighbourhood, and considerable quarrying has taken place in the hillside below the old watch-house called le Guet.

At its northern end Cobo is divided into creeks by reefs or rocks running out almost at right angles from the shore. In one of these, at a certain state of tide, bathing is dangerous because of the undertow, but this spot is prominently marked with warning boards. Saline Bay, like Vazon, once boasted a rifle range, with butts on the flanks of Grandes Rocques.

The headland of Grandes Rocques, despite the damage inflicted upon it by the Germans, still boasts some magnificent rock scenery, and enough of its old defences remain to show how these have been modified in every age to meet the requirements of ever-changing military technique.

The low-lying land bordering Saline Bay and Grandes Rocques was once a marshy area known as the Mare de Carteret; this is now being tackled by an extensive drainage scheme.

THE CASTEL HOSPITAL. This solid and pleasing building, with its fine front and its extensive land around, was established in 1751, on what is quaintly named La Neuve Rue, as a country counterpart to the Town Hospital. There the aged and infirm of the country parishes were to be looked after, and the farm and land helped to contribute to the cost of running the establishment. Since the Second World War it has been adapted to care for the mentally ill.

ST GEORGE'S. The arable land in the neighbourhood of the fine 18th century mansion of St George suggests that this area was probably that of the original settlement in the parish. Further hints are the existence in the grounds of a chapel and a sacred spring, both of which go with the original house cluster in other parishes.

The surroundings have much of the character of an English park. An old building at the entrance gate, now used as the seat of the court of *Fief le Comte*, may well once have been the gatekeeper's lodge.

Of the chapel, not far from the entrance, little now remains save a few stones. In 1675, Marie Guille, wife of the first Guille seigneur of St George, made a gift of the chapel to the inhabitants of the Câtel, to serve as a schoolhouse. In 1736, however, when a more convenient building was given by Marie de Sausmarez, the parishioners still claimed a right of way to the chapel, although it was no longer used as a public building. This question of right of way had been a bone of contention for centuries. It was finally settled in 1759 by the Royal Court in favour of John Guille, who had the chapel pulled down.

Near the ruins of the chapel is a small cemetery, said to be haunted, and not far away is the famous "Holy Well of St George", reported efficacious for the cure of *Maladie de la Fontaine* (eczema) and invaluable to the maiden seeking a lover, provided she adhere rigidly to the conditions imposed by the saint.

Here St George and St Patrick are said to have met and contended for saintly sway over the Holy Isle. With Christian resignation, St Patrick is said to have abandoned his claim in favour of St George. On his departure he filled his wallet with venomous toads and reptiles, which, legend says, he later dropped over Jersey.

Portions of the mansion are old, but the present front was added by William Guille in 1787. The estate passed out of the possession of the Guilles, by sale, in 1920.

SAUMAREZ PARK. The original part of this dignified mansion, the nearest approach in Guernsey to a French Château, was built by William le Marchant in 1721. He travelled with his wife to England to collect materials and furniture to equip it. The le Marchants were one of the leading island families of that period, who had already bought the old Henry family house of Haye du Puits not far away.

In 1783 Saumarez Park passed by marriage to James Saumarez, later Lord Saumarez, the most famous island seaman, who was second-in-command to Nelson at the Battle of the Nile. The third Lord Saumarez, who had served as Ambassador to Japan, enlarged the house, and extended and improved the beautiful grounds. He even brought over Japanese workmen to build a pagoda. At his death in 1938 the property was bought by the States of Guernsey, but before they could decide on a use for it, the Germans occupied the island. The house was used, or rather misused, by the Organisation Todt, the German labour force, and at the liberation was found to be in an appalling condition. The States allowed the St John's Ambulance Brigade to use the house for a home for the aged, and the Brigade set to work to clean and re-equip it. By June 1945 it was ready to be opened as a Hostel, and now is run by a board of management, who depend on voluntary contributions and any payments the residents can make for all the day-to-day expenses. The Hostel is run by a warden and matron, and accepts up to 55 elderly men and women as residents. It is a happy place, as not only do the old people enjoy the spacious house, but they can wander in the grounds, with the lake and the lovely gardens which are maintained by the States as a public park. In what were the stables, grouped round a courtyard, is now housed the Guernsey Folk Museum, of wagons, tools, and household utensils and other items, run by the National Trust of Guernsey in collaboration with the Hostel.

THE PARISH CHURCH OF ST MARIE DU CASTRO. The square tower of the Câtel church, surmounted by a tall octagonal spire, is one of the most conspicuous landmarks in Guernsey.

The church is built on an eminence, which may not unlikely have been the shrine of an earlier paganism. The carved menhir in the churchyard, closely resembling, but not so fine as, that at St Martin's, strongly suggests this.

There is a strong probability, too, that the menhir itself, before the Reformation, may have been used and regarded as a statue of the Virgin.

Tradition asserts the site of the church to have been that of a castle, the Château du Grand Sarrasin, Geoffroi. This Geoffroi may have been a piratical Dane who, from this stronghold, made forays upon the island. It is said that Duke William of Normandy, previous to the invasion of England, sent Sampson d'Anneville to expel the pirate from this stronghold.

This was effected, and Geoffroi was either killed or fled. His castle was demolished and the church erected upon the site. It was dedicated, as was meet in the circumstances, to Our Lady of Deliverance.

Another tradition states that the church was begun at les Eturs. But, as in the case of other island churches, the attempt was sabotaged by demoniacal forces and the site abandoned in favour of the present one.

Part of the old castle walls (if these ever existed) were incorporated into the walls of the church. Mrs Lane Clarke says:

". . . the north and east walls of the church appear more ancient than the rest, and of a different structure, wherein some stones are still seen projecting, with a hole at the end, and other marks of strong gates having been there."

Of the interior of the church little need be said. There are two naves and chancels of equal length. During the past century the south chancel has been raised above the original level, as is shown by the piscina on the south side. The arcades are fine and massive. The font is new, the pre-Reformation one, after having been cast out of the church, having found a permanent resting-place in the garden of Rosenheim, at St Andrew's.

There are a number of interesting frescoes in the church, but these are no longer very clear. One depicts three skeletons admon-

138

ishing the Seigneur of Coutances for hunting on the sabbath. Another is reputed to be a portrait of St Thomas à Becket, while a third is a mural painting of the Lord's Supper. The vestry was once a lady chapel. There is a hole, too, through which, it is said, a cannon could be fired in time of peril. Certainly, churches were once not only depositaries for arms, but also defensible points.

Belonging to the church or presbytery was the house known as la Fontaine. This possessed a holy well, a rood cross, a round chimney, and many carvings of an ecclesiastical character.

One legend of the Câtel Church is interesting, though probably not older than the 16th century. It is that if a married couple remain in the church after their wedding, until Matins begin, their marriage becomes illegal.

The Câtel provides one instance of the probability that the people of this island did not lightly or willingly abandon the old faith in the 16th century. At the end of 1579 or early in 1580 the Presbyterian authorities ordained a general fast for January 22, 1580, "to appease the anger and wrath of God against His people". Hellier la Perre, constable of the parish (and who should therefore have known better), not only ignored the fast, but did not scruple to give a banquet and to absent himself from church both morning and evening. His punishment was condign. He was condemned to the dungeon, on bread and water, fined 100 sous, and made to do public penance in the church of his parish.

The part played by the church in the public life of the parish is illustrated by the functions which used to take place in the churchyard. Here the Court of the Fief St Michel used to meet once a year. *Après la prêche*, too, the verger would mount a stone near the porch and announce the *publications*. It was he, too, but not on the sabbath, who sold to the highest bidder the rector's pigs and tithes.

The Parish of the Vale and the Parish of St Sampson's go together, partly because they are mixed up geographically in the north-east corner of the island, and partly because they have an atmosphere and a fierce local pride of their own, pride of "the North". Between them, they total 3,718 acres, with a large population, and they contain a considerable diversity of scene and activity. There are the biggest concentrations of glasshouses in the island. There are many granite quarries, a few working, most worked out. There are industrial and power works to the north and south of St Sampson's. As a contrast there is a scattering of farms in the Vingtaine de L'Epine and the Clos du Valle, there is Lancresse Common with its golf course, and there are the fishing-boats moored in Grande Havre, Bordeaux, and St Sampson's.

THE PARISH CHURCH OF ST MICHEL DU VALLE. The church of the Vale is dedicated to St Michael. It stands on a hillock through which sea-worn rock protrudes, and at the foot of this eminence, but on the other side of the road, is the small and shallow lake known as the Vale Pond. This may be regarded as the last vestige of the Braye du Valle.

A century and a half ago the church was cut off from the main island at every high tide, and boats were often pressed into use to convey people to service.

There is little doubt that there was a Benedictine priory here, but the date of its foundation has yet to be substantiated. Traces of monastic buildings still exist near the church. Berry, writing in 1814, says:

"There are some pointed arches on the south wall of the Vale Church, which might probably have been part of the chapel."

Dicey, a far more reliable historian (1751), says:

"Some small part of the ruins thereof are at this time to be seen."

A clue to the probability that there was a church on the site before the Benedictines arrived lies in the existence in the church of a big stone, marked with a cross and Alpha and Omega, and dated to the 7th century. Benedictine monks from Mont St Michel in Normandy are said to have established themselves at the Vale as early as 966. Tupper discounts this story on the grounds that, previous to the charter of Duke Robert, father of the Conqueror, the Benedictines had no possessions whatever in Guernsey.

This priory was in a ruinous condition and apparently abandoned by the year 1406, for we find Sir John de Lisle, the Governor, asking permission to use the timber of the buildings to repair Castle Cornet, "as the Priory had fallen into decay".

The abbot of the mother abbey, in Normandy, however, must have still remained in possession of the Fief St Michel, which covered practically half the island, west of a line drawn from Fort Doyle to Pleinmont. To this day, at the Court of Chief Pleas, the Abbot of Mont St Michel is summoned in the same way as all the seigneurs of fiefs, and the King's Procureur (Attorney-General), with a vehemence suggesting that it is surely time the Court realised that all church fiefs have escheated to the Crown, replies: "*Sa Majesté*".

The fief formerly held a court of its own, not abolished until the middle of the last century. It had gallows rights and market rights, the latter exercised at les Landes du Marché.

The Vale Church consists of two naves and chancels of equal length, with a tower at the western end of the southern nave. On this side of the church there is some evidence of Norman work. On the south side of the chancel there is a row of sedilia, and in the northern chancel will be found the finest piscina in the church, as well as an ancient window containing the original pre-Reformation tracery of which the windows of other churches have been almost entirely denuded. An ancient slab in the northern chancel bears the words:

"Orate pro anima Galfridi."

The identity of Galfridi is unknown. He may have been one of the priors of the Vale. But it is singular that the "popish" inscription has survived.

The pillars of the arcade bear corbels, but one only of these is perfect. There is a 15th century porch, which is not complete. The row of canopies over the northern windows is rather remarkable and dates, perhaps, to the 14th century. There are some ancient bells in the tower.

ST SAMPSON'S CHURCH. Like the Town Church, St Sampson's was probably a fishermen's church in origin, on the seashore of the inlet which cut across to Grande Havre and made a virtual island of the Clos du Valle.

The statement that St Sampson's is the oldest church in the island is probably incontestable. The easily remembered date ascribed to it, 1111, is again based on the misleading *Dédicaces*. Its consecration on the same day as that of St Brelade's, in Jersey, as the *Dédicaces* asserts, is a physical impossibility. There is, however, a strong resemblance between the two churches.

There can be no doubt whatever that a church stood on this same site at a far earlier date than 1111. With many other churches in the island, it was granted by William the Conqueror, long before the Conquest, to the Abbey of Marmoutier.

Its reputed founder, St Sampson, is claimed as the apostle of Christianity in the Channel Islands. Of illustrious birth, he is said to have been Bishop of St David's, Wales. Driven out by the Saxon invasion, he sought refuge in Brittany, about the year 520, during the reign of Childebert, son of Clovis.

There it is claimed that he became Bishop of Dol. But, as no bishops were established in Brittany until the 9th century, his position could have been only a nominal one.

St Sampson, accompanied by Judual, a kinsman, duke of the northern Gallician Bretons, and a selection of monks from the community of Pentale, in what was later to become Normandy, landed at the only natural harbour in Guernsey. On the south side of this inlet he caused a chapel to be erected.

Temporarily the islands may have been attached to the dioceses of Avranches and Dol, but they were quickly transferred to that of Coutances.

Regarded as the patron saint of Guernsey, the feast day of St Sampson is held to be July 28. It is not in the least remarkable that numerous miracles are ascribed to him.

It may be assumed, then, that from a wooden structure, built as early, perhaps, as the 6th century, the present church gradually developed until the 14th century.

Not very long ago the whole church was overgrown with ivy and had a most picturesque appearance. In the interests of the preservation of the fabric, however, this was removed.

Among Guernsey churches, the tower is unique. Quaint, pyramidal, and saddle-back, it stands roughly midway of the length of the church, on the north side.

Like most of the old Guernsey churches, St Sampson's is built of granite, some of which is not of local origin. The Chausey Islands are known to have been used extensively as a source of material for Channel Islands churches.

The chancel, nave, and north aisle are vaulted with rubble and pebbles, in keeping with many local churches. The fact that the south aisle is not vaulted marks this portion of the church as of considerably later date than the remainder of the building, probably the 14th century.

The north aisle has three arcades in the outer wall containing tombs, one of which has a long cross deeply cut into the stone.

In these archways now stand several pre-Reformation ornaments discovered not many years ago during renovations to the church. They include a crucifix, two altar candle-sticks, part of a thurible, and a branch candlestick for three candles.

The glass of the windows is uniformly good, but it is all modern.

THE NORTH-WEST COAST. On the north of the Vingtaine de L'Epine are four tiny bays, known respectively as Port Soif, Portinfer, Pecquerie, and Port Grat. Between Pecquerie and Port Grat is the miniature bay of Pulias, having between it and the coast road a bank of shingle forming the boundary of a stagnant salt-water pond.

Grand Havre, the last of the great bays of the west coast, does not belie its name. At high tide it is, indeed, a noble expanse of water, sheltered from the full force of Atlantic gales by two inward curving horns, each of which is crowned by a Martello tower. The southern horn is known as la Rousse and the northern as Chouet.

At the point where Grand Havre bites deepest into the land is Pont St Michel, between the sea-shore and the Vale Pond. This marks the western end of that old arm of the sea, filled in by Doyle, called the Braye. This bridge of the past gave access to the Vale Church. Other relics of the Braye are preserved in the names La Grève and le Marais.

The Pont St Michel marks the entry into the Clos du Valle, originally cut off by the sea from the remainder of the island. This low-lying district has the reputation of being more bracing than the highlands of the south.

It abounds in quarries, a few still worked, most abandoned and filled with water. The area is also extremely rich in dolmens and other prehistoric remains.

This is particularly true of Lancresse Common, that sandy, undulating plain which covers the whole of the northernmost portion of Guernsey, from Mont Cuet on the west to Fort Doyle on the east. A story, of the truth of which there is but slender evidence, accounts for the name. Duke Robert, father of the Conqueror, is said to have set sail for England in 1031 to help his cousins, Alfred and Edward, against Canute. He met with contrary winds and was obliged to put into Guernsey. His fleet cast anchor in a northern bay, henceforth called Lancresse, a possible corruption of *l'ancrage*.

Other doubtful stories told of Duke Robert are that he was responsible for the building of such important local fortifications as the Vale Castle, Jerbourg Castle, and the Château des Marais. But the most apocryphal of all ascribes to him the introduction of the Guernsey breed of cattle into the island, through the instrumentality of the Benedictine monks who settled at the Vale.

Nowhere else in the island are so many Martello towers to be seen as at Lancresse. From Chouet to Fort Doyle the whole of the coast-line is dotted with them.

Until well into the present century the Common approaches were barred by gates. Upon it sheep and cattle were grazed. The gates were finally removed in 1920.

The Golf Links, of 18 holes, suffered badly during the years of the occupation. These have now been fully restored.

Forts le Marchant and Doyle, on the eastern side of Lancresse Bay, are creations of the last century. Both are now disused. Fort Pembroke, on the western side, bears many of the marks of antiquity.

THE BRAYE DU VALLE. In old charts Guernsey is shown as two islands, the northern and very much smaller one being separated from the remainder at high water by a narrow channel, the eastern end of which was St Sampson's harbour and the western Grand Havre Bay, near the Vale Church. This small island was known as the Clos du Valle, and that part of the quay at St. Sampson's named the Bridge was so called because at this point a bridge spanned this narrow channel.

The filling of this channel, at the expense of the British Government, was undertaken under the governorship of Sir John Doyle in 1806. The result was the reclamation of approximately 300 English acres. At first these acres were little better than a bed of sand. They were disposed of by order of the Crown, and realised £5,000, which sum was utilised by Doyle in his great road-construction programme.

As the result of drainage and careful cultivation, this reclaimed sea-bed has become good arable and pasture land.

This narrow inlet was 20 feet deep at high tides, and it is now impossible to ascertain where the material came from to fill it. The Braye du Valle, as it was called, was much wider and larger than is nowadays commonly believed. The deepest part of the lowlands was where the Braye and the Route Militaire now intersect.

There were extensive salt-pans in two parts of the Braye, one group near Grand Fort and another at the present Salt-pans.

At dead low tide the Braye could be crossed only by stepping-stones. At high tide a ferry was necessary. It is said, however, that there was at one time a bridge from l'Islet to the Vale Church, known as St Michael's Bridge.

Changes in the level of the sea-bed are well illustrated by the Braye. The bones of a whale were once found near Pleinheaume, and the keel of a boat, said to be neolithic, was once unearthed at the Coutanchez.

It has been pointed out, with some justice, that Doyle in no way foresaw the development of the granite trade in the 19th and 20th centuries. Had he done so, he would, instead of filling the Braye, have converted it into a canal with locks, so that ships could have been loaded directly, or almost directly, from the quarries and stone yards. This would have involved little or no deepening, for the locks would have been closed at the appropriate times.

THE ORMER. Around this part of the coast, as in most other parts where there are large stones or rocky crevices, can be found the ormer. What feelings of nostalgia the mere mention of that word will raise in the exiled Guernseyman! Not that the ormer is peculiar to this island. In New Zealand a larger and coarser variety, 6 inches by 4 inches, is fairly common. It is eaten by the Maoris (who, from the flavour of the flesh, call it the *mutton-fish*), but not by the white population. A variety found on the coast of California is still larger, measuring 8 inches by 6 inches. A good-sized ormer in Guernsey is from 3 to 4 inches long by 2 to 3 inches wide.

The word ormer is a contraction of *oreille-de-mer*, from the resemblance of the shell to the human ear, and the scientific name *haliotis* bears the same meaning. Its distribution in the area of the Channel is fairly wide, extending from Barfleur southwards. Generally speaking, its home is fairly shallow water, near to low water of spring tides, but it is probably never entirely uncovered.

The ormer is not a sluggish animal. It moves at the rate of 5 to 6 yards per minute. If placed on its back it is active in righting itself. If its shell is removed it creeps about as usual and the heart can be seen beating actively. It grows another shell, and if that falls off again another, but the new shells are abnormal. Pearls are sometimes produced in ormers.

The ormer lives apparently chiefly on the green weed growing on the under-surface of boulders. Its chief enemies are the octopus, star-fish, and probably the oyster-catcher (sea-pie). Frost has a bad effect upon it. In 1901 there was a severe frost coincident with a low spring tide. As a result, thousands of ormers were killed, or so numbed that they loosed their hold and were easily picked up.

The ages-old popularity of the ormer is evidenced by the following extract from a book written in 1673, entitled *News from the Channel; or the Discovery and perfect Description of the Island of Sark, by a gentleman now inhabiting there, to his friend and kinsman in London*, and quoted by Ansted:

". . . as also a large shel-fish, taken plentifully at low tides, called an Ormond, that sticks to the rocks, whence we beat them off with a forck or iron hook. 'Tis much bigger than an oyster, and like that, good, either fresh or pickled, but infinitely more pleasant to the gusto; so that an epicure would think his pallat in paradice, so he might but always gormandise on such delitious ambrosia."

LES DÉHUS DOLMEN. The whole of the Clos du Valle abounds in megalithic monuments. The most striking of these is the dolmen of les Déhus at Paradis.

In the closing years of the 18th century, when the granite trade of the island was beginning to develop, the exposed capstones were in imminent danger of being broken up for export. Fortunately, the *hougue* and the plot of land on which it stood were bought by Mr John de Havilland, and thus one of the most important and most interesting megalithic structures in the Channel Islands was preserved.

Les Déhus was investigated by Lukis as early as 1837, and the pottery and skeletons discovered by him are now in the island museum. But it was not until 1917 that one of the most remarkable features of the dolmen was noticed for the first time. This was a figure cut on the under-surface of the second capstone.

Since 1917 further researches have been made, the passage grave thoroughly explored and the covering of earth replaced. The whole has been scheduled as an ancient monument.

In connection with les Déhus an interesting point of folklore arises, not confined to Guernsey alone. Early in the present century, when the dolmen was being thoroughly examined, there was widespread feeling among the inhabitants of the northern parishes that ill-luck would follow the desecration of the tomb. A series of robberies and assaults, culminating in a murder, and the death (from natural causes) of one of the excavators of the tomb, were ascribed "to the evil spirit that had escaped from its imprisonment in the tomb".

THE VALE CASTLE. From the sea the approaches to St Sampson's harbour are both narrow and dangerous. Nevertheless, both as a settlement and a haven, St Sampson's possibly pre-dates St Peter Port.

The mouth of the harbour is covered from both sides by fortresses, the Vale Castle or Château de St Michel to the north and Mont Crevelt to the south. Of the history of Mont Crevelt little is known. In Napoleonic times it boasted a Martello tower and a series of gun-platforms and breastworks. A good deal of this old work still remains. But the Germans during the occupation marred its mediaeval appearance with their unsightly concrete additions. A more recent contrast is the battery of oil-storage tanks and the warehouses which have gone up on the reclaimed land to the south.

The Vale Castle, standing on a considerable eminence rendered still more prominent by the quarrying away in recent years of the granite slopes surrounding it, is probably older than Castle Cornet. Its outer works bear every mark of antiquity, and the round arched gateway, with its portcullis, is a particularly fine example of mediaeval military architecture. The dungeons, pierced in its thick walls, utilised as shelters by the occupying forces, are now spoiled.

Like Castle Cornet, the Vale Castle has been used for military purposes in all centuries. After the First World War there was some danger of the Castle falling into the hands of a granite company, and of the whole hill being quarried away. It was acquired by the States, and its barrack buildings used for a time to alleviate the housing shortage.

To the Vale Castle belongs the dubious honour of mention in the *Dédicace des Eglises*, which dates its foundation, by monks, as A.D. 966. Needless to say, this is as spurious as the history of the churches recorded in that publication. Tupper, with his customary caution, says:

"Some portion of the Vale Castle is thought to be the work of the Normans, although certainly not so ancient as the tenth century."

The Treaty of Neutrality of 1484 led to the disuse of the Vale Castle, and it was allowed to fall into ruin. Under the Stuarts it came again into use, being garrisoned and equipped by the five low parishes.

The tiny cemetery, on the slope leading up to the main entrance, contains the graves of Russian troops, of whom 6,000 were quartered in the island towards the close of the year 1799. They had fought side by side with English troops in Holland, and their presence in the island is accounted for by the Bill of Rights, which prohibited the introduction of foreign troops into England. Many of these were quartered in barracks at Delancey. A disease, contracted by exposure to the marshy conditions of Holland, carried off several hundreds of them, hence the small enclosure on the flank of the hill.

ST SAMPSON'S HARBOUR. The history of St Sampson's as a second town and a seaport dates only from the beginning of the 19th century, when the breach through the northern part of the island, known as the Braye du Valle, was closed.

Before that time it was used by fishermen, and there existed on the Col du Mont Crevelt some kind of ancient breakwater. In 1820 the States voted £800 to repair this and to build a quay on the north side.

Road-building on a scale hitherto unknown had begun in England, and a Scottish engineer, named MacAdam, who was to add a new word to the English language, advocated the use of cracked stones to make a durable road surface. Here was a material that Guernsey could supply. It existed in unlimited quantity in the neighbourhood of St Sampson's harbour. It was therefore inevitable that the harbour should develop.

Between 1839 and 1841 the North Quay was extended as far as the Maisonette rock, the South Quay was built and the breakwater lengthened. These works cost £7,000, and this expenditure was met by the imposition of certain dues on the exportation of stone.

The extension of the breakwater led to the reclamation of a considerable area of foreshore. This was claimed by the Crown. It was, however, ceded to the States in 1841 in consideration of the sum of £100.

In 1842 the South Quay was extended and a head built at right angles to it. This cost £3,340.

Nearly ten years elapsed, and then the Mont Crevelt breakwater was further lengthened and a quay provided on the north-east side. £9,000 was spent on this.

The harbour was beginning to asume its present shape. Not until 1862, however, were any further changes made, and these were chiefly of an ameliorative nature. The centre of the harbour was deepened and trenched, rocks inside the breakwater were removed and the wall of the new North Quay was built.

In 1864 rebuilding of the west and south walls of the old North Pier was undertaken, the old bridge and South Quay were widened and a new slip was provided on the north side.

The bay between the old and new North Quays was excavated and deepened, the Crocq was enlarged and a Careening Hard and patent slip constructed on its eastern side.

It is not always realised how large an area has been reclaimed from the sea in the neighbourhood of St. Sampson's harbour. In 1857 a wall 529 feet long was built over the rocks to the east of the new North Pier. Another wall, 350 feet in length, was built in the bay of the Longue Hougue, between Mount Crevelt and the Rocher Fortu. These works resulted in the reclamation of some 11 *vergées* of land, which in the course of time were levelled by the deposit of ballast. In the case of these reclamations the Crown apparently waived its rights.

The proprietors of the reclaimed land of the Braye du Valle were under an obligation to keep the bridge in repair. In 1872 they made a proposition to the States for the redemption of this liability. This was accepted for the sum of £50.

On the south-west corner of the Crocq, near the harbour-master's office, stands a massive stone, 13 feet in height, which once formed part of a dolmen. One face bears an inscription to the memory of

Daniel de Lisle Brock, Bailiff and President of the States when the first works were begun.

At the eastern end of the Crocq is another obelisk, 27 feet high, of local granite. This bears on one face the names of the Committee of the States which in 1872 was responsible for the harbour, and on another the name of the Bailiff, Sir Peter Stafford Carey.

The new north arm was for a very long time known as Abraham's Bosom. This biblical expression is, in fact, a nautical phrase for a place where vessels may lie snug and comfortable in all weathers while awaiting a favourable opportunity, after loading, to put to sea.

During the heyday of the stone trade St Sampson's was frequently crowded with shipping, and after a ship was loaded she was often moved away from the quay to make room for another, and moored fore and aft to ground rings in this, the part of the harbour with the softest bottom.

To this day some of these rings and chains can still be seen at low tide, and the aptness of the expression Abraham's Bosom realised. Most of the vessels used in the stone trade were sailing-ships which, when laden, were warped out of the harbour as far as the breakwater, and sometimes farther, by steam tugs, the names of which are now scarcely more than a memory. There were the *Queen of the Isles* and the *Watt*, and, later, the *Alert* and *Assistance*. Once out of the harbour, of course, these old windjammers proceeded under their own sail.

To this day a visitor to St Sampson's cannot fail to be struck by the magnificent granite work. The most striking of all are perhaps the shapely granite bollards.

During the past thirty years the stone trade has progressively declined, and St Sampson's is not the busy place it used to be. It would today be very quiet indeed, had not some of the cargo traffic of St Peter Port been diverted there.

In St Peter Port the stretch from the Albert Pier to the old North Pier was formerly known, for obvious reasons, as the coal quay. Now all coal, whether for domestic consumption or for greenhouse heating, is discharged at St Sampson's, and many old stone-cracking yards are depôts for coal. Labour shortage, an acute problem since the end of the occupation, has been partially met by the installation of electric cranes and mechanical grabs. Improvements in this direction are still going on, but it may even now be claimed that few ports of the size of St Sampson's are better equipped to deal with the whole of the island's imports of coal, a substantial portion of its oil, and a fair part of its timber.

Another aspect of St Sampson's cannot be ignored. For rather

149

more than half a century, beginning in 1840 and ending in 1897, it was an important ship-building centre. Yards, none of them large, extended right round the present harbour, and tales are still told of the launching of many goodly ships.

Not far from the wall of the churchyard, the good ship *Concordia* stuck as she was being launched. For three and a half days she remained immovable. Witchcraft being suspected, for a bird was observed flying continually over the vessel, a white wizard was sent for. He scattered salt over the deck, and the vessel immediately glided into the water.

The *Golden Spur*, the largest vessel built and owned in Guernsey, sprang into being in a yard not far from the bridge. The ketch *Sarnia*, the last vessel to be built in the island, wrecked on the Ferrières, refloated, and finally lost on the English coast, also came from this yard.

Between 1840 and 1897 a hundred vessels were built in Guernsey, while 70 were lengthened and rebuilt in the same period. Island shipping during these years comprised 90 ships in the foreign trade, including a number which went to the Mediterranean for dried fruit.

BULWER AVENUE—THE TOMATO BOARD DEPOT. The advent of steam reduced the shipyards, of which there were no fewer than 13 between St Peter Port and St Sampson's, to silence. But a further period of comparative prosperity followed, with the development of the stone trade. At the beginning of the present century the island exported half a million tons of granite annually, mostly to England, for road-making.

Coincidentally with the stone trade arose the growing industry, now the mainstay of the island. It began with the culture of grapes under glass, followed by that of figs, melons, and other luscious fruits. Not until the seventies did the tomato come into the picture.

Glasshouses appeared overnight, and just before the Germans landed in 1940 approximately 1,000 acres of Guernsey soil were covered by glass. Air raids, the concussion of A.A. gunfire, and unavoidable neglect reduced this area during the occupation by some 120 acres. The industry picked up again quickly after the war, but there was one difference. To deal with the controls imposed by the English Ministry of Food, the Tomato Marketing Board was established, to a majority of growers this seemed to work well, and after some controversy it was set up on a permanent basis with statutory powers in 1951.

The next big step in the rationalisation of the industry came 10

150

years later. Experiments had been carried out on the handling and bulk cartage of the tomato crop, and it was decided to use shallow 12 lb. trays which could fit on each other instead of the more picturesque but old-fashioned baskets. These trays could be wired together in threes, and then blocks of them could be stacked on a large flat tray to eliminate individual handling and help mechanical loading. This method is known as palletisation, and it necessitated the building of the Central Depot, to which the carters could bring the trays from the vineries, and where the trays could be inspected, wired, covered with their paper wrapping and placed on pallets before being carried by lorry to the docks in St Peter Port.

The wisdom of this industrial approach has been proved, as each year some 50,000 tons, about nine and a half million packages, pass through the great sheds of the Depot, and are sent on their way to markets in the United Kingdom from Penzance to Inverness, and to Northern Ireland and Eire.

The sheer size of the enterprise fascinates visitors, as they watch in their hundreds from the Visitors' Gallery.

All these tomatoes are produced from approximately 1000 acres of glass, almost exactly the same acreage as in 1939 produced 32,000 tons.

BULWER AVENUE TO LES BANQUES. A light railway once connected St Sampson's with St Peter Port. At the end of the last century electric trams were substituted for this, and, so that the track might be level throughout its whole length, a cutting was made through the hillock of Hougue à la Perre. Later an extension of the tram-sheds led to the removal of the remainder of the hillock on the landward side and the destruction of the Martello tower which stood upon it. Hougue à la Perre, a fortification from time immemorial, remained, however, between the road and the beach. During the occupation the Germans adapted it to modern warfare, honeycombed it with tunnels and strengthened it with concrete. Trams had finally faded away in 1934, in competition with buses, and the Germans relaid this track for a light railway, extending it at the northern end to Lancresse Common, and at the southern to the breakwaters of the Town Harbour.

The road between St Sampson's and St Peter Port, though wide, is on the whole dull and uninteresting. It runs in a sweeping curve of some 3 miles round Bellegrève Bay, which, admittedly beautiful at high tide, leaves an impression, largely false, of dirt and neglect at low tide.

A sea-wall bounds Bellegrève Bay throughout almost its entire length. At the St Sampson's end the area won from the sea by the tipping of quarry rubbish on the beach is particularly noticeable from the fact that the road has a sea-wall on both its sides, the landward one being the old and now unnecessary one.

This was the track originally followed to St Sampson's by the trams, which entered that port along the south side. The bus route now follows the Grandes Maisons Road, thus cutting off two sides of a triangle, and emerges at St Sampson's on the bridge.

DELANCEY HILL. The coast road and the Grandes Maisons Road skirt the base of a grassy eminence known as Delancey Hill. This is a public park belonging to St Sampson's. It possesses quite a number of megalithic remains, many of which have unfortunately been removed.

The military importance of the hill has been recognised in every age, and old batteries of Napoleonic times dot the seaward flank. Germans, too, have left a number of indelible concrete marks upon it. But their greatest act of vandalism was to fell the granite obelisk, erected in 1876, immortalising the exploits of Admiral Lord Saumarez, a contemporary of Nelson. The four bronze plaques depicting his exploits were fortunately saved, and are now displayed on the walls of the Outer Bailey of Castle Cornet.

THE CHÂTEAU DES MARAIS. On the border between St Sampson's and St Peter Port, in an area which was once a marshy waste but is now being reclaimed for housing development, rise two hillocks. That nearest the sea is crowned by the mouldering walls of an old castle, now usually known as Ivy Castle. In old records it is sometimes referred to as Château d'Orgueil and sometimes as Château des Marais. It is well worth a visit. It covers an area of about four acres. Within the outermost wall, whose outline is still traceable, is a moat, parts of which are still flooded. From the upper works a good view is obtainable of the country all round, including the other hillock, whose flank has been scarred by quarrying. The keep can still be traced, and there are vestiges of an old chapel, Notre Dame des Marais. In spite of encroachments by the modern world, the Château keeps its old air of seclusion, as it looks out north over the marshes from which it takes its name.

ALDERNEY

ALDERNEY is a kidney-shaped island, if the extensive indentations of its coast be ignored, with its greatest length, of about 3 miles and two thirds, from north-east to south-west. Its breadth nowhere exceeds a mile and a half.

Anyone approaching Alderney from Guernsey by air cannot fail to notice that practically the whole of the south-eastern coast is made up of lofty and abrupt cliffs. These approximate in height to those of Guernsey's southern coast, and landing on the airport from this direction is rather like fluttering down on a shelf, the outer rim of the airport being necessarily very near the edge of the cliff.

But long before Alderney is reached the observant air traveller will realise why, in the past, when the method of transport he now enjoys was at the most a dream, Napoleon spoke of Alderney as "le bouclier d'Angleterre". Ansted uses the no less striking simile of "the Ehrenbreitstein of the Channel". To the British Foreign Office of the 18th and 19th centuries, when Anglo-French rivalry was at its zenith, it was indeed the key of the Channel.

To the east, and running almost due north and south, is the coast of Normandy, terminating in Cape la Hague. From the rocks that fringe this cape to those that fringe Alderney is a distance of 6 miles only, and of these 6 miles little more than 2 exceed 20 fathoms in the depth. This channel is called the Race of Alderney, and the extreme distance across it from land to land is some $8\frac{1}{2}$ miles.

About a mile to the north-west of Alderney is a very extensive shoal, $2\frac{1}{2}$ miles long from north-east to south-west and $1\frac{1}{2}$ miles wide. There are one or two islands, the largest of which, called Burhou, is half a mile long. None of these islands is inhabited. On Burhou, however, a haunt of the stormy petrel, are the remains of a house, erected to provide shelter for fishermen and others driven there by stress of weather.

The channel between Alderney and the Burhou group is called the "Passe au Singe", which has, in course of time, become corrupted into the "Swinge". It is a dangerous passage, navigable for only a few hundred yards of its width, and not more than 10 fathoms deep.

Another rock to the north-west of Alderney, which is also often visible from Guernsey, is called the Ortach. This islet of solid rock rises 60 feet out of water. On its south side it descends vertically into the sea to a depth of 60 or 70 feet, but its western face has an out-cropping ledge at a depth of 14 feet below low-water level. It, and the Garden Rocks off the western point of the island, are now the breeding grounds of great colonies of Gannets, a truly wonderful sight for anyone who can get close or use a powerful pair of field-glasses.

BRAYE HARBOUR. The approach to Alderney by sea, though providing a less extensive view than that by air, is none the less picturesque. The only landing, for a ship of any size, is at the harbour in Braye Bay, on the north-western coast of the island. This coast bears some resemblance to the west coast of Guernsey, in that the bays are wide, sandy, and shallow, and have an extensive foreshore. The westernmost, Clonque Bay, is a typical example of this.

It was in 1847 that the British Government, casting an apprehensive eye at the naval works under construction at Cherbourg, projected a harbour at Alderney capable of accommodating far more than the British fleet of those days. From Cape Grosnez, and running in an east north-easterly direction across Braye Bay, a breakwater was constructed. It was a gigantic task, involving a large amount of work in water more than 20 fathoms in depth. More than £1,500,000 sterling were expended, and the work was then abandoned. From 1872 onwards considerable breaches were made by the sea, despite continued efforts at preservation, efforts which have been maintained to the present day.

The submerged remains of half the completed work now form a reef which renders the entrance to the harbour most dangerous. Before the breakwater was built, the harbour in Alderney was regarded as a refuge for small vessels during south-westerly gales, but Cherbourg has now displaced Alderney in this respect.

At the landward end of the Admiralty breakwater is the old harbour. From its extremity a jetty runs out roughly parallel with the breakwater, and it is here that goods and passengers are landed in Alderney. It was from this jetty that the whole population of the island was evacuated on June 23, 1940, in face of the threat of enemy occupation. But the complete evacuation had one advantage. Though scattered throughout Great Britain, the islanders remained one community. The Court and States of Alderney ceased to act as such, but both bodies were replaced by a voluntary relief committee composed exclusively of Alderney people, centred in London, and elected by a post-card vote of all adult Alderney evacuees. Again and again this post-card referendum was utilised for the settlement of special questions affecting the whole exiled community.

154

THE TOWN OF ST ANNE. The five years of German occupation left the island derelict and destitute, and the islanders who returned in a steady trickle after liberation were faced with great difficulties. A little of this can still be seen today as one lands on the jetty to make one's way up the hill to the Town. The 50-yard German steel jetty is rotting and dangerous, the remains of a granite-crushing works stand gaunt and hideous, and the surface of the road is rough and uneven. But the row of tall 18th century houses through which one passes in Braye Street are bright and repainted, and when one climbs up to St Anne, one finds an attractive small town, with an atmosphere all its own. All cobbled, Victoria Street joins the High Street at a T-junction, other little streets branch off on one side or the other, and all is neat, clean, and mostly freshly painted. Solid square house abuts on solid square house, a visible expression of the sturdiness of the island's character.

THE CHURCH OF ST ANNE. The peaceful centre of the Town is Royal Connaught Square, with on one side the Island Hall, an 18th century mansion which was built by John Le Mesurier, Governor of Alderney, and is now used to house the Island Library and Museum, and on another the wall of the cemetery. In this rises the clock tower of the old chapel of St Anne—all that remains of the old structure which, dilapidated and ruinous, was pulled down when the new church was built. This new church of St Anne, which was consecrated in 1850, was built by the Rev. John Le Mesurier, son of the last hereditary Governor, as a memorial to his parents and his family. The architect was Sir George Gilbert Scott, and it is a fine example of his work, cruciform, of local granite, with Caen stone used for the carved portions.

The peal of six bells in the sturdy tower was removed by the Germans, but luckily after the liberation they were discovered in Cherbourg and were brought back to be recast and rehung.

The occupation forces, who used the building as an oil-store, did other damage, removing the pews and fittings and breaking many of the windows. Through the generosity of islanders and many others, the pews and other furniture has now been replaced and a number of fine stained-glass windows have been put in.

THE COURT HOUSE. Half-way along New Street stands the Court House, a plain and dignified building which was built in 1850. On the ground floor are the offices and the Committee room, above is the Court room itself, with its stylish wooden horseshoe table and desk at the centre for the Court and the States of Alderney. At this table sit the seven *Jurats* each week, and the President and nine Deputies of the States at such times as there is business to transact.

The existence of a Court in Alderney goes back to Norman times. Then, the laws were enforced by a Prevot and six *Jurats* at a time when the King owned half the island and the Bishop of Coutances owned the other half. During the Hundred Years War with France, the island suffered severely from raids, and the Black Death no doubt decreased the population. But, unlike Sark, there were always a number of residents in the area around the Trigalle and St Martins, and these were added to in the 15th century by new immigrants from Guernsey and Normandy.

In the 16th century the island came to have some strategic importance in the eyes of the English Government, owing to the activities of privateers and uneasy relations with the French. Two successful raids by a French soldier of fortune, Captain Malesart, led the Governor of Guernsey, Sir Leonard Chamberlain, to send a relief force in 1558, and from this developed a long, if not particularly happy relationship between Alderney and the Chamberlain family. The Crown granted a fee-farm lease of the island to various members of the family between this date and the beginning of the Civil War. This was not a popular measure with the islanders as the Chamberlains were Catholics and the islanders were largely Calvinists, who with a strongly democratic tradition objected to the way in which they were often treated.

At the Restoration the lease of the island was granted to Sir George Carteret of Jersey, whose widow sold her rights to Sir Edmund Andros, a Guernseyman who was Governor of New York. He delegated his powers to another Guernseyman, Thomas le Mesurier, and this led to considerable friction between the acting-Governor and Thomas Le Cocq, Judge of the Alderney Court and a member of a leading island family. In spite of island opposition the control of the island finally passed into the hands of the Le Mesurier family in 1721, Henry being appointed hereditary Governor a few years later.

The Le Mesuriers had a difficult time trying to control opposition in the Court and the States, but their period of rule coincided with a prosperous time for the wild islanders. With the new harbour at Braye as a base, some sailed the seas around as privateers, while others made money from the export of Alderney cattle and the manufacture of the little kegs so useful in smuggling. The independent spirit of the islanders remained unaltered, and they resisted successfully the assumption of the title of "Seigneur" by General John Le Mesurier, the new Governor, in 1803. He it was who finally closed the family's association with the island in 1825, by surrendering his grant. He was led to this step by his struggles with the islanders, and by the economic depression which fell on the island at the end of the Napoleonic War when the garrison was withdrawn and privateering and smuggling became more and more difficult.

This withdrawal of the Governor's household aggravated the position that the Court and States of the island had to face. But in the Victorian period two factors helped the economy, the labour and garrison which came in as a result of the "harbour of refuge" scheme, and the development of the granite industry. The years passed, with agriculture and granite as the mainstays of the island, but the German occupation ended these centuries of history abruptly.

After the islanders' return, it was felt that their age-old constitution required to be adapted to the present day, and this was done in the Government of Alderney Law of 1948. This abolished the feudal survivals of the Court of Chief Pleas and the Douzaine, and separated the Court from the States. The Court, of a Chairman and six other *Jurats*, is solely concerned with judicial business, and is appointed by the Home Secretary acting for the Crown. The States of Alderney now consist of a President and nine deputies; these are elected by universal suffrage, and there is no bar of sex or property qualification.

THE FORTS. When the British Government in the 1840s decided on the construction of the Breakwater to protect their new "harbour of refuge", they set to work to make the island impregnable as well. The steep cliffs protected the south and east coasts, but the more gentle north and west coasts with their sweeping sandy bays were to be guarded by 10 forts. A large labour force was brought in; houses were built for them and by 1861 the forts, in a half-circle from Fort Clonque to Essex Castle were ready for the garrison. Now they have been handed over to the States of Alderney, some to be used as interesting private dwellings, one to be used by the Army when it returns on occasion to the island for training, the rest left as picturesque empty shells, reminders of the grandiose scheme which the Victorians dreamed up.

ESSEX CASTLE AND LONGY BAY. Although Essex Castle was included in the Victorian ring of forts, its history goes back to Tudor times. Henry VIII, who had a shrewd understanding of the importance of a Navy and Naval bases, issued orders for the construction of a fort to protect Longy Bay, the only naval base and refuge in Alderney at that time. Work was begun in 1547, and was carried on energetically by Protector Somerset who had a labour force of 200 and a garrison of 200 sent over. The project was abandoned at the accession of Queen Mary, but by that time a rectangular outer wall had been built, enclosing an area of refuge for the islanders and their flocks, and dominated by a central fort. The only Tudor remains today are the north and west side of the outer wall, for the rest was razed by the Victorians to make way for their fort. There is no reason to suppose that the fort, named Essex Castle by the Le Mesuriers in the 1790s and adorned with the pepper-pot tower, had any link with the Earl of Essex.

But the area of Longy Bay has much older historical associations than those with Protector Somerset. On Longy Common was the biggest concentration of Megalithic remains, dolmens, cists, hoards of stone axes and other weapons and implements, a bronze foundry, and, the most recent discovery on the site of the new golf-course, an Iron-Age pottery works. Most of these remains were destroyed as a result of quarrying and Army building, but records still exist. Recently too the dolmen of Les Pourciaux has been rediscovered, although half of it is still hidden beneath the concrete of a German machine-gun post. This wealth of recorded remains supports the tradition that Alderney, with Lancresse Common in Guernsey, was a sacred resting place for the dead in that remote period.

Later in time is the building now known as the Nunnery, the nickname given to it by soldiers in the Napoleonic War. This building, rectangular with round bastions, was almost certainly a Roman fort and signal-station of about A.D. 350, built as one of the system of intercommunicating forts which the Romans used to help their fleet of the Saxon Shore in its endless patrols against pirates and raiders. The area near the Nunnery still has the name of the Old Town, an area which was overwhelmed by great sandstorms at an unrecorded date.

THE BLAYE. West and south of St Anne spreads the plateau of good soil known as the La Grande and La Petite Blaye. This area has been the main arable land of the island from prehistoric times, and has been farmed on the open-field system up to the present day. This meant that the area was enclosed only during the sowing and growth of the crops; after harvest the island farmers removed the temporary hedges and grazed their cattle and flocks in common during the winter.

After the German surrender on May 16, 1945, the islanders

gradually returned to find their farms derelict and their fields a wasteland. The English Government was generous with subsidies, and an attempt was made to restore the island's agriculture on a communal basis. This communalism was too great a strain for the individuality of the islanders, and the former farmers were then assisted to set themselves up again, the land was resurveyed and registered, and Guernsey cattle were brought over to restart the herds. There were a number of experiments in market-gardening, but the main crop today is carrots, exported to England.

One area of the Blaye had however already been turned to another use, as an airport. This airport is the oldest in the Channel Islands, dating back to the spring of 1935. At that time it was simply a level field, with a tin shed as a terminal building, which housed the only woman airport-controller in the world, Miss W. Le Cocq. After the War the service was reopened, more adequate terminal buildings were put up, and the runway was first extended and then very recently given a hard surface. This airlink, with Guernsey through the "Islander", and directly with England is increasingly seen as Alderney's life-line, of vital significance as the number of summer tourists increases.

SARK

When Tennyson wrote:

> *Our little systems have their day,*
> *They have their day and cease to be,*

he could not have had Sark in mind, for in that island we have still an example of active feudalism. It is feudalism, however, which the student will find full of contradictions. It is a revival of mediaeval feudalism, dating back to 1565, a time when feudalism in England was well on the road to decay, and in its governmental institution, the Court of Chief Pleas, or Cour de Chef Plaids, as it is more accurately known, we have an example of democracy—if the use of this much-abused term is permissible—based not on the rights, but on the duties of man.

It was in the year 1565 that Queen Elizabeth granted "the Island of Sark in our Dutchy of Normandy" to Helier de Carteret, Seigneur of St Ouen in the island of Jersey. He was to hold it as tenant-in-chief of the Crown, by the twentieth part of a Knight's fee and an annual payment of 50s. The conditions attached to the grant were that within two years he was to see that the island was continually inhabited, dwelt in, or occupied by at least 40 tenants, subject of the Crown, or "such as should oblige themselves by oath to the Captain of the Island of Guernsey or Jersey, to be faithful, true or obedient to the Queen, her heirs or successors". There is still perpetuated in the Deed the requirement that the "tenant" must provide "Un homme ménager soit lui-même ou un autre demeurant sur le dit héritage avec mousquet et amunition pour la défense de l'Ile."

In default of compliance with this obligation, a fine of £10 was to be imposed. Persistence in default, after six months admonition, raised the fine to £20. A third default was to be met by a fine of £40, and upon a fourth, by which time we may suppose the patience of the Crown to be exhausted, the grant was to be revoked, and the Queen, her heirs and successors might re-enter upon the said Island.

The settlement of Sark, which was virtually derelict, by a group of 40 families, must have been, in the 16th century, an adventure of no mean order. True, Helier de Carteret entered Sark with a ready-made constitution, which all his followers had sworn to uphold. But the immediate establishment of an economy in an island devastated by war, devoid of cattle, crops, and dwellings, must have entailed herculean tasks of organisation and improvisation.

160

There are unfortunately, no records of this first year, but the recolonisation of Alderney after the Liberation forms a useful parallel.

Helier de Carteret drew most of his future tenants from St Ouen. But he did apply for assistance to *"son trèsfeal amy"* (his very true friend) Nicholas Gosselin, eldest son of that notorious Bailiff of Guernsey who had ordered the throwing back into the flames of the babe born to a woman while being burnt at the stake for heresy during the reign of Queen Mary. Gosselin was connected with Jersey through his wife, Peronelle Lempriere. This lady was remarkable, for those days, in that she *"scavoit lire et escrire"* (could read and write). Gosselin sent over some Guernsey families and was, as a token of gratitude, granted the hunting rights of Beauregard, situated above the inlet called, in his honour, Havre Gosselin.

In 1673 there appeared in print a letter written by a Mr F. Wearis, an Englishman, who spent several years in Sark, and who wrote an account of the island to his "dear Cozen" in London. The book is entitled: *News from the Channel, or the Discovery and perfect Description of the Isle of Serke, appertaining to the English Crown, and never before publickly discussed of.*

This letter gives a picture of Sark which lovers of that island will find fresh today. It is, moreover, an unsolicited testimonial to the success of the experiment made by Helier de Carteret and to the durability of the political constitution which he established.

Wearis begins by thanking his cousin for the "treasure of your more welcome letter" which had reached Sark by the "Anne of Bristol, touching here homeward bound". He is living, he says, "in a place where my native tongue is almost a stranger", where a "barbarous" kind of French is generally spoken. His English friends had been astonished when they heard he had gone to live in Sark, "some inquiring in which of the Indies that strange island lies, others offering wagers that there is no such place in the world. Scarce one Englishman of a thousand hath heard or can give any good account of it." This is the justification for his letter. So, "to satisfie the curiosity of my friends . . . I shall venture on a brief description of this little part of the world where Providence hath allotted me a present and (I thank Heaven) no uncomfortable habitation".

His geography is somewhat at fault, for he describes Sark as "an island situate in the Channel betwixt England and France . . . about four leagues to the south-west of Guernsey". Sark, of course, lies only half that distance south-east of Guernsey.

As to its size, he says that it "can yield no great temptation to any Prince's ambition to make himself master of it. . . . Yet nature, as if she had here stored up some extraordinary treasure, seems to have been very solicitous to render it impregnable, being on every side surrounded with vast rocks and mighty cliffs, whose craggy tops, braving the clouds with their stupendous height, bid defiance to all that shall dream of forcing an entrance."

"Two only ascents or passages there are into it, the first where all goods and commodities are received . . . and where for a large space through a solid rock there is a causeway cut by art down to the sea, with two strong gates for its defence, wherein most of the storage for navigation, as masts, sails, anchors, etc., are kept."

This is a reference to the old tunnel, bearing the date 1588. The new (Creux Harbour) tunnel was made in 1868.

"And two pieces of Ordnance above," he continues, "always ready planted to prevent any surprise."

These guns are still to be seen at the Seigneurie. One of them, a bronze culverin, bears the inscription "Don de sa Majesté, la Royne Elizabeth au Seigneur de Serq, A.D. 1572".

"Our Heaven and our sky" [he goes on to say] "are generally free from that nasty dish-clout of fogs and clouds which in your city are wont to muffle up the sun's glorious face. . . . I know not one physician in the island (and perhaps we live the longer for their absence), yet to meet here a hearty old man of four-score is nothing rare nor infrequent."

Water is "sometimes not very ready, and yet we have in the island six very fine springs generally running, whose water, purified in its underground passage, bubbles up free from any snack of brackishness".

The soil "is for the most part hot and sandy, yet excellent for bearing all kinds of roots, as parsneps, turneps, etc., and very well stored with fruit trees, furnishing us with cyder".

"Corn we have of most sorts, but not in any extraordinary quantity. Our pasture is but short, but exceedingly sweet, and therefore we have rare mutton, but no great plenty of beef, and cows only enow to supply us with milk and butter, for our cheese we have generally from England."

Fuel is scarce, "for the most part furzes and sometimes turf, for we have but little wood, and no timber at all growing throughout the whole island, so that we are forced to make shift with old apple trees for our houses, or furnish ourselves as well as we can with deal."

Food, however, is plentiful. Of fish, we have "a hundred sorts, particularly a large fish we call a vrack fish, which we split, and nailing it to our walls, dry it in the sun for part of our winter provision". This is apparently a reference to conger. On the ormer, he expatiates like a gourmet.

162

Fowl includes "woodcocks and widgeons, besides the abundance of duck, mallard, teal and other wild fowl, with clift pidgeons, with which at some seasons almost the whole island is covered".

"Of conies we have everywhere exceeding plenty, and yet, lest we should want, a small island near (Brecquou) is inhabited by nothing else, whither we go a-ferretting, and some families here have made £15 or £20 a year only of their skins. And if this rich fare will not content you, we have a most excellent pottage, made of milk, bacon, coleworts, mackerel and gooseberries boyled together, all to pieces."

"For our defence," he says, "we have a Captain with about 40 soldiers, who continually keep guard, and are maintained by contribution of the inhabitants."

Their Court "is held every Tuesday, where an honest fisherman we call the Judge, another (at present his son) that is entitled Monsieur le Prevost, a person that has the gift of writing, with five other sage Burgers, that are Justices, or some of them, meet . . . and briskly determine all causes, according to their mother wit and grave discretions, except in criminals, when life is concerned, in which case the offenders are immediately sent for tryal and punishment to Guernsey."

The minister in Wearis' time was a Huguenot. He himself was an Anglican, and he says that "the discipline which beyond the seas they call Reformed, wants much of that beauty and decent order wherewith the Church of England entertains her children". He does acknowledge, however, that the incumbent was "a person of more industry and parts than could be hoped for among such people, and hath lately begun teaching Grammar to the children, with Writing and Arithmetic, erecting a school for that purpose, so that who knows to what prodigious learning we may here one day arrive!"

Sark dress was simple. "The apish variety of fantastic fashions, wherewith Paris is justly accused to infect Europe, has no footing." Men wore "vast blue trunk breeches". Women wore "hospital gowns of the same colour, wooden sandals and red petticoats". For festival occasions, both sexes wore large ruffs, and the women, "instead of hats or hoods, truss up their hair, the better class in a sort of cabbidge net, the poorer in a piece of linen, perhaps an old dish-clout turned out of service, or the tag-end of a tablecloth". This was tied on the top like a turban and allowed to hang down behind like a veil.

Trade appears to have been more or less confined to "Bristol and some other of your Western ports, for the grand, and almost only manufacture of our island is knitting, which our people perform with a wonderful dexterity both for stockings, gloves, caps and wastecoats, men, women and children being brought up to it: so that you may commonly see thirty or forty of them assembled in a barn, which you would take for a conventicle of your sweet singers of Israel, for though all ply their knitting devoutly, yet at the same time they tune their pipes and torture some old song with distracted notes".

Wearis ends with an apology to his relative for the length of his letter and drinks his health in "a black jack of french wine, which paying no costome, we have here as plentiful cheap as in France itself".

In a footnote to the chapter on Sark in *The Channel Islands*, Miss Edith F. Carey says that:

"The memory still survives of the occasion when the Lords of the Admiralty, wishing to land and inspect the defences of Sark before the harbour was built, sailed round and round the island vainly seeking for a landing-place, and finally sailed away, declaring that it was inaccessible."

Yet, despite its apparent inaccessibility and impregnability, the island was a veritable cockpit from the 12th to the 16th century.

Up to that date no two historians are agreed upon the history of this "small, sweet world of wave-encompassed wonder". Relics of prehistoric man have been found in Sark, such as stone celts, known as *coins de foudre* (thunder-bolts), stone discs or amulets, called *rouettes de fêtiaux* (fairies' spinning-wheels) and diminutive pipes with tiny bowls named *pipes des fêtiaux*. Illustrations of these occur in Kendrick's *Archæology of the Channel Islands*, Vol. 1. Of dolmens, so common in Herm and Guernsey, scarcely a vestige remains, though there is ample evidence that these once existed and that they were destroyed in the search for building material.

Evidence of a Visigothic occupation, at about the beginning of the 5th century, was discovered in 1718, when five inhabitants declared upon oath that in making a hedge they had found an earthen pot bound with an iron hoop. In this pot were 13 pieces of metal, 12 shaped like plates, but varying in size, and the remaining one oblong and fish-shaped. There was also a little ingot, of about 2 oz. in weight and of a yellow colour, and finally 18 small coins, rudely engraved with a lion, the badge of the Visigothic dynasty.

This find was surrendered to the Procureur of the Seigneur of Sark, but its subsequent fate is unknown. Kendrick suggests that this "treasure" may have been the hoard of a bronze founder.

Christianity, according to tradition, was brought to Sark by the Breton missionary, St Magloire, who founded there a chapel and a monastery. The site of the latter is still known as La Moinerie, not far from l'Eperquerie; at that time probably the only landing in Sark. There is a little stream close by, upon which a water-mill was erected. The bay below is, to this day, known as Port-du-Moulin.

Sixty monks, from Normandy, Brittany, and Britain, are said to have followed St Magloire to Sark. This flourishing community, however, was swept away by northern pirates, led by the Danish Jarl, Hâtenai, of whom Wace writes and whose name is perpetuated in Guernsey as that of its highest point, Hâtenez, in St Martin's, a hillock now crowned by the reservoir of the Water Board.

Traces of Scandinavian occupation exist in entrenchments at Grand Fort and le Château, and mediaeval pottery, fragments of weapons and gold and silver ornaments have been found here.

In the 12th century, Sark was in the hands of the Norman family of de Vernon. A century later, in the reign of King John, the de Vernons took the part of Philip Augustus of France, and Sark became forfeit to the English Crown.

The renegade Fleming, Eustace the Monk, then ravaged the island. His ally was Geoffrey de Lucy, once Seigneur des Isles, but then a deserter from the cause of the English king. After severe fighting, they were defeated and driven off, leaving behind as prisoners the men who had garrisoned Sark and a brother and an uncle of Eustace.

Early in the 14th century there were disputes between the Bishop of Avranches and the King about seigneurial rights in Sark. At that time, too, Sark was a separate bailiwick, with a bailiff and *Jurats* of its own. There were numerous fiefs, whose tenants owed "carriage of the corn of the champart of the lord the King in Normandy, wheresoever the officers of the lord the King shall wish, between Mount St Michael and Cherbourg". The tenants were further obliged to provide the linen cloths and sacks, besides the boats in which the corn was carried. They were also responsible for "the prisoners of the lord the King, in the aforesaid fees".

Then began, in the reign of Edward III, the Hundred Years' War, in which every Channel Island suffered, but Sark perhaps most of all. Not only were its fields ravaged and its peaceful inhabitants destroyed, but it acquired a reputation as a haunt of pirates and wreckers, who became a menace to commerce in the Channel. These pirates were expelled in 1356, and although there were later French landings, it is broadly true that Sark remained an unoccupied island for 200 years.

THE BAILIWICK OF GUERNSEY

It was an act of political expediency which led Helier de Carteret to occupy Sark. He realised the danger to Jersey and the Channel Islands in general, and to his own domains in St Ouen in particular, if the French should reoccupy the island or if it should again become the lair of pirates.

It is probable that he went to Sark some two years before receiving the Letters Patent from Queen Elizabeth which created him Seigneur. Sark was in a deplorable condition, "so full of rabbit-holes and heather, briars, brambles, bracken, and undergrowth, that it looked impossible to cultivate. There were no tracks down which a cart could pass, nor harbour where a boat could unload safely."

His wife, who was also his first cousin, Margaret de Carteret, widow of Clement Dumaresq, Seigneur of Samarès, accompanied him. He had married her when he was only 19 years of age.

She was a veritable helpmeet to him. A ruined chapel was used for accommodation, while space was being cleared for a house. Building materials were brought from Jersey and carried up precipitous cliff-tracks on the backs of men. Ground was cleared and corn and vegetables planted. Horses, cattle, pigs, and farm implements were brought in. In an incredibly short space of time 40 dwellings were erected, each on its own *enclos*.

Lists of the 40 tenants have been compiled again and again, and it is interesting to find many of the same names occurring in each. There are Hamons, de Carterets, Guilles, and le Couteurs in a list taken from the registers from 1570–1603. The same names, with the addition of Maugers, Le Pelleys, Mollets, and Vaudins, appear in John Oxenham's romance, *Carette of Sark*, the period of which is the end of the 18th century. In 1875 we find such names as Carré, Baker, Le Page, and Girard. In 1908, however, there are no fewer than 12 English names among the 40 tenants. These include Baker, Henry, Kinnersley, Pickthall, Riley, and Taylor. When Helier de Carteret conferred the government of Sark upon his son Philippe in 1579, a new constitution for the island was adopted, modelled on that of Jersey. A bailiff, *Jurats*, and other officials were appointed, and Sark became a bailiwick.

This new constitution was, however, short-lived. By the terms of the original grant, Sark came under the suzerainty of Guernsey. The Royal Court refused to recognise the new régime, and summoned Helier de Carteret to appear in Guernsey to explain by what authority he had acted.

Helier ignored this summons, whereupon the Bailiff and four Guernsey *Jurats* called upon him in Sark and, after holding an enquiry, ordered the Sark Bailiff, Edward de Carteret, cousin of

The rock arch at Dixcart Bay, Sark

The parish church

SARK

The prison

Jethou, seen from Herm

The shell beach

HERM

The Manor House

Helier, and two of his *Jurats*, to proceed at once to Guernsey to explain this establishment of a rival jurisdiction.

The trial took place in 1582. The two *Jurats* were sent back to Sark, but Edward de Carteret was condemned "as a usurper" and sent to Castle Cornet. He was kept prisoner there for some seven weeks and then released on bail. The Royal Court of Guernsey, having vindicated its rights, took no further proceedings against Edward. He did not return to Sark, but spent the remaining part of his life, poor and obscure, in Guernsey. Here he died in 1601, and was buried in the Town Church.

It was not until the reign of Queen Anne, in 1713, that Sark passed out of the hands of the de Carterets. With the permission of the Queen, Sir Charles, who was heavily in debt, sold it to the Milner family. This family held it for a comparatively short time. In 1730 the island was purchased by a Sark woman, Dame Suzanne le Gros, widow of Nicholas le Pelley. The le Pelleys, an old Guernsey family, held it until 1852.

That was a period when bright hopes were entertained of fortunes from silver, lead, and copper deposits in Guernsey, Herm, and Little Sark. At first the Sark's Hope Mining Company looked a promising venture, with five shafts sunk in Little Sark, and loading facilities at Port Gorey. Remains can be seen today. But in 1845 the sea flooded the profitable lower galleries, and the Company, including the Seigneur, Ernest le Pelley, was ruined. He was compelled to mortgage the island to a Mr John Allaire for £4,000. On the death of the latter, the bond was foreclosed by his daughter, Mrs Thomas Guerin Collings, whose great grand-daughter is now Dame de Serk.

THE HARBOURS AND HARBOUR HILL. The Aval Creux, that steep hill winding up from both the Creux Harbour—the smallest in the world—and the new Maseline breakwater, to the summit of the table-land, is flanked by cliff land which in spring is covered with the tender green fronds of bracken interspersed with bluebells, which give an illusion of mist-covered azure netting of the finest weave.

But, like Christina Rossetti's road, the Aval Creux winds uphill all the way, and the only alternative to climbing it on foot is riding in a carriage or trap, drawn by one of Sark's fine horses.

For the motor car is taboo in Sark. Such is the decree of the Court of Chief Pleas, made some years ago. It was then argued, not without wisdom, that the tiny island was quite unsuited for fast traffic and that its peaceful charm would be lost should cars and motor-cycles be allowed to career along the few roads and lanes where such progression is possible.

Attempts have been made again and again to secure the modification of this ukase. A few years ago a doctor settling in Sark felt that an automobile was an indispensable item of medical equipment. Although warned of the taboo, his car was, by his orders, put ashore on the harbour quay. There he was again warned that he would not be allowed to move the car from that spot to his dwelling under its own power. Ignoring this warning, however, his daughter drove the car up the hill.

The outcome was a prosecution before the Chief Pleas, the imposition of a fine, and a ban upon the appearance of the car upon the public roads, *unless it were drawn by a horse*.

Representations made later to the Chief Pleas that an exception might reasonably be made in this case were of no avail. It was dangerous, it was argued, to create a precedent.

And even in the summer of 1949, when H.R.H. the Princess Elizabeth, accompanied by her husband, the Duke of Edinburgh, arrived in the island to open, officially, the new Maseline Harbour, the taboo was not lifted, and Their Royal Highnesses rode from the landing-place to the Seigneurie in a one-horse chaise.

There have, however, been two concessions to 20th century forms of travel. Farm tractors are allowed on the roads and lanes, and are allowed down to the Maseline jetty to pick up stores for the hotels and shops, and to collect the luggage of the increasing number of visitors. The other more recent concession has been in the interests of humanity—a few electrically-driven chairs are now allowed for those who are crippled to drive about on the public roads.

THE VILLAGE AND THE CHURCH. At the top of the hill is a rough rectangle of lanes, their banks covered with wild flowers in the spring. Scattered in this area are cottages and houses, some of granite, some in less harmony with the landscape. Along the "Avenue", now replanted with trees in an effort to repair the damage done during the Occupation, are shops and the Post Office, branches of banks, and the granite Prison Cell. Farther along, the Rue de Moulin rises to the highest point of the island, 348 feet, and there the old mill stands, a mill no longer, defaced by a German observation slit, but still a vital sea-mark for yachtsmen and fishermen.

Around the corner from the "Avenue" is the Church of St Peter. Some letters, written by General Bayley, Lieutenant-Governor of

Guernsey, and dated 1818, show that it was he who advocated the building of a new church in Sark. The existing one he described as "an old rotten barn" and, mindful that example should be wedded to precept, he offered the sum of £25 towards the cost of a new building.

The le Pelleys, the seigneurial family of the island, then on the crest of a wave of prosperity, gave the land and a grant of money. The Church Building Society contributed £400 on condition that half of the sittings should be free. The remaining half of the sittings were divided into closed pews, containing three, four, or five sittings, which were sold to those who wished to have a closed pew. These pews, like sittings in the parish churches of Guernsey, were then attached to the proprietor's farm, to form part thereof, to be inherited with the farm, and never to be separated or sold away from it. An annual rent of fivepence (half a franc) on each sitting was fixed for the repair and maintenance of the church.

The church cost rather more than £1,000. The foundation stone was laid, in the presence of the Dean of Guernsey, by Peter le Pelley, son of the seigneur. It was licensed for divine service in 1821 by the Bishop of Winchester, who consecrated it in 1829.

Eleven years before, Dr Fraser, Bishop of Salisbury, visited Sark to administer the sacrament of Confirmation. He was the first bishop who had set foot on the island since the Reformation.

A vicarage worthy of the new church was provided by the le Pelleys. The old house, known as la Perronerie, which they had inherited from the le Gros family, was rebuilt and converted into the present Seigneurie, and the Manoir became the vicarage.

Until 40 years ago the services of the Sark church were conducted in French. It is interesting to note that Sark was the last of the Channel Islands to abandon Presbyterianism, although the first to adopt the chanting of the liturgical hymns, the *Venite*, *Te Deum*, etc., sung in French to English compositions.

Dr Pusey, one of the most eminent leaders of the Oxford Movement, resided for some months in Sark, when suspended from his duties in Oxford. He created two precedents, in that he conducted the service in English—the island was then full of miners—and wore a surplice. This surplice he left behind in the vicar's care for the use of any visiting clergyman who might perform a service.

The addition of a chancel in 1878 greatly improved the interior of the church. Among the tablets on the walls is one to the memory of Helier de Carteret, a belated tribute to the founder of this miniature feudal State.

169

THE BAILIWICK OF GUERNSEY

THE SCHOOL AND THE CONSTITUTION. On the north side of the rectangle of lanes is the solid building of the School. This is also the seat of the administration of the island, and the meeting place of the Parliament, the Court of Chief Pleas, three times a year, or more frequently if necessary. Over this Court presides the Seneschal, who is nominated by the Seigneur, but is then sworn in before the Royal Court of Guernsey and is virtually irremoveable from office. To assist him he has the Greffier, or Registrar, and the Prevot, or Sheriff, appointed by the Court of Sark. Up to 1951 the remaining members of Chief Pleas were the Seigneur and the other tenants, holders of the 40 farms into which the island was originally divided by Helier de Carteret. Although, by an amendment to the Constitution in 1922, there were supposed also to be 12 popularly elected People's Deputies, this attempt to introduce some democracy into the island was largely ignored. In 1951 however, agitation by a more radical element led to the holding of a genuine General Election, and to the passing of the Reform (Sark) Law. This stipulated the proper auditing of accounts, and the consent of Her Majesty in Council to taxation, and it considerably circumscribed the Seigneur's ancient right of veto on any Ordinance passed by the Chief Pleas.

Subsidiary to the island Parliament and its executive Committees are the Douzaine, as in the Guernsey parishes, and the two executive officers, the Constable and the Vingtenier, who retain their ancient powers of police action.

THE SPINE ROAD. A glance at the map of Sark will show a road running, with one slight deviation, north and south, over what may be described as the backbone of the island. This is in all probability the track originally driven by Helier de Carteret, who thereupon invited his 40 tenants to peg out their claims on either side, so that each should have access to the sea. Each tenant thus obtained both arable and cliff land, although a reasonable area of common was also preserved.

The road starts in the north at the edge of the attractive wild bare area known as L'Eperquerie Common, which stretches away to the line of humpy islets known as La Grune, Courbee du Nez, and Bec du Nez. Down a steeply-winding path on the east side is L'Eperquerie landing, the little rock-strewn cove where Helier de Carteret first brought his settlers ashore. Farther along the road one comes to a path which leads away down through a little wood and a charming glen to Port du Moulin, and its beach. From here is a fine panorama, with the island of Brecqhou on the left, and in front Les Autelets, the three strange pinnacles of rock which rise abruptly from the sea.

On down the road a little way and the mansion of La Dame, La Seigneurie, can be seen in the trees on the right. This fine granite house in the local style looks out on a forecourt and lawns, and through an iron grille one can glimpse the flowers and vegetables in the walled garden. Rising above the house itself is a Victorian tower, and behind are barns and storehouses and the pigeon-cote, with its cooing inhabitants.

Beyond the crossroads of La Vauroque the road runs straight down to La Coupée.

LA COUPÉE. La Coupée, that natural and precarious bridge connecting Great with Little Sark, has exerted a magnetic influence on devotees of nearly every branch of art. The genius of Turner has reproduced it in water-colour. Its savage grandeur was the inspiration of many of the romances of John Oxenham. Its sheer beauty evoked some of Swinburne's finest lines.

Its safety was assured, soon after the Liberation, by a party of Royal Engineers, who strengthened its weaknesses in several places with reinforced concrete. A firm iron rail runs along each side. Nevertheless, when a strong wind blows across the isthmus, anyone with no head for heights might well be excused from making the crossing. When no rail existed, previous to the 19th century, that crossing, especially on horseback, must have demanded a very high degree of courage or a complete lack of imagination.

On the southern side of this natural viaduct is a sheer precipice of some 300 feet; the northern side is steep, but there is a winding path and steps down to Grande Greve Bay, the best sandy beach in the island, where the curious can find Sark stones and pebbles of many colours and shapes.

LITTLE SARK. Beyond La Coupée the Spine Road rises again to the plateau of Little Sark, and passing between fields comes to an end at the cluster of farm buildings and cottages by the attractive La Sablonnerie Hotel. Round by the well a path carries on due south to the bare headland where the silver was mined, where rabbits run, and where, hidden away beneath the cliff, lies Venus Pool, a beautiful natural diving-pool about 40 feet wide and 18 feet deep.

THE VALLEYS. One of the attractions for the walker in Sark is to come upon one of the little valleys which slip away from the main plateau down to the sea.

One of the most beautiful and lush is the Dixcart Valley, rich with flowers and shrubs and trees, and with its stream gurgling along beside the path. This path comes out at Dixcart Bay, a beach part sand, part pebbles, almost divided by a natural arch of rock. To the left of this valley stretches the long grass and black-thorn-covered bluff of the d'Os d'Ane, and beyond that again is the more inaccessible Derrible Bay. In the cliff above this bay is the great 100 foot hole of the Creux Derrible.

The word *creux* is associated in all the islands with a chimney-like formation, brought about by the wearing away of soft material surrounded by harder rock. A *creux* ends at sea level, where a natural tunnel connects it with the sea. The rising tide, rushing up this tunnel, forces air and foam up the chimney, and in stormy weather the sound and sight of this phenomenon are wonderful and awe-inspiring. In action, the *creux* is known as a *souffleur* or blow-hole.

THE CAVES. A side-road from La Vauroque crossroads leads past the Sark duck-pond, past the lovely garden of the house next door, round near the Beauregard Hotel, and on through fields to the cliff-edge and the Pilcher Monument.

This granite obelisk, on the summit of the cliffs above Havre Gosselin, commemorates a tragedy of 1868, when Jeremiah Giles Pilcher, of London, and several others were drowned, when at-tempting to cross from Sark to Guernsey.

From this point one can look right down to the old haven below and think of those who land there and have to climb with their baggage up and up the steps to the top. In front lies Brecqhou and to the right is the bare headland honeycombed by the Gouliot caves.

The caves of Sark figure largely in the many romances which have that island for their setting. Summer is the season of the year to explore these, and this should not be undertaken without the services of a competent guide and boatman.

Caves honeycomb not only the wild west coast, but are to be found on every side of Sark. Through intricate passages and over the green swell of a great wave the boatman guides his craft into the very heart of the cliff. Here it rides through a deep channel of crystal-clear water. The rock coloration is marvellous and in-describable. The Red Cave, for example, is of deepest crimson, soft and warm. The extremity of some of the caves rises perpen-dicularly, the colours of the rock face glowing like those of the back curtain of a scene in some classic opera.

One of the most interesting of the caverns is that named after Victor Hugo. It has a wide channel entrance, fringed with *Asplenium marinum*. Its chief interest, however, lies in the probability that Hugo made use of his knowledge of the Sark caves for his descriptions of the rock scenery and caverns of the Douvres in *Travailleurs de la Mer*. The cave in which Gilliatt fought his life-and-death struggle with the giant pieuvre was miles nearer Hauteville House than the Douvres, and the giant pieuvre was perhaps a nightmare version of a small Sark octopus.

The Gouliot caves, perhaps the best known, are approachable from the land. The farthermost cave has a narrow channel entrance to the sea which, when the tide is low, flows gently in over the purple floor, glistening like a stream of emeralds in the dimmed light of the sun. A fairy palace, the walls of these caves are everywhere fretted and frescoed with an unstinted wealth of marine life. Scarce a square inch of their surface but is covered by shell, sponge, or coralline. Sea anemones, plum, green, and red, with every shade of brown and olive in between, stud roof and walls. There are plant-like polypes, shedding embryo medusae from their capsuled branches. The floor and walls are liberally strewn with acorn-shells and barnacles, and masses of seaweed of every hue carpet the floor.

The dim twilight of these caves and the sound of echoing water, now near, now distant, sometimes above, sometimes below, must fill the visitor of imagination with awe and reverence.

The most romantic of the caves are the Boutiques. They begin as a tunnel in the cliffs to the extreme north of the island, reached by a rough climb over rocks. The floor of this tunnel, some 200 feet long, is composed of black and white pebbles. This tunnel ends in a wide opening, which looks out to sea. There is no need, however, to return the same way. A giant staircase in the bowels of the earth, known as the Boutiques Chimney, emerges, after a perilous ascent, on a steep path in the cliffs just beyond the Eperquerie Common.

Brecqhou, the tiny island lying midway off the west coast of Sark, was formerly known as l'Ile des Marchands. The le Marchant family, who held it, did so, however, as vassals or tenants of Sark.

To this day the owner of Brecqhou, in his capacity of tenant, has a seat in the Sark Chief Pleas and when the island changes hands, as it has done on several occasions during the past 100 years, the purchaser has to pay the *congé*, or one-thirteenth of the purchase price, to the Seigneur of Sark.

The area of the island is roughly 160 acres—one quarter of a square mile. Of this, between 60 and 70 acres only can be classed as arable or pasture-land.

Its coast, like that of Sark, is wild and rocky, and the interior plateau rises rather more than 100 feet above sea level.

Landing in Brecqhou, except in calm weather, is no easy matter. Le Port, a small bay on the west, forms a natural harbour, and here a landing has been built. From this a flight of steps climbs the face of the cliff. These steps meet a roadway leading to the house.

There is an alternative landing to the north, known as Jacob's Ladder. Here, too, is a flight of steps leading to the summit of the island.

The one house on Brecqhou is a new one, built just prior to the Second World War. It is a dwelling harmonising with its surroundings, built of stone with half-timber upper elevation.

There are other, farm, buildings on the island, and it has been farmed to a degree by both its post-war owners, Mr Donaldson and Mr Leonard Matchan.

Herm. Three miles across the Little Russel from Guernsey lies the charming island of Herm. Only 1 and a half miles long and half a mile wide it has interesting variations of scenery, and it has had an interesting history too.

As in the other islands of the Bailiwick, its first inhabitants were Neolithic people, who reached it in dug-out canoes and left their memorial in a number of burial-chambers, cromlechs, and cists, and a varied assortment of objects found on the sites. The large number of sites supports the tradition that Herm had special sanctity as the burial-ground for the dead from Guernsey and Normandy. The feeling of restfulness and peace is still there today, so that Mrs Compton Mackenzie, the wife of a former tenant, could write, "Propitiate at all costs the spirit of the island", and the present owner is conscious of a guardian spirit, especially at night among the tombs in the north of the island.

In Christian times, hardy monks from St Magloire's foundation in Sark crossed over to explore Herm, and a small chapel was built on the Pierre Percée reef between Herm and Jethou. This was dry land in that area, as the sea level was some 30 feet lower. Later, as the sea level rose, this chapel was abandoned, and a new one was built on the high ground of Herm. Benedictine monks served this for a few years, and then William the Conqueror gave Herm to the Augustinian Order of Cherbourg. The Abbot instituted quite a colony, laymen as well as monks, who laid out a considerable farm of cattle and sheep. The Prior of the community had a difficult task, for Herm's inhabitants were not all religious and saintly men. One of these, John Charnethous, in the 13th century, was indicted before the Abbot's Assize on many charges; stealing, concealing criminals, conspiracy to pervert the course of justice, and acquiring wreckage without licence. He only escaped his just desserts by appealing to the English Crown.

With the increase of lawlessness and aggressive Protestantism in the 15th and 16th centuries, the religious community declined, and in 1569 Queen Elizabeth annexed Herm and Jethou to the see of Winchester. There is a tradition that more than 20 years earlier all the Roman Catholics fled to Herm and tried to make it their final stronghold, that they were overcome, and that the honourable terms of surrender were ignored and the monks and other refugees were slaughtered.

A few families lingered as inhabitants for a time, but by the middle of the 17th century the island was deserted. Heylin, a local historian, records in 1656, "the island of Herm is now only inhabited by pheasant and good plentie conies". During the next 150 years there were periodic attempts to farm the island again, as the monks had done, and it was also used as a shooting area by the Lieutenant-Governors of Guernsey. Then in 1815 the quarrying of Herm granite became an important business. First Colonel Lindsay, and then his son-in-law, John Duncan, invested in and built up the industry, and the Herm Granite Company prospered. In its heyday some 400 people lived and worked on the island, and cottages, shops, an inn and a school were provided for them. The small bee-hive-shaped gaol, which still stands near the White House Hotel, was built as a lock-up for the drunken workmen.

By the 1860s the granite industry had declined, and a succession of new tenants appeared, wealthy men attracted by the chance of owning an island. First a Colonel Fielden, who improved the buildings and set up the White House Hotel as a commercial venture. He spent lavishly too on the gardens, but he was caught trying to recoup his expenditure by smuggling brandy into England, and left for South Africa where he died penniless.

After a brief period when an Order of Trappist Monks leased the island and a Scottish fish-canning company had a scheme to dry and salt fish there, Herm passed in 1891 into the control of Prince Blücher, a man of great wealth with a passion for islands. He made great changes, converting the manor and its outbuildings into a large castellated mansion, and planting groves of pine, spruce and eucalyptus trees. The hotel was turned into a private residence for his son; the chapel of St Tugual was restored, and roadways were laid down.

This happy period was ended by the First World War, when Prince Blücher was interned. In 1920 Sir Compton Mackenzie, the novelist, became the new tenant, and he was followed three years later by a motor-manufacturer, Sir Percival Perry. His lease was virtually ended by the German Occupation, during which Herm was used by the States of Guernsey as a pasture for sheep and cattle, and as a source of rabbits for the hungry Guernsey population. In June 1940 Herm had only Mr Dickson, one of Lord Perry's employees, in residence. He was joined by his wife, and later by the Le Pages, and this little community lived happily and fairly uneventfully on the island for the period of the War.

In December 1946 the States of Guernsey bought the island from the Treasury for £15,000, and leased it under rather onerous terms to Mr Jefferies. He made valiant efforts to put the island to rights, but it was an unprofitable business, and in 1949 he passed on his interest to the present tenants, Major and Mrs Peter Wood.

THE COMMON AND BAYS. Of Herm's 500 acres approximately a quarter is covered by the Common at the northern end of the island. This undulating tract of sandy land gives a great feeling of freedom as one wanders over its criss-crossing paths. Its springy turf is studded with burnet roses, and cropped close by a teeming rabbit population. Clumps of bracken and blackberries, and bushes of willow and honeysuckle break up the landscape, and in many places can be found remains of Neolithic tombs. Unfortunately many of the great capstones were broken up by the quarrymen in the days of Herm's granite trade. Their most notable act of spoliation was to remove a large menhir, the Pierre aux Rats, on the north coast. This was an important sea-mark, and the protests of local fishermen led to its replacement by the stone obelisk which stands up today in the centre of the sand-dunes above the great sweep of Mouisonnière beach.

On the west of the Common is another sandy beach, a favourite rendezvous for Guernsey yachtsmen when the wind is in the east. But the most famous beach is the eastern one, the Shell Beach; onto its 700 yard stretch the tides have deposited over the centuries myriads of shells. Although its store has been picked over by countless enthusiasts, there are still rare specimens to be found. As the visitor makes his way from the harbour to the Common and the Shell Beach, he passes on its outskirts a tiny cemetery, where two cholera victims from a passing ship were buried in 1832.

Farther on, the path passes between two hillocks, Le Grand Monceau, to the east, and Le Petit Monceau to the west, from both of which a wonderful view can be had of the Humps, the series of rocky islets which run away to the north-east of Herm.

THE CLIFFS AND POINT SAUZEBOURGE. From the south end of the Shell Beach round the island to above the landing place of Rosière Steps the cliffs are steep and in places precipitous, barer than in Guernsey and a haunt of rabbits. The southernmost promontory, Point Sauzebourge, is a wild area, of heather and bracken and furze, penetrated by few paths, but with the opportunity for those who seek of finding a Megalithic Cromlech half hidden in the undergrowth. In the cliffs of this promontory is the deep blow-hole, the Creux Pigeon; up into its shaft at high tides the seas boom and hiss. The only real gap in the ring of cliffs is found in the cutting which takes one down to Belvoir Bay, between the big rock Caquorobert and the southern end of the Shell Beach. A well-made track leads down through lush undergrowth, past Belvoir House, where the first modern-style tenant, Colonel Fielden, used to live, to the warm sandy enclosed cove. At high water the beach shelves steeply, so that the swimmer is soon afloat; at low water great stretches of sand are exposed, a place where little sand-eels and many other creatures can be found.

THE FARM AND UPLANDS. From the Common a narrow dirt road leads one uphill along the spine of the island, past the farm and between the high pastures on either side. The farm itself is based in the castellated mansion of Prince Blücher's days; after the neglect of the war years, the buildings have been renovated and restored inside, some to house the workers and their families, others as cattle-byre, milking parlour, store-shed, machine-shop, and electric power house. This plant drives the modern milking machinery for the herd of 95 pedigree Guernseys which Major Wood is building up into one of the largest herds in the Bailiwick. Each day a surplus of milk is exported to Guernsey.

The farm has an acreage of 120, and it is a fine sight to see the beautiful golden herd in one or other of the big fenced pastures, green against the background of the blue seas of the Great Russel between Herm and Sark. In the farmland area are one or two small woods, mostly of fir; these, with the woods which slope down behind the Tavern and the Hotel, are carefully tended, and each year more firs, and willow, Norwegian maple and eucalyptus are planted.

st tugual's chapel. Adjoining the farm is the ancient chapel, dating back to the days of the mediaeval monks. The first historical record of it occurs in a Latin MS of 1480; it refers to the appointment of Jean Guyffart, a friar of Cherbourg, to the incumbency and states, "we give you the administration and prioryship pertaining to the parochial church of St Tugual of Herm, at present free and vacant through the simple resignation of a discreet man of the Lord, John le Jolis". Information about St Tugual himself is rather vague, but the most likely account is that he was a Bishop of Dol in Brittany, whose name was given to the chapel by missionary monks from St Magloire's religious house in Sark.

The chapel itself was unfurnished and in poor condition when Major Wood took over in 1949. It has been restored in simple good taste. Now one turns the corner from the farm buildings to enter a delightful peaceful courtyard. There is a garden of grass and flowers and shrubs enclosed by a low wall, and at the back a higher protective wall with a tiled top—like so many of the walls in the island. In the corner, from a small tower, hangs the chapel bell, which was rehung some years ago.

One enters, through the arched doorway with its good wooden door, into the simple rectangle which is the chapel proper. Before the little altar are set the chairs for the congregation. There, islanders and visitors meet to worship in a non-denominational service, led by Major Wood, with one of his children playing the organ. Periodically they are honoured by the presence of the Bishop of Winchester, who takes the simple service when he stays in the island. Onto the altar fall rainbow colours from a new window let into the south wall. As is appropriate for Herm, the theme of the window is that of Christ stilling the waves, "And he arose and rebuked the wind and said unto the sea 'Peace, be still' " (St Mark 4). Opposite this window is a minute side chapel.

To the south of the chapel is now a pleasant open space of grass leading up to the owner's modernised house, its wide windows looking out south-west over the sea to Guernsey.

the hotel and harbour. A good road leads down from the farm through the eucalyptus and other trees to the cluster of hotel, tavern, shops, and cottages which is the centre of the visitor-side of Herm's life. The White House Hotel itself fits snugly below the rising hillside, and looks out over a grass plot and a little beach to the sea. It is a pleasant country house, and in it, and in the cottages nearby, 100 guests can stay. For them and for the thousands of day-visitors who come across from Guernsey in launches the island provides up-to-date amenities—a tested water-supply from bore-holes and wells, electricity from the AC generators, and an up-to-date sewage system. Supplies for the hotel, the Mermaid Tavern, and the three beach cafés are brought over from Guernsey in the island's own 40 foot launch. This launch, which has its own ship-to-shore radio, and direction-finding equipment, operates all the year round, but it is helped out in the summer by a chartered fishing boat which brings over bulk supplies.

Another link with the outside world is the radio-telephonic link with Guernsey, which enables Herm's own telephone exchange, with 17 lines, to function as part of a much vaster network. This is a considerable improvement on the pigeon-post service operated by the previous tenant, Mr Jefferies. He too inaugurated a postal service by launch, with his own stamps to cover the expense, as he was refused official postal facilities. This is carried on today, and Herm stamps find themselves despatched all over the world.

But the main link is the small harbour on the west coast below the White House Hotel. The stout pier was originally built by Lindsay of the Herm Granite Company, and to its shelter can come the launches from Guernsey from roughly half-tide up to half-tide down. At low water the landing-place at the Rosaire Steps has to be used, an attractive but rather laborious method of reaching the island.

Jethou. The small island of Jethou, about $1\frac{1}{4}$ miles in circumference, is reputed to have been joined to Herm until a great storm of A.D. 709; but today it is separated from its larger neighbour by the Percée Passage. It rises like a great hummock, some 267 feet high, from the sea, with a plateau of about 20 acres on the top, and it has a small hummock, the rock Crevichon, to its north, and another granite hummock, Grande Fauconniere, to its south. Both these rocks are topped by white sailing-marks. The sea-approaches to Jethou are not easy, and there is only one real landing-place, at the landing-ramp by Crevichon.

Signs of early inhabitants are a few capstones, the site of a cromlech, two menhirs, two kitchen-middens of limpets and other shells, and a strange stone wall of boulders some 3 feet high. The island's first recorded history is its donation by Robert Duke of Normandy to Restald, his ship-master, who on his retirement bequeathed the island to the Benedictines of Mont St Michel. Later the island became and has remained a Crown possession, though its practical use in the 16th and 17th centuries seems to have been as a haunt of pirates.

In 1717 the Crown leased the island to a Mr Nowall of London, and other tenants followed him, all of whom had to sign a clause in the lease concerning "the rights of the inhabitants of Guernsey to go upon the coasts of the said small island to fish and cut vraic, and to fetch from this stones for building and other uses, in the same manner they have hitherto done".

There was probably some sort of house on the island in the early 18th century, but the present Manor House, which nestles on the west side, can only be dated back to about 1825, an infant compared to the ancient mulberry tree in its grounds.

In the 19th century there was some quarrying of granite from two small quarries, and also from Crevichon; tradition has it that the steps of St Paul's are of Crevichon granite. This exploitation ended in the 1860s, and later tenants, including Sir Compton Mackenzie, were left undisturbed to enjoy its simple charms, the cliff paths, the wild flowers, the wood and the grove, and the fields. Today visitors from Guernsey can come over by launch for a few hours to enjoy the sights and sounds of Jethou.

KEY TO THE MAPS

GUERNSEY

Les Adams	B6	Fort Richmond	C5	Priory of St Mary	A6	
Airport	E7			Princess Elizabeth		
Albecq	D4	Le Gouffre	F9	Hospital	G6	
		Grandes Rocques	E3			
Bailiff's Cross	F6	Grand Havre	F2	Reservoir	D6	
Bec du Nez	H7			Rocquaine Bay	B7	
Bellegrève Bay	H4	Havelet Bay	H5	Route Militaire	G3	
La Bette	G8	Havilland Hall	G5			
Blanchelande Convent		Le Havre de Bon Repos		Saints Bay	G8	
	G7		D9	Saumarez Park	E4	
Bordeaux	H2			St Andrew	F6	
Le Bourg	F7	Icart Point	G8	St Andrew's Church	F6	
		L'Islet	G3	St Apolline Chapel	C6	
Calais	H7			St George	E5	
Castel Church	F5	Le Jaonnet	F8	St Martin	G7	
Castle Cornet	H5	Jerbourg	H7	St Martin's Church	G6	
Catel	D5			St Martin's Point	J7	
Catioroc	B6	Kings Mills	E5	St Matthew's Church		
Château de Marais	G4				E4	
Clarence Battery	H6	Lancresse Bay	G1	St Peter Port	H5	
Cobo Bay	D4	Lancresse Common	G2	St Peter's Church	D8	
La Corbière	E9	Lihou Island	A6	St Pierre-du-Bois	C7	
Creux Es Fées Dolmen				St Sampson	H3	
	B6	Mont Crevelt	J3	St Saviour	D6	
Creux Mahie Cave	C8	Moulin Huet	H7	St Saviour's Church	D7	
		La Moye Point	F9			
Déhus Dolmen	H1			Talbot Valley	F6	
Delancey Park	H3	Paradis	J1	Torteval	B8	
Dolmen	G1	Pea Stacks	H8	Torteval Church	C8	
Doyle Column	H7	Pembroke Fort	G1			
		Pequeries	E2	Vale	E3, G2	
L'Erée	B6	Perelle Bay	C5	Vale Castle	J2	
		Petit Bot Bay	F8	Vale Church	G2	
Fermain Bay	H7	Petit Port	H7	Le Vallon	H7	
Forest	E8	Pleinmont Point	A8	Le Varclin	H7	
Forest Church	E8	Portinfer	E3	Les Vauxbelets	E6	
Fort Doyle	J1	Portelet Bay	F8	Vazon Bay	D5	
Fort George	H6	Portelet Harbour	B8	Vingtaine de l'Epine	F4	
Fort Grey	B7	Port Grat	F2			
Fort Houmet	D4	Port Soif	E3	Watch House (Torteval)		
Fort le Marchant	H1	Prevoté Watch House			B8	
Fort Pézéries	A8		D8	Watch House	E4	

ALDERNEY

Braye Bay	Fort Doyle	Nunnery
Braye Harbour	Fort Tourgis	Parish Church
Breakwater	Garden Rocks, Les Etacs	Raz Island
Château a l'Etoc	La Grande Blaye	St Anne
Clonque Bay	La Petite Blaye	Telegraph Bay
Essex Castle	Longy Bay	The Race
Fort Albert	Longy Common	The Swinge
Fort Clonque		

THE BAILIWICK OF GUERNSEY

HERM

Belvoir Bay
Caquorobert
Chapel
Herm Harbour
Hotel

Le Creux Pigeon
Le Petit Monceau
Le Grand Monceau
Le Manoir

Mouisonnière Beach
Pierre aux Rats
Rosière Steps
Shell Beach

SARK

Beau Regard
Brechou
Church
Creux Harbour
Derrible Bay
Dixcart Bay

Eperquerie Landing
Gouliot Caves
Havre Gosselin
La Coupée
La Seigneurie
Les Autelets

Little Sark
Maseline Harbour
Mill
Pilcher Monument
School
Silver Mines

THE CHANNEL ISLANDS

Alderney
Casquets
Chausey Islands
Dirouilles

Guernsey
Herm
Jersey

Minquiers
Paternosters
Sark